To search in our daily cognition for the concepts, which do not rest upon particular experience, and yet occur in all cognition of experience, where they as it were constitute the mere form of connection, presupposes neither greater reflexion nor deeper insight, than to detect in a language the rules of the actual use of words generally, and thus to collect elements for a grammar. In fact both researches are very nearly related. . . .—IMMANUEL KANT, *Prolegomena to any Future Metaphysics.*

ESSAYS IN CONCEPTUAL ANALYSIS

ESSAYS IN CONCEPTUAL ANALYSIS

By

H. BROTMAN, E. DAITZ, ANTONY FLEW
PETER HERBST, JOHN HOSPERS
D. F. PEARS, J. J. C. SMART, P. F. STRAWSON
STEPHEN TOULMIN, J. O. URMSON
and G. J. WARNOCK

Selected and Edited by
ANTONY FLEW

LONDON
MACMILLAN & CO LTD
NEW YORK · ST MARTIN'S PRESS
1960

MACMILLAN AND COMPANY LIMITED
London Bombay Calcutta Madras Melbourne

THE MACMILLAN COMPANY OF CANADA LIMITED
Toronto

ST MARTIN'S PRESS INC
New York

PRINTED IN GREAT BRITAIN

PREFACE

THIS is by no means the first collection of philosophical reprints in roughly the same *genre* to have been published in the last few years. Furthermore, the majority of the papers included originally appeared in still recent issues of the least inaccessible philosophical journals. Nevertheless it seems reasonable to hope that there are needs which it may help to fill. The articles included are all sufficiently important to be constantly referred to in discussions and regularly recommended to students. Even when it originally appeared in a journal to which a library subscribes there is still considerable point in having such an article available there in a second place, and in a form convenient for vacation reading. Even where an individual philosopher subscribes to the journal concerned it often happens, human nature and particularly student human nature being what it is, that the issues containing the most important articles have gone missing. Students, too, need to be able to buy and to own their own copies of the papers which are most useful to them. And it is even possible that some who are not either as teachers or as students professionally concerned with philosophy may wish to take a look into the workshop to see the sort of things the philosophers are doing nowadays: though in making this selection no concessions have been made for the sake of popular appeal.

All the subjects treated fall within the field covered by Oxford 'Logic' examination papers: morals, politics, aesthetics, the philosophy of science and of religion [1] have thus been excluded; but within that deliberately restricted field

[1] For a collection of articles in the same philosophical *genre* but confined to this field, see *New Essays in Philosophical Theology* (S.C.M. Press, 1955), edited by Antony Flew and Alasdair MacIntyre.

CONTENTS

Chapter I

PHILOSOPHY AND LANGUAGE[1]

BY ANTONY FLEW

I PROPOSE to attack a miscellany of popular misconceptions, trying incidentally to illuminate various possibly puzzling practices. A very typical passage from Aristotle's *Nicomachean Ethics* will serve as a text:

We must also grasp the nature of deliberative excellence — εὐβουλία — and find whether it is a sort of knowledge, or of opinion, or of skill at guessing — εὐστοχία — or something different from these in kind. Now it is not knowledge: for men do not investigate — ζητοῦσι — matters about which they know, whereas deliberative excellence is a sort of deliberation, and deliberating implies investigating and calculating. But deliberation is not the same as investigation: it is the investigation of a particular subject [*i.e.* conduct — A. F.]. Nor yet is it skill at guessing: for this operates without conscious calculation, and rapidly, whereas deliberating takes a long time. . . . Correctness cannot be predicated of knowledge, any more than can error, and correctness of opinion is truth (Bk. VI, ch. ix: 1142 a 32 ff.).

Objections: (i) 'But imagine that a man knew that there was a body buried in his back garden, and nevertheless joined with the police in their investigations: would that not be investigating a matter about which he already knew?'

(ii) 'But surely it is sometimes all right to speak of erroneous knowledge: as when sarcastically I say: "He knew the winner of the two-thirty: but he knew wrong"?'

---

[1] This paper was originally commissioned by the *Philosophical Quarterly* as a cross between a survey of work of a certain sort published since the end of the Second German War and an *apologia pro philosophia nostra contra murmurantes*. Hence it was to a quite exceptional degree both polemical in tone and burdened with footnotes. For this reprinting the tone has been softened and the burden lightened a little. But the former is considerably sharper and the latter very much heavier than they would be if I had been writing now and for this present purpose.

Replies: (i) 'No, it would in his case, but not that of the police, only be *pretending* to investigate, a matter of "investigating" (in inverted commas, making the protest that this is a bogus case of investigation). To anyone who knows that the man knows that the body is there, and yet sincerely persists in saying that that man is investigating, and not pretending to investigate or "investigating" (in snigger quotes): what else can we say but "You just do not know the meaning of the word 'investigate'"?'

(ii) 'You are quite right, of course: but your exception is one which, properly understood, only helps to reinforce Aristotle's thesis. For the whole sarcastic point of the use of the expression "knew wrong" and of saying "he 'knew'" (in that sniggering inverted comma tone of voice) depends absolutely on the (logical) fact that "He knows p" entails "p"; that it is incorrect to say "He knows p" unsarcastically if you or he to your knowledge have reason to doubt p.[1] And, again, if anyone has reason to doubt p (or, still better, knows not p); and yet sincerely and unsarcastically insists "He (there) knows p": what else can we say but "Either you do not know the meaning of the word 'know' and are ignorantly misusing it; or else you have your own peculiar use for the word which I wish you would explain and try to justify"?'

Notes: (i) It is appropriate to build our basic example here upon a passage of the *Nicomachean Ethics*: since most of the *avant-garde* of Oxford philosophy since the war (Austin, Hart, Hare and Urmson, for instance) are soaked in this book; and there is a very strong analogy between their work and it.

[1] See J. L. Austin's classic 'Other Minds' in *Logic and Language*, Vol. II (ed. A. Flew, Blackwell, Vol. I, 1951, Vol. II, 1953), and also § III of S. E. Toulmin's 'Probability', Chapter VIII below. I shall use *LL*, I and *LL*, II as abbreviations for *Logic and Language*, First and Second Series, respectively. I apologize for the frequency of these references: but those wishing to look up some of the articles mentioned here will presumably be glad to reduce the number of volumes with which they have to deal; while certainly no one will wish to have repeated anything I have said before.

When someone like Ryle says 'We don't say' or 'We can't say' or uses any of the semi-equivalent expressions of the material mode of speech ; and we can think of occasions on which we might and do intelligibly and not incorrectly say precisely what he says we cannot say : it is a good rule to consider whether these exceptions do not in fact actually reinforce the point he is really concerned to make, or whether, if not, they are really relevant to it, involving the same use of the word. No one is infallible, and certainly not Ryle in this matter, but we should allow for the fact that a self-contradictory or otherwise logically improper expression *may* get a piquancy precisely as such; and can thus acquire a use, a point, which depends entirely on the fact that it is a misuse, and is thus parasitical on the logico-linguistic rule to which it is an exception. 'He knew but he knew wrong', 'bachelor husband', and 'the evidence of my own eyes' all get their piquancy in this way.

(A) 'But Aristotle was not concerned with *mere words* : whereas your replies to objections involve nothing else.' A closer look at the example will show that and how this anti-thesis is here crucially misleading. The replies are not about words in the way in which protests at the replacement of 'men (and women)' or 'people' by '(male and female) personnel' are about words.[1] Nor do they concern English words to the exclusion of equivalents in Greek or Chocktaw. Nor do they even concern words as opposed to non-verbal signs doing the same jobs. (Consider the camp-fire version of 'Underneath the spreading chestnut tree', of which our late King was so fond, in which gestures replace some of the words.) Rather they are about the *uses* of certain words, the *jobs* they do, the *point* of employing them : their *meaning*, and the *implications* which they carry.

Thus it would be no more necessary to mention the particular English words 'investigate' and 'know' in trans-lating the replies into another language than it is to mention ζήτησις and ἐπιστήμη in rendering Aristotle's argument from

[1] 'God created personnel in his own image' (Sir Alan Herbert)

the Greek. Though English-speaking philosophers sometimes speak of correct or standard English this must not be
mistaken to imply that they are concerned with English as
opposed to other languages (usually : but see (B) below).[1]
The replies, like Aristotle's theses and the objections to them,
are all equally concerned with logic as much as with language. The whole enquiry is logical rather than philological,
an examination of the 'informal logic'[2] of two workaday
concepts. Hence the fashion for expressions such as 'the
logic of (our) language', '*logic* and language', 'the *logic* of
"probable"', 'the *logical* behaviour of "God"-sentences',
and even '*logical* geography' is not necessarily just a pointless irritating fad ; though nothing we have to say will do
anything to justify 'The Logic of British and American
Industry' or 'The Logic of Liberty' when used of enquiries
neither in the linguistic idiom nor even conceptual.

(B) This suggests why philosophers given to talking about
correct English 'seem to take little account of the existence
of other languages whose structure and idiom are very
different from English . . . but which seem equally if not
more capable of engendering metaphysical confusion'.[3]
Being, like their colleagues, concerned with conceptual
matters, their protests against the misuse of English are not
primarily motivated by a concern for correct *English* as
opposed to faultless Eskimo. But the matter should not be
allowed to rest there. The existence of other natural languages whose structure, idiom, and vocabulary are not
completely congruent with those of our own is philosophically
relevant in at least three ways.

(i) They provide concepts not available in the stock of
our language group. Notoriously there are in all languages
words untranslatable into English : no English words, that
is, have precisely the same use. And many of the concepts

---

[1] Cf. L. J. Cohen, 'Are Philosophical Theses relative to Language?' in
Analysis, 1949.
[2] G. Ryle, 'Ordinary Language', *Philosophical Review*, 1953.
[3] *PQ*, 1952, p. 2 (top).

concerned are of philosophic interest : either directly in
themselves ; or indirectly because it is necessary to master
them in order to understand some philosopher who used or
discussed the concept in question. Perhaps the best examples
are ethical, such as ὕβρις, ἀρετή, or *tabu*.

(ii) Different languages offer different temptations. J. S.
Mill must have been beguiled into his disastrous argument
from what is in fact desired to what is in morals desirable
by the 'grammatical' analogy between English words like
'audible' and 'visible' and the English word 'desirable'.[1]
(There might be a language in which there was no such
morphological analogy between a class of words meaning
'able as a matter of fact to be somethinged' and one meaning
'ought as a matter of value to be somethinged'.) The misconstruction of 'infinity' as being the word for a gigantic
number is made attractive by the morphological analogy
between the expression 'to infinity' and such as 'to one
hundred'. If we always said 'for ever' or 'indefinitely'
instead of 'to infinity', and if 'aleph-nought' did not happen
to sound like the word for a colossal number, then this
temptation would disappear.[2] It has been said that it is
hard to make Hegel's dialectic plausible or even intelligible
in English for the lack of any word with ambiguities parallel
to those of the German *aufheben*.[3] Kant, in a significantly
phrased passage, noted:

The German language has the good fortune to possess expressions which do not allow this difference [between the opposites of
das Übel and *das Böse* — A. F.] to be overlooked. It possesses two
very distinct concepts, and especially different expressions, for that
which the Latins express by a single word *bonum*.[4]

While the Greek way of forming abstract noun substitutes

---

[1] *Utilitarianism* (Everyman), p. 32 (bottom) : Mill argues from this morphological analogy, explicitly. Though even here it is doubtful if this was more
than the occasion for a mistake, the true cause of which was the quest for a
'scientific ethics'.
[2] See *P.A.S.*, Supp. Vol. XXVII, pp. 42-3 and 47-8, for a recent example
of this howler and its criticism.
[3] T. D. Weldon, *The Vocabulary of Politics* (Pelican, 1953), p. 107.
[4] *Critique of Practical Reason*, trans. T. K. Abbott, p. 150.

from the neuter of the definite article and the adjective does something, though not of course very much, to explain the attractions for Plato of the Theory of Forms.[1]

(iii) The existence of natural languages with radically different logical characteristics gives the opportunity for logical explorations of ways of thinking far more diverse than those embraced in most of these singly : for, as it were, logico-linguistic travel, which can broaden the mind and stimulate the imagination and so provide benefits of the sort which alert people are able to get from physical travel.

Consider, for example, the analogy between the recognition of the legitimate existence of non-Euclidean geometries which helps to undermine rationalist hopes of a quasi-geometrical deductive system of knowledge about the world based on self-evident necessary premises; and the realization that there actually are natural languages to which the subject-predicate distinction can scarcely be applied, which are not saturated with the concept of cause, and which provide words to pick out different differences and likenesses from those which English, and indeed most European languages, are equipped to mark. To realize this is to discredit ideas that the subject-predicate distinction must be inextricably rooted in the non-linguistic world,[2] that the notion of cause is an indispensable category of thought,[3] and that language must reflect the ultimate nature of reality.[4] Of course, it is theoretically possible to imagine other conceptual systems and categories of concept.[5] But this is excessively

[1] For some of the many more worthy attractions see D. F. Pears, 'Universals', in *LL*, II. For Aristotle's battle against the temptations of this idiom, in which he had to express his definition of goodness, see the early chapters of *Nic. Eth.*, Bk. I.

[2] This point was originally made by Sayce; and reiterated by Russell, *Analysis of Mind*, p. 212.

[3] See articles by D. D. Lee mentioned below, though her interpretation of Trobriand thought is disputed.

[4] See *Republic*, 596 A 6-8 for a suggestive admission : 'We have been in the habit, if you remember, of positing a Form, wherever we use the same name in many instances, one Form for each many'.

[5] Cf. the 'language games' of Wittgenstein, imaginary truncated languages used as diagrams in *Philosophical Investigations* : and the Newspeak of George Orwell's *1984*, Appendix.

difficult, as witness the calibre of some of the philosophers who have assumed or even asserted contingent, though perhaps admirable, characteristics of their particular languages to be necessities of thought. In any case there is actual material waiting to be studied,[1] and there is much to be said for the use of real, as opposed to imaginary, examples in philosophy. It can add vitality to discussion and help to break down the idea that philosophical training and philosophical enquiry can have no relevance or value in the world outside our cloistered classrooms.

(C) The *use* of a word is not the same as, though it is subtly connected with, the *usage* of that word. The former (see above) is language-neutral: if we enquire about the *use* of 'table' then we are simultaneously and equally concerned with the *use* of 'tavola' and other equivalents in other languages; with, if you like, the concept of table. The latter is language-specific: if we enquire about the *usage* of 'table' then we are concerned with how that particular *English* word is (or ought to be) employed by those who employ that word, and not 'tavola'.

But the two are crucially related. No word could be said to have a use except in so far as some language group or sub-group gives it a use and recognizes as correct the usage appropriate to that use: for the sounds we use as words are all, intrinsically and prior to the emergence of any linguistic conventions about them, almost equally suitable to do any linguistic job whatever. Whereas a knife, say, could not be used, or even misused, as a tent, 'glory' might have been given the use we have in fact given to 'a nice knock-down argument'.

The *uses* of words depend subtly on the correct *usages* of words. Humpty Dumpty can only be accused of *misusing* 'glory' because the accepted, standard, correct *usage* of Lewis Carroll's language group was radically different from

[1] See *LL*, II, p. 3: to the references given there in the second note can be added D. D. Lee in *Psychosomatic Medicine*, Vol. XIII, 1950, and in *The Journal of Philosophy*, 1949.

his private usage. It was perverse, ill-mannered, misleading, and endangered the possibility of linguistic communication, thus wantonly and without explanation to flout the linguistic conventions. (No doubt, like contemporary 'prophets of a new linguistic dispensation',[1] he regarded such linguistic conventions as 'preposterous restrictions upon free speech'.[2]) Furthermore, as academic philologists[3] and people concerned with maintaining and increasing the efficiency of the English language[4] (and others) have often urged, what is *correct* usage of any language group depends ultimately upon *actual* usage. It is because *use* depends on *correct usage* while this in turn depends ultimately upon *actual usage* that changes in actual usage can enrich or impoverish the conceptual equipment provided by a language. If a new usage is established by which a new use is given to a word, a use not previously provided for, then to that extent the language concerned is enriched.[5] Whereas if an old usage whereby two words had two different uses is replaced by a new one in which one of them loses its job to become a mere synonym of the other, then similarly there is a proportionate impoverishment. Since the actual usage of any language group or sub-group is never in fact completely static, both processes are usually going on, and together constitute a considerable part of the history of any language. ('The history of language . . . is little other than the history of corruptions': Lounsbury was writing as a grammarian, but the same is true from a logical point of view; though 'corruption' must be taken as value-neutral here.)

To come at the matter from a new angle: consider how the historical theologian studies the concept of *nephesh* in Israel. He has and can have no other method but the

---

[1] *PQ*, 1952, p. 12.   [2] *PQ*, 1952, p. 2.
[3] To the point here would be references given by P. L. Heath, *PQ*, 1952, p. 2, *n.*
[4] See Sir Alan Herbert's *What a Word!* Sir Ernest Gowers' *Plain Words* and *ABC of Plain Words*, etc.
[5] This point is developed by F. Waismann in his 'Analytic-Synthetic', and stressed to a point at which some might complain that it encouraged anarchic Humpty-Dumptyism (*Analysis*, 1950, Vol. X ff.).

examination of the occurrences of the word '*nephesh*' in his texts : the attempt to discover from a survey of usage what was its use, what job this word did in the vocabulary of the people who employed it. Or, again, consider how Professor H. J. Paton objects decisively to the translation of *abgeleitet* as 'deduced' because 'an examination of Kant's usage will show that it seldom or never means this' (*The Categorical Imperative*, p. 134, *n*.). Or consider how the cryptographer tries to discover the meaning of an unknown element in a code. He has and can have no other method but a similar examination of its occurrences, hoping by a study of usage to hit upon its use, its meaning. Appeals to *use* and *usage* in creative philosophy can be regarded as a belatedly explicit application of the tried and necessary methods of the historians of ideas.

Before passing to section (D), various minor points: First, 'linguistic conventions' here means those by which we use 'pod' rather than 'pid' or 'nup' to mean pod ; and so forth. Second, 'language group or sub-group' is not here a precise expression. It is intended to cover the users of recognized languages, of their dialects, of jargons and private languages of all kinds, down to and including individuals who develop terminologies private to themselves and their readers and interpreters, if any. Our point is one about the presuppositions of linguistic communication. Third, not all features of the usage of a word will be relevant to questions about its use : that the personal pronouns 'I', 'he', and 'she' are subject to radical morphological transformation in other cases is of concern to Fowler, but not to the philosopher ; for their use would be unaffected if usage were to send these transformations the way of other unnecessary case-indications. But this is a matter for caution, for it is hard to be sure without examination what will turn out to be relevant : Fowler would be concerned with the spread of the usage which makes 'contact' a transitive verb ; but perhaps this change also subtly affects the notion of contact.[1]

[1] On the analogous difficulty of knowing in advance the 'logical breaking strains of concepts' see Ryle's Inaugural, *Philosophical Arguments* (Oxford, 1945).

Fourth, it is possible for people to communicate, in a way which depends partly on words (or other conventional signs), in spite of misusing many of the words (or other conventional signs) they employ : for the intelligent appreciation of context (in the widest sense) can do much to compensate for such deficiencies. But to the precise extent to which it needs to, communication is thereby not depending upon words (or other conventional signs). Fifth, this stress on *use* derives mainly from Wittgenstein : the idea is present unexploited in the *Tractatus Logico-Philosophicus* : 'In philosophy the question "For what purpose do we really use that word . . . ?" constantly leads to valuable results' (6.211, cf. also 3.328, 3.326, and 5.47321); and it became the slogan 'Don't ask for the *meaning*, ask for the *use*' in the early thirties after his return to Cambridge.[1] The explicit concern with correct *usage* as the determinant of *use* seems to derive mainly from J. L. Austin.[2]

(D) Notoriously there is often a gap between actual and correct usage. It is possible for some usage which is (even much) more honoured in the breach than the observance to be one which defaulters are prepared to acknowledge as correct, mainly because certain people and reference books are recognized as generally authoritative : there is still, in Britain at any rate, no question as to what is the correct usage of such non-technical logical terms as 'refute', 'imply', and 'infer', but it seems most unlikely that the actual usage of the majority even of first-year university students conforms with it. This gap is of the greatest importance to anyone who wishes to understand 'what is at the bottom of all this terminological hyperaesthesia, and all the whistle-blowing and knuckle-rapping and scolding that goes along with it'.[3]

(i) It enables a piece of 'logical geographizing', telling

[1] See the *Philosophical Investigations*, especially *ad init.* for his own account of the reasons for this maxim.

[2] See M. Weitz, 'Oxford Philosophy', *Philosophical Review*, 1953 : and *P.A.S.*, Supp. Vol. XVIII, for Austin's first characteristic publication.

[3] *PQ*, 1952, p. 5 (top).

us only what most of us in a way know, making no distinction
not already provided for in familiar words, to be an exercise
in precisification of thought and in improvement of usage
for all those who work through it ; and not merely for those,
like the students mentioned above, whose word training has
been conspicuously deficient.   Consider the effects of describing the differences and analogies between *threats*,
promises, and *predictions* ; to draw example from a recent
Oxford examination paper.   Though often such examina-
tions of present correct usage will show that we need not
only to bring our actual usage more into line with correct
usage, but also to go further by suggesting improvements.
'Essential though it is as a preliminary to track down the
detail of our ordinary uses of words, it seems that we shall
in the end always be compelled to straighten them out to
some extent' (Austin).[1]

(ii) It gives ground for hope that philosophers, including
always and especially ourselves, who misuse or tolerate the
misuse of certain words and expressions,[2] or who give or
accept incorrect accounts of their *rationes applicandi*, may
be led by suitable attention to their correct usage and actual
use to realize and remedy their mistakes.   This phrase
ratio applicandi is modelled deliberately upon the *ratio
decidendi* of the lawyers : the principle under which all
previous decisions can be subsumed and upon which, as the
fiction has it, they were in fact made.   For just as it is perfectly possible to make decisions consistent with such a
principle without having actually formulated it : so it is
possible, and even usual, to be able to apply a word correctly in unselfconscious moments, without being able to
discern its *ratio applicandi*, or even to do so when positively
in error about it ; though of course anyone making such a
mistake will have some inclination to misuse the word.

(iii) But it also makes it possible to misrepresent present

---

[1] 'How to Talk' in *P.A.S.*, 1952–3, p. 227.
[2] For some subtle and very important examples of a sensitivity to ordinary
correct usage see G. J. Warnock's *Berkeley*, especially in chaps. 7-10.

the rest of this book provides many others.) Perhaps Kant was discouraged from recognizing the merit in Hume here by Hume's own misleading talk about mere words as well as by the aggressive way in which he misrepresented a good start as the end of the affair. Certainly we find him two pages later very grudgingly conceding part of Hume's point, but insisting that at any rate *transcendental* freedom cannot thus be reconciled with scientific determinism.[1]

(v) After so much has been said about misuses and misconstructions, it must be mentioned that interest originally directed at the uses of words only inasmuch as this brought out what were misuses and misconstructions, is sometimes, by a familiar psychological process, partly diverted to the study of use for its own sake. Before suggesting that, however psychologically understandable, such interests do not become a philosopher in his working hours we should cast our minds back to Aristotle and reflect whether all his studies of the concepts of moral psychology were in fact wholly directed to some ulterior end even within philosophy; or, more generally, ask ourselves whether an interest in concepts is not one of the things which makes a philosopher.

But whatever are the rights and wrongs about ulterior and ultimate ends and whatever the jurisdictional proprieties, disputes about these here turn out to be largely unnecessary. For in elucidating the ordinary uses (as opposed to philosophers' suspected misuses) of some of the rather limited range of words around which our controversies tend to cluster,[2] it has been noticed that the conceptual equipment provided by ordinary (here opposed particularly to technical) language is amazingly rich and subtle; and that even the classical puzzles cannot be fully resolved without elucidating not merely the formerly fashionable élite of notions but also all their neglected logical hangers-on.

[1] *Loc. cit.* p. 190.
[2] See Waismann, 'Language Strata' in *LL*, II, and Ryle, 'Ordinary Language', for suggestions about this clustering.

In formulating and attacking free will puzzles, philosophers, with the outstanding exception of Aristotle, have been inclined to concentrate on a few ideas : *free will, compulsion, choice, necessity, responsible*, and one or two others. Whereas we have available in our ordinary vocabulary of extenuation and responsibility a great range of notions, which it would be wise to master and exhaust before thinking of adaptation or invention : [1] *automatically, by mistake, unintentionally, by force of habit, involuntarily, unwillingly, on principle, under provocation*, to mention a few. Philosophers have tended to ignore all this richness and variety, assuming that it could all be satisfactorily assimilated to a few most favoured notions. But to do this is clumsy and slovenly. While proposals to jettison ordinary language in favour of new-minted terms overlook the crucial primacy of the vernacular : ordinary, as opposed to technical, language is fundamental in the sense that the meaning of terms of art can only be explained with its aid ; and it is a perennial complaint against such lovers of jargon as Kant and the Scholastics that this essential work is so often botched, skimped, or altogether neglected. The upshot of all this is that it is improbable that the elucidation of the logic of any term at all likely to engage any philosopher's attention will fail some day to find application to some generally recognized philosophical problem, however 'pure' his own interests may have been : the implied comparison with the pure scientific research which so frequently finds unexpected and unintended application is suggestive and, up to a point, apposite. It is to such often seemingly indiscriminate interest in the uses of words that we owe such fruitful logical explorations of neglected territory as R. M. Hare's 'Imperative Sentences',[2] and J. L. Austin on performatory language in 'Other Minds'. Contrast the old 'fetich of the indicative sentence' (Ryle)

[1] Not that such adaptation or invention may not be called for : see P. D. Nowell-Smith in *The Rationalist Annual*, 1954, for suggestions designed to accommodate the discoveries of psychoanalysis.

[2] *Mind*, 1949: and incorporated with additions and improvements into his *The Language of Morals*.

said, 'Napoleon was the greatest French soldier', I should be using the word 'Napoleon' to mention a certain individual, but I should not be using the phrase, 'the greatest French soldier', to mention an individual, but to say something about an individual I had already mentioned. It would be natural to say that in using this sentence I was talking *about* Napoleon and that what I was *saying* about him was that he was the greatest French soldier. But of course I *could* use the expression, 'the greatest French soldier', to mention an individual; for example, by saying: 'The greatest French soldier died in exile'. So it is obvious that at least some expressions belonging to the classes I mentioned *can* have uses other than the use I am anxious to discuss. Another thing I do not want to say is that in any given sentence there is never more than one expression used in the way I propose to discuss. On the contrary, it is obvious that there may be more than one. For example, it would be natural to say that, in seriously using the sentence, 'The whale struck the ship', I was saying something about both a certain whale and a certain ship, that I was using each of the expressions 'the whale' and 'the ship' to mention a particular object; or, in other words, that I was using each of these expressions in the uniquely referring way. In general, however, I shall confine my attention to cases where an expression used in this way occurs as the grammatical subject of a sentence.

I think it is true to say that Russell's Theory of Descriptions, which is concerned with the last of the four classes of expressions I mentioned above (*i.e.* with expressions of the form 'the so-and-so'), is still widely accepted among logicians as giving a correct account of the use of such expressions in ordinary language. I want to show in the first place, that this theory, so regarded, embodies some fundamental mistakes.

What question or questions about phrases of the form 'the so-and-so' was the Theory of Descriptions designed to answer? I think that at least one of the questions may be illustrated as follows. Suppose someone were now to utter the sentence, 'The king of France is wise'. No one would say that the sentence which had been uttered was meaningless. Everyone would agree that it was significant. But everyone knows that there is not at present a king of France. One of the questions the Theory of Descriptions was designed to answer was the question: How can such a sentence as 'The king of France is wise' be significant even when there is nothing which answers to the description it contains, *i.e.*, in this case, nothing which answers to the description 'The king of France'? And one of the reasons why Russell thought it important to give a correct answer to this question was that he thought it important to show that another answer which might be given was wrong. The answer that he thought was wrong, and to which he was anxious to supply an alternative, might be exhibited as the conclusion of either of the following two fallacious arguments. Let us call the sentence 'The king of France is wise' the sentence S. Then the first argument is as follows:

(1) The phrase, 'the king of France', is the subject of the sentence S.

Therefore (2) if S is a significant sentence, S is a sentence *about* the king of France.

But (3) if there in no sense exists a king of France, the sentence is not about anything, and hence not about the king of France.

Therefore (4) since S is significant, there must in some sense (in some world) exist (or subsist) the king of France.

And the second argument is as follows:

(1) If S is significant, it is either true or false.

(2) S is true if the king of France is wise and false if the king of France is not wise.

(3) But the statement that the king of France is wise and the statement that the king of France is not wise are alike true only if there is (in some sense, in some world) something which is the king of France.

an expression used in the uniquely referring way, fall into neither of these two classes. Expressions used in the uniquely referring way are never either logically proper names or descriptions, if what is meant by calling them 'descriptions' is that they are to be analysed in accordance with the model provided by Russell's Theory of Descriptions.

There are no logically proper names and there are no descriptions (in this sense).

Let us now consider the details of Russell's analysis. According to Russell, anyone who asserted S would be asserting that :

(1) There is a king of France.

(2) There is not more than one king of France.

(3) There is nothing which is king of France and is not wise.

It is easy to see both how Russell arrived at this analysis, and how it enables him to answer the question with which we began, viz. the question : How can the sentence S be significant when there is no king of France ? The way in which he arrived at the analysis was clearly by asking himself what would be the circumstances in which we would say that anyone who uttered the sentence S had made a true assertion. And it does seem pretty clear, and I have no wish to dispute, that the sentences (1)-(3) above do describe circumstances which are at least *necessary* conditions of anyone making a true assertion by uttering the sentence S. But, as I hope to show, to say this is not at all the same thing as to say that Russell has given a correct account of the use of the sentence S or even that he has given an account which, though incomplete, is correct as far as it goes ; and is certainly not at all the same thing as to say that the model translation provided is a correct model for all (or for any) singular sentences beginning with a phrase of the form 'the so-and-so'.

It is also easy to see how this analysis enables Russell to answer the question of how the sentence S can be significant, even when there is no king of France. For, if this analysis is correct, anyone who utters the sentence S to-day would be jointly asserting three propositions, one of which (viz. that there is a king of France) would be false ; and since the conjunction of three propositions, of which one is false, is itself false, the assertion as a whole would be significant, but false. So neither of the bad arguments for subsistent entities would apply to such an assertion.

II

As a step towards showing that Russell's solution of his problem is mistaken, and towards providing the correct solution, I want now to draw certain distinctions. For this purpose I shall, for the remainder of this section, refer to an expression which has a uniquely referring use as 'an expression' for short ; and to a sentence beginning with such an expression as 'a sentence' for short. The distinctions I shall draw are rather rough and ready, and, no doubt, difficult cases could be produced which would call for their refinement. But I think they will serve my purpose. The distinctions are between :

(A1) a sentence,
(A2) a use of a sentence,
(A3) an utterance of a sentence,

and, correspondingly, between :

(B1) an expression,
(B2) a use of an expression,
(B3) an utterance of an expression.

Consider again the sentence, 'The king of France is wise' It is easy to imagine that this sentence was uttered at various times from, say, the beginning of the seventeenth century onwards, during the reigns of each successive French monarch ; and easy to imagine that it was also uttered during the subsequent periods in which France was not a monarchy. Notice that it was natural for me to speak of 'the sentence' or 'this sentence' being uttered at various

times during this period; or, in other words, that it would
be natural and correct to speak of *one and the same* sentence
being uttered on all these various occasions. It is in the sense
in which it would be correct to speak of one and the same
sentence being uttered on all these various occasions that I
want to use the expression (A1) 'a sentence'. There are,
however, obvious differences between different *occasions of
the use* of this sentence. For instance, if one man uttered it
in the reign of Louis XIV and another man uttered it in the
reign of Louis XV, it would be natural to say (to assume)
that they were respectively talking about different people;
and it might be held that the first man, in using the sentence,
made a true assertion, while the second man, in using the
same sentence, made a false assertion. If on the other hand
two different men simultaneously uttered the sentence (*e.g.*
if one wrote it and the other spoke it) during the reign of
Louis XIV, it would be natural to say (assume) that they
were both talking about the same person, and, in that case,
in using the sentence, they *must* either both have made a
true assertion or both have made a false assertion. And
this illustrates what I mean by *a use* of a sentence. The
two men who uttered the sentence, one in the reign of
Louis XV and one in the reign of Louis XIV, each made
a different use of the same sentence; whereas the two men
who uttered the sentence simultaneously in the reign of
Louis XIV, made the same use [1] of the same sentence.
Obviously in the case of this sentence, and equally obviously
in the case of many others, we cannot talk of *the sentence*
being true or false, but only of its being used to make a true
or false assertion, or (if this is preferred) to express a true
or a false proposition. And equally obviously we cannot
talk of *the sentence* being *about* a particular person, for the
same sentence may be used at different times to talk about

---

[1] This usage of 'use' is, of course, different from (*a*) the current usage in
which 'use' (of a particular word, phrase, sentence)=(roughly) 'rules for
using'=(roughly) 'meaning'; and from (*b*) my own usage in the phrase
'uniquely referring use of expressions' in which 'use'=(roughly) 'way of
using'.

quite different particular persons, but only of *a use* of the sentence to talk about a particular person. Finally it will make sufficiently clear what I mean by an utterance of a sentence if I say that the two men who simultaneously uttered the sentence in the reign of Louis XIV made two different utterances of the same sentence, though they made the same *use* of the sentence.

If we now consider not the whole sentence, 'The king of France is wise', but that part of it which is the expression, 'the king of France', it is obvious that we can make analogous, though not identical distinctions between (1) the expression, (2) a use of the expression, and (3) an utterance of the expression. The distinctions will not be identical; we obviously cannot correctly talk of the expression 'the king of France' being used to express a true or false proposition, since in general only sentences can be used truly or falsely; and similarly it is only by using a sentence and not by using an expression alone, that you can talk about a particular person. Instead, we shall say in this case that you *use* the expression to *mention* or *refer to* a particular person in the course of using the sentence to talk about him. But obviously in this case, and a great many others, the *expression* (B1) cannot be said to mention, or refer to, anything, any more than the *sentence* can be said to be true or false. The same expression can have different mentioning-uses, as the same sentence can be used to make statements with different truth-values. 'Mentioning', or 'referring', is not something an expression does; it is something that someone can use an expression to do. Mentioning, or referring to, something is a characteristic of *a use* of an expression, just as 'being about' something, and truth-or-falsity, are characteristics of *a use* of a sentence.

A very different example may help to make these distinctions clearer. Consider another case of an expression which has a uniquely referring use, viz. the expression 'I'; and consider the sentence, 'I am hot'. Countless people may use this same sentence; but it is logically impossible

D

for two different people to make *the same use* of this sentence :
or, if this is preferred, to use it to express the same proposition. The expression 'I' may correctly be used by (and
only by) any one of innumerable people to refer to himself.
To say this is to say something about the expression 'I':
it is, in a sense, to give its meaning. This is the sort of thing
that can be said about *expressions*. But it makes no sense
to say of the *expression* 'I' that it refers to a particular
person. This is the sort of thing that can be said only of a
particular use of the expression.

Let me use 'type' as an abbreviation for 'sentence or
expression'. Then I am not saying that there are sentences
and expressions (types), *and* uses of them, *and* utterances of
them, as there are ships *and* shoes *and* sealing-wax. I am
saying that we cannot say *the same things* about types, uses
of types, and utterances of types. And the fact is that we
do talk about types; and that confusion is apt to result
from the failure to notice the differences between what we
can say about these and what we can say only about the
uses of types. We are apt to fancy we are talking about
sentences and expressions when we are talking about the
uses of sentences and expressions.

This is what Russell does. Generally, as against Russell,
I shall say this. Meaning (in at least one important sense)
is a function of the sentence or expression; mentioning and
referring and truth or falsity, are functions of the use of the
sentence or expression. To give the meaning of an expression (in the sense in which I am using the word) is to
give *general directions* for its use to refer to or mention
particular objects or persons; to give the meaning of a
sentence is to give *general directions* for its use in making
true or false assertions. It is not to talk about any particular
occasion of the use of the sentence or expression. The
meaning of an expression cannot be identified with the
object it is used, on a particular occasion, to refer to. The
meaning of a sentence cannot be identified with the assertion
it is used, on a particular occasion, to make. For to talk

about the meaning of an expression or sentence is not to talk about its use on a particular occasion, but about the rules, habits, conventions governing its correct use, on all occasions, to refer or to assert. So the question of whether a sentence or expression *is significant or not* has nothing whatever to do with the question of whether the sentence, *uttered on a particular occasion*, is, on that occasion, being used to make a true-or-false assertion or not, or of whether the expression is, on that occasion, being used to refer to, or mention, anything at all.

The source of Russell's mistake was that he thought that referring or mentioning, if it occurred at all, must be meaning. He did not distinguish B1 from B2; he confused expressions with their use in a particular context; and so confused meaning with mentioning, with referring. If I talk about my handkerchief, I can, perhaps, produce the object I am referring to out of my pocket. I cannot produce the meaning of the expression, 'my handkerchief', out of my pocket. Because Russell confused meaning with mentioning, he thought that if there were any expressions having a uniquely referring use, which were what they seemed (*i.e.* logical subjects) and not something else in disguise, their meaning must *be* the particular object which they were used to refer to. Hence the troublesome mythology of the logically proper name. But if someone asks me the meaning of the expression 'this' — once Russell's favourite candidate for this status — I do not hand him the object I have just used the expression to refer to, adding at the same time that the meaning of the word changes every time it is used. Nor do I hand him all the objects it ever has been, or might be, used to refer to. I explain and illustrate the conventions governing the use of the expression. This *is* giving the meaning of the expression. It is quite different from giving (in any sense of giving) the object to which it refers; for the expression itself does not refer to anything; though it can be used, on different occasion, to refer to innumerable things. Now as a matter of fact there is, in

English, a sense of the word 'mean' in which this word does approximate to 'indicate, mention or refer to'; *e.g.* when somebody (unpleasantly) says, 'I mean you'; or when I point and say, 'That's the one I mean'. But *the one I meant* is quite different from *the meaning of the expression* I used to talk of it. In this special sense of 'mean', it is people who mean, not expressions. People use expressions to refer to particular things. But the meaning of an expression is not the set of things or the single thing it may correctly be used to refer to: the meaning is the set of rules, habits, conventions for its use in referring.

It is the same with sentences: even more obviously so. Everyone knows that the sentence, 'The table is covered with books', is significant, and everyone knows what it means. But if I ask, 'What object is that sentence about?' I am asking an absurd question — a question which cannot be asked about the sentence, but only about some use of the sentence: and in this case the sentence has not been used to talk about something, it has only been taken as an example. In knowing what it means, you are knowing how it could correctly be used to talk about things: so knowing the meaning has nothing to do with knowing about any particular use of the sentence to talk about anything. Similarly, if I ask: 'Is the sentence true or false?' I am asking an absurd question, which becomes no less absurd if I add, 'It must be one or the other since it is significant'. The question is absurd, because the *sentence* is neither true nor false any more than it is *about* some object. Of course the fact that it is significant is the same as the fact that it *can* correctly be used to talk about something and that, in so using it, someone will be making a true or false assertion. And I will add that it will be used to make a true or false assertion *only* if the person using it *is* talking about something. If, when he utters it, he is not talking about anything, then his use is not a genuine one, but a spurious or pseudo-use: he is not making either a true or a false assertion, though he may think he is. And this points the way

to the correct answer to the puzzle to which the Theory of
Descriptions gives a fatally incorrect answer. The important
point is that the question of whether the sentence is significant
or not is quite independent of the question that can be raised
about a particular use of it, viz. the question whether it is a
genuine or a spurious use, whether it is being used to talk
about something, or in make-believe, or as an example in
philosophy. The question whether the sentence is significant
or not is the question whether there exist such language
habits, conventions or rules that the sentence logically could
be used to talk about something; and is hence quite independent of the question whether it is being so used on a
particular occasion.

III

Consider again the sentence, 'The king of France is wise',
and the true and false things Russell says about it.

There are at least two true things which Russell would
say about the sentence :

(1) The first is that it is significant; that if anyone were
now to utter it, he would be uttering a significant sentence.

(2) The second is that anyone now uttering the sentence
would be making a true assertion only if there in fact at
present existed one and only one king of France, and if he
were wise.

What are the false things which Russell would say about
the sentence ? They are :

(1) That anyone now uttering it would be making a true
assertion or a false assertion ;

(2) That part of what he would be asserting would be
that there at present existed one and only one king of France.

I have already given some reasons for thinking that these
two statements are incorrect. Now suppose someone were
in fact to say to you with a perfectly serious air : 'The king
of France is wise'. Would you say, 'That's untrue' ? I

think it is quite certain that you would not. But suppose he went on to *ask* you whether you thought that what he had just said was true, or was false; whether you agreed or disagreed with what he had just said. I think you would be inclined, with some hesitation, to say that you did not do either; that the question of whether his statement was true or false simply *did not arise*, because there was no such person as the king of France. You might, if he were obviously serious (had a dazed astray-in-the-centuries look), say something like: 'I'm afraid you must be under a misapprehension. France is not a monarchy. There is no king of France.' And this brings out the point that if a man seriously uttered the sentence, his uttering it would in some sense be *evidence* that he *believed* that there was a king of France. It would not be evidence for his believing this simply in the way in which a man's reaching for his raincoat is evidence for his believing that it is raining. But nor would it be evidence for his believing this in the way in which a man's saying, 'It's raining', is evidence for his believing that it is raining. We might put it as follows. To say 'The king of France is wise' is, in some sense of 'imply', to *imply* that there is a king of France. But this is a very special and odd sense of 'imply'. 'Implies' in this sense is certainly not equivalent to 'entails' (or 'logically implies'). And this comes out from the fact that when, in response to his statement, we say (as we should) 'There is no king of France', we should certainly *not* say we were *contradicting* the statement that the king of France is wise. We are certainly not saying that it is false. We are, rather, giving a reason for saying that the question of whether it is true or false simply does not arise.

And this is where the distinction I drew earlier can help us. The sentence, 'The king of France is wise', is certainly significant; but this does not mean that any particular use of it is true or false. We use it truly or falsely when we use it to talk about someone; when, in using the expression, 'The king of France', we are in fact mentioning someone.

The fact that the sentence and the expression, respectively, are significant just is the fact that the sentence *could* be used, in certain circumstances, to say something true or false, that the expression *could* be used, in certain circumstances, to mention a particular person ; and to know their meaning is to know what sort of circumstances these are. So when we utter the sentence without in fact mentioning anybody by the use of the phrase, 'The king of France', the sentence does not cease to be significant : we simply *fail* to say anything true or false because we simply fail to mention anybody by this particular use of that perfectly significant phrase. It is, if you like, a spurious use of the sentence, and a spurious use of the expression ; though we may (or may not) mistakenly think it a genuine use.

And such spurious uses [1] are very familiar. Sophisticated romancing, sophisticated fiction,[2] depend upon them. If I began, 'The king of France is wise', and went on, 'and he lives in a golden castle and has a hundred wives', and so on, a hearer would understand me perfectly well, without supposing *either* that I was talking about a particular person, *or* that I was making a false statement to the effect that there existed such a person as my words described. (It is worth adding that where the use of sentences and expressions is overtly fictional, the sense of the word 'about' may change. As Moore said, it is perfectly natural and correct to say that some of the statements in *Pickwick Papers* are *about* Mr. Pickwick. But where the use of sentences and expressions is not overtly fictional, this use of 'about' seems less correct ; *i.e.* it would not *in general* be correct to say that a statement was about Mr. X or the so-and-so, unless there were such a person or thing. So it is where the romancing is in danger of being taken seriously that we might answer the question, 'Who is he talking about?' with 'He's not talking about anybody' ; but, in saying this, we are not

---

[1] The choice of the word 'spurious' now seems to me unfortunate, at least for some non-standard uses. I should now prefer to call some of these 'secondary' uses.

[2] The unsophisticated kind begins : 'Once upon time there was . . .'

saying that what he is saying is either false or nonsense.)

Overtly fictional uses apart, however, I said just now that to use such an expression as 'The king of France' at the beginning of a sentence was, in some sense of 'imply', to imply that there was a king of France. When a man uses such an expression, he does not *assert*, nor does what he says *entail*, a uniquely existential proposition. But one of the conventional functions of the definite article is to act as a *signal* that a unique reference is being made — a signal, not a disguised assertion. When we begin a sentence with 'the such-and-such' the use of 'the' shows, but does not state, that we are, or intend to be, referring to one particular individual of the species 'such-and-such'. *Which* particular individual is a matter to be determined from context, time, place, and any other features of the situation of utterance. Now, whenever a man uses any expression, the presumption is that he thinks he is using it correctly : so when he uses the expression, 'the such-and-such', in a uniquely referring way, the presumption is that he thinks both that there is *some* individual of that species, and that the context of use will sufficiently determine which one he has in mind. To use the word 'the' in this way is then to imply (in the relevant sense of 'imply') that the existential conditions described by Russell are fulfilled. But to use 'the' in this way is not to *state* that those conditions are fulfilled. If I begin a sentence with an expression of the form, 'the so-and-so', and then am prevented from saying more, I have made no statement of any kind ; but I may have succeeded in mentioning some-one or something.

The uniquely existential assertion supposed by Russell to be part of any assertion in which a uniquely referring use is made of an expression of the form 'the so-and-so' is, he observes, a compound of two assertions. To say that there is a ϕ is to say something compatible with there being several ϕs ; to say there is not more than one ϕ is to say something compatible with there being none. To say there is one ϕ and one only is to compound these two assertions. I have so far been concerned mostly with the alleged assertion of existence and less with the alleged assertion of uniqueness. An example which throws the emphasis on to the latter will serve to bring out more clearly the sense of 'implied' in which a uniquely existential assertion is implied, but not entailed, by the use of expressions in the uniquely referring way. Consider the sentence, 'The table is covered with books'. It is quite certain that in any normal use of this sentence, the expression 'the table' would be used to make a unique reference, *i.e.* to refer to some one table. It is a quite strict use of the definite article, in the sense in which Russell talks on p. 30 of *Principia Mathematica*, of using the article '*strictly*, so as to imply uniqueness'. On the same page Russell says that a phrase of the form 'the so-and-so', used strictly, 'will only have an application in the event of there being one so-and-so and no more'. Now it is obviously quite false that the phrase 'the table' in the sentence 'the table is covered with books', used normally, will 'only have an application in the event of there being one table and no more'. It is indeed tautologically true that, in such a use, the phrase will have an application only in the event of there being one table and no more *which is being referred to*, and that it will be understood to have an application only in the event of there being one table and no more which it is understood as being used to refer to. To use the sentence is not to assert, but it is (in the special sense discussed) to imply, that there is only one thing which is *both* of the kind specified (*i.e.* a table) *and is being referred to* by the speaker. It is obviously not to assert this. To refer is not to say you are referring. To say there is *some table or other* to which you are referring is not the same as referring to a particular table. We should have no use for such phrases as 'the individual I referred to' unless there were something which counted as referring. (It would make no sense to say you had pointed if there were nothing which counted as pointing.) So once more I draw the conclusion that referring to or mentioning a particular thing cannot be dissolved into any kind of assertion. To refer is not to assert, though you refer in order to go on to assert.

Let me now take an example of the uniquely referring use of an expression not of the form, 'the so-and-so'. Suppose I advance my hands, cautiously cupped, towards someone, saying, as I do so, 'This is a fine red one'. He, looking into my hands and seeing nothing there, may say : 'What is ? What are you talking about ?' Or perhaps, 'But there's nothing in your hands'. Of course it would be absurd to say that, in saying 'But you've got nothing in your hands', he was *denying* or *contradicting* what I said. So 'this' is not a disguised description in Russell's sense. Nor is it a logically proper name. For one must know what the sentence means in order to react in that way to the utterance of it. It is precisely because the significance of the word 'this' is independent of any particular reference it may be used to make, though not independent of the way it may be used to refer, that I can, as in this example, use it to *pretend* to be referring to something.

The general moral of all this is that communication is much less a matter of explicit or disguised assertion than logicians used to suppose. The particular application of this general moral in which I am interested is its application to the case of making a unique reference. It is a part of the significance of expressions of the kind I am discussing that they can be used, in an immense variety of contexts, to make unique references. It is no part of their significance to assert that they are being so used or that the conditions of their being so used are fulfilled. So the wholly important distinction we are required to draw is between

(1) using an expression to make a unique reference ; and

(2) asserting that there is one and only one individual which has certain characteristics (*e.g.* is of a certain kind, or stands in a certain relation to the speaker, or both).

This is, in other words, the distinction between

(1) sentences containing an expression used to indicate

or mention or refer to a particular person or thing ; and
(2) uniquely existential sentences.

What Russell does is progressively to assimilate more and
more sentences of class (1) to sentences of class (2), and consequently to involve himself in insuperable difficulties about
logical subjects, and about values for individual variables
generally : difficulties which have led him finally to the
logically disastrous theory of names developed in the *Enquiry
into Meaning and Truth* and in *Human Knowledge*. That
view of the meaning of logical-subject-expressions which
provides the whole incentive to the Theory of Descriptions
at the same time precludes the possibility of Russell's ever
finding any satisfactory substitutes for those expressions
which, beginning with substantival phrases, he progressively
degrades from the status of logical subjects.[1] It is not
simply, as is sometimes said, the fascination of the relation
between a name and its bearer, that is the root of the trouble.
Not even names come up to the impossible standard set.
It is rather the combination of two more radical misconceptions : first, the failure to grasp the importance of the
distinction (section II above) between what may be said of
an expression and what may be said of a particular use of
it ; second, a failure to recognize the uniquely referring use
of expressions for the harmless, necessary thing it is, distinct from, but complementary to, the predicative or ascriptive
use of expressions. The expressions which can in fact occur
as singular logical subjects are expressions of the class I
listed at the outset (demonstratives, substantival phrases,
proper names, pronouns) : to say this is to say that these
expressions, together with context (in the widest sense), are
what one uses to make unique references. The point of the
conventions governing the uses of such expressions is, along
with the situation of utterance, to secure uniqueness of
reference. But to do this, enough is enough. We do not,
and we cannot, while referring, attain the point of complete

---

[1] And this in spite of the danger-signal of that phrase, '*misleading* grammatical form'.

explicitness at which the referring function is no longer performed. The actual unique reference made, if any, is a matter of the particular use in the particular context; the significance of the expression used is the set of rules or conventions which permit such references to be made. Hence we can, using significant expressions, pretend to refer, in make-believe or in fiction, or mistakenly think we are referring when we are not referring to anything.[1]

This shows the need for distinguishing two kinds (among many others) of linguistic conventions or rules : rules for referring, and rules for attributing and ascribing ; and for an investigation of the former. If we recognize this distinction of use for what it is, we are on the way to solving a number of ancient logical and metaphysical puzzles.

My last two sections are concerned, but only in the barest outline, with these questions.

IV

One of the main purposes for which we use language is the purpose of stating facts about things and persons and events. If we want to fulfil this purpose, we must have some way of forestalling the question, 'What (who, which one) are you talking about ?' as well as the question, 'What are you saying about it (him, her) ?' The task of forestalling the first question is the referring (or identifying) task. The task of forestalling the second is the attributive (or descriptive or classificatory or ascriptive) task. In the conventional English sentence which is used to state, or to claim to state, a fact about an individual thing or person or event, the performance of these two tasks can be roughly and approximately assigned to separable expressions.[2] And in such a

[1 This sentence now seems to me objectionable in a number of ways, notably because of an unexplicitly restrictive use of the word 'refer'. It could be more exactly phrased as follows : 'Hence we can, using significant expressions, refer in secondary ways, as in make-believe or in fiction, or mistakenly think we are referring to something in the primary way when we are not, in that way, referring to anything'.]

2 I neglect relational sentences; for these require, not a modification in the principle of what I say, but a complication of the detail.

sentence, this assigning of expressions to their separate rôles corresponds to the conventional grammatical classification of subject and predicate. There is nothing sacrosanct about the employment of separable expressions for these two tasks. Other methods could be, and are, employed. There is, for instance, the method of uttering a single word or attributive phrase in the conspicuous presence of the object referred to ; or that analogous method exemplified by, *e.g.*, the painting of the words 'unsafe for lorries' on a bridge, or the tying of a label reading 'first prize' on a vegetable marrow. Or one can imagine an elaborate game in which one never used an expression in the uniquely referring way at all, but uttered only uniquely existential sentences, trying to enable the hearer to identify what was being talked of by means of an accumulation of relative clauses. (This description of the purposes of the game shows in what sense it would be a game : this is not the normal use we make of existential sentences.) Two points require emphasis. The first is that the necessity of performing these two tasks in order to state particular facts requires no transcendental explanation : to call attention to it is partly to elucidate the meaning of the phrase, 'stating a fact'. The second is that even this elucidation is made in terms derivative from the grammar of the conventional singular sentence ; that even the overtly functional, linguistic distinction between the identifying and attributive rôles that words may play in language is prompted by the fact that ordinary speech offers us separable expressions to which the different functions may be plausibly and approximately assigned. And this functional distinction has cast long philosophical shadows. The distinctions between particular and universal, between substance and quality, are such pseudo-material shadows, cast by the grammar of the conventional sentence, in which separable expressions play distinguishable rôles.[1]

To use a separate expression to perform the first of these

[1 What is said or implied in the last two sentences of this paragraph no longer seems to me true, unless considerably qualified.]

tasks is to use an expression in the uniquely referring way. I want now to say something in general about the conventions of use for expressions used in this way, and to contrast them with conventions of ascriptive use. I then proceed to the brief illustration of these general remarks and to some further applications of them.

What in general is required for making a unique reference is, obviously, some device, or devices, for showing both *that* a unique reference is intended and *what* unique reference it is; some device requiring and enabling the hearer or reader to identify what is being talked about. In securing this result, the context of utterance is of an importance which it is almost impossible to exaggerate ; and by 'context' I mean, at least, the time, the place, the situation, the identity of the speaker, the subjects which form the immediate focus of interest, and the personal histories of both the speaker and those he is addressing. Besides context, there is, of course, convention ; — linguistic convention. But, except in the case of genuine proper names, of which I shall have more to say later, the fulfilment of more or less precisely stateable contextual conditions is *conventionally* (or, in a wide sense of the word, *logically*) required for the correct referring use of expressions in a sense in which this is not true of correct ascriptive uses. The requirement for the correct application of an expression in its ascriptive use to a certain thing is simply that the thing should be of a certain kind, have certain characteristics. The requirement for the correct application of an expression in its referring use to a certain thing is something over and above any requirement derived from such ascriptive meaning as the expression may have ; it is, namely, the requirement that the thing should be in a certain relation to the speaker and to the context of utterance. Let me call this the contextual requirement. Thus, for example, in the limiting case of the word 'I' the contextual requirement is that the thing should be identical with the speaker ; but in the case of most expressions which have a referring use this requirement cannot be so precisely specified. A further, and perfectly general, difference between conventions for referring and conventions for describing is one we have already encountered, viz. that the fulfilment of the conditions for a correct ascriptive use of an expression is a part of what is stated by such a use ; but the fulfilment of the conditions for a correct referring use of an expression is never part of what is stated, though it is (in the relevant sense of 'implied') implied by such a use.

Conventions for referring have been neglected or misinterpreted by logicians. The reasons for this neglect are not hard to see, though they are hard to state briefly. Two of them are, roughly : (1) the preoccupation of most logicians with definitions ; (2) the preoccupation of some logicians with formal systems. (1) A definition, in the most familiar sense, is a specification of the conditions of the correct ascriptive or classificatory use of an expression. Definitions take no account of contextual requirements. So that in so far as the search for the meaning or the search for the analysis of an expression is conceived as the search for a definition, the neglect or misinterpretation of conventions other than ascriptive is inevitable. Perhaps it would be better to say (for I do not wish to legislate about 'meaning' or 'analysis') that logicians have failed to notice that problems of use are wider than problems of analysis and meaning. (2) The influence of the preoccupation with mathematics and formal logic is most clearly seen (to take no more recent examples) in the cases of Leibniz and Russell. The constructor of calculuses, not concerned or required to make factual statements, approaches applied logic with a prejudice. It is natural that he should assume that the types of convention with whose adequacy in one field he is familiar should be really adequate, if only one could see how, in a quite different field — that of statements of fact. Thus we have Leibniz striving desperately to make the uniqueness of unique references a matter of logic in the narrow sense, and Russell striving desperately to do the same thing, in a different way, both for the implication of uniqueness and for that of existence.

It should be clear that the distinction I am trying to draw is primarily one between different rôles or parts that expressions may play in language, and not primarily one between different groups of expressions; for some expressions may appear in either rôle. Some of the kinds of words I shall speak of have predominantly, if not exclusively, a referring rôle. This is most obviously true of pronouns and ordinary proper names. Some can occur as wholes or parts of expressions which have a predominantly referring use, and as wholes or parts of expressions which have a predominantly ascriptive or classificatory use. The obvious cases are common nouns; or common nouns preceded by adjectives, including participial adjectives; or, less obviously, adjectives or participial adjectives alone. Expressions capable of having a referring use also differ from one another in at least the three following, not mutually independent, ways :

(1) They differ in the extent to which the reference they are used to make is dependent on the context of their utterance. Words like 'I' and 'it' stand at one end of this scale — the end of maximum dependence — and phrases like 'the author of *Waverley*' and 'the eighteenth king of France' at the other.

(2) They differ in the degree of 'descriptive meaning' they possess : by 'descriptive meaning' I intend 'conventional limitation, in application, to things of a certain general kind, or possessing certain general characteristics'. At one end of this scale stand the proper names we most commonly use in ordinary discourse ; men, dogs, and motor-bicycles may be called 'Horace'. The pure name has no descriptive meaning (except such as it may acquire *as a result of* some one of its uses as a name). A word like 'he' has minimal descriptive meaning, but has some. Substantival phrases like 'the round table' have the maximum descriptive meaning. An interesting intermediate position is occupied by 'impure' proper

names like 'The Round Table' — substantival phrases which have grown capital letters.

(3) Finally, they may be divided into the following two classes : (i) those of which the correct referring use is regulated by some *general* referring-cum-ascriptive conventions ; (ii) those of which the correct referring use is regulated by no general conventions, either of the contextual or the ascriptive kind, but by conventions which are *ad hoc* for each particular use (though not for each particular utterance). To the first class belong both pronouns (which have the least descriptive meaning) and substantival phrases (which have the most). To the second class belong, roughly speaking, the most familiar kind of proper names. Ignorance of a man's name is not ignorance of the language. This is why we do not speak of the meaning of proper names. (But it won't do to say they are meaningless.) Again an intermediate position is occupied by such phrases as 'The Old Pretender'. Only an old pretender may be so referred to ; but to know which old pretender is not to know a general, but an *ad hoc*, convention.

In the case of phrases of the form 'the so-and-so' used referringly, the use of 'the' together with the position of the phrase in the sentence (*i.e.* at the beginning, or following a transitive verb or preposition) acts as a signal *that* a unique reference is being made ; and the following noun, or noun and adjective, together with the context of utterance, shows *what* unique reference is being made. In general the functional difference between common nouns and adjectives is that the former are naturally and commonly used referringly, while the latter are not commonly, or so naturally, used in this way, except as qualifying nouns ; though they cán be, and are, so used alone. And of course this functional difference is not independent of the descriptive force peculiar to each word. In general we should expect the descriptive force of nouns to be such that they are more efficient tools

E

for the job of showing what unique reference is intended when such a reference is signalized; and we should also expect the descriptive force of the words we naturally and commonly use to make unique references to mirror our interest in the salient, relatively permanent and behavioural characteristics of things. These two expectations are not independent of one another; and, if we look at the differences between the commoner sort of common nouns and the commoner sort of adjectives, we find them both fulfilled. These are differences of the kind that Locke quaintly reports, when he speaks of our ideas of substances being *collections* of simple ideas; when he says that 'powers make up a great part of our ideas of substances'; and when he goes on to contrast the identity of real and nominal essence in the case of simple ideas with their lack of identity and the shiftingness of the nominal essence in the case of substances. 'Substance' itself is the troublesome tribute Locke pays to his dim awareness of the difference in predominant linguistic function that lingered even when the noun had been expanded into a more or less indefinite string of adjectives. Russell repeats Locke's mistake with a difference when, admitting the inference from syntax to reality to the extent of feeling that he can get rid of this metaphysical unknown only if he can purify language of the referring function altogether, he draws up his programme for 'abolishing particulars'; a programme, in fact, for abolishing the distinction of logical use which I am here at pains to emphasize.

The contextual requirement for the referring use of pronouns may be stated with the greatest precision in some cases (*e.g.* 'I' and 'you') and only with the greatest vagueness in others ('it' and 'this'). I propose to say nothing further about pronouns, except to point to an additional symptom of the failure to recognize the uniquely referring use for what it is; the fact, namely, that certain logicians have actually sought to elucidate the nature of a variable by offering such *sentences* as 'he is sick', 'it is green', as examples of something in ordinary speech like a *sentential*

function. Now of course it is true that the word 'he' may
be used on different occasions to refer to different people or
different animals : so may the word 'John' and the phrase
'the cat'. What deters such logicians from treating these
two expressions as quasi-variables is, in the first case, the
lingering superstition that a name is logically tied to a single
individual, and, in the second case, the descriptive meaning
of the word 'cat'. But 'he', which has a wide range of
applications and minimal descriptive force, only acquires a
use as a referring word. It is this fact, together with the
failure to accord to expressions, used referringly, the place
in logic which belongs to them (the place held open for the
mythical logically proper name), that accounts for the misleading attempt to elucidate the nature of the variable by
reference to such words as 'he', 'she', 'it'.

Of ordinary proper names it is sometimes said that they
are essentially words each of which is used to refer to just
one individual. This is obviously false. Many ordinary
personal names — names *par excellence* — are correctly used
to refer to numbers of people. An ordinary personal name
is, roughly, a word, used referringly, of which the use is *not*
dictated by any descriptive meaning the word may have,
and is *not* prescribed by any such general rule for use as a
referring expression (or a part of a referring expression) as
we find in the case of such words as 'I', 'this' and 'the', but
is governed by *ad hoc* conventions for each particular set of
applications of the word to a given person. The important
point is that the correctness of such applications does not
follow from any *general* rule or convention for the use of the
word as such. (The limit of absurdity and obvious circularity
is reached in the attempt to treat names as disguised description in Russell's sense ; for what is in the special sense implied,
but not entailed, by my now referring to someone by name
is simply the existence of someone, *now being referred to*,
who is *conventionally referred to* by that name) Even this
feature of names, however, is only a symptom of the purpose
for which they are employed. At present our choice of names

is partly arbitrary, partly dependent on legal and social observances. It would be perfectly possible to have a thorough-going *system* of names, based *e.g.* on dates of birth, or on a minute classification of physiological and anatomical differences. But the success of any such system would depend entirely on the convenience of the resulting name-allotments for the purpose of making unique references; and this would depend on the multiplicity of the classifications used and the degree to which they cut haphazard across normal social groupings. Given a sufficient degree of both, the selectivity supplied by context would do the rest; just as is the case with our present naming habits. Had we such a system, we could use name-words descriptively (as we do at present, to a limited extent and in a different way, with some famous names) as well as referringly. But it is by criteria derived from consideration of the requirements of the referring task that we should assess the adequacy of any system of naming. From the naming point of view, no kind of classification would be better or worse than any other simply because of the kind of classification — natal or anatomical — that it was.

I have already mentioned the class of quasi-names, of substantival phrases which grow capital letters, and of which such phrases as 'the Glorious Revolution', 'the Great War', 'the Annunciation', 'the Round Table' are examples. While the descriptive meaning of the words which follow the definite article is still relevant to their referring rôle, the capital letters are a sign of that extra-logical selectivity in their referring use, which is characteristic of pure names. Such phrases are found in print or in writing when one member of some class of events or things is of quite outstanding interest in a certain society. These phrases are embryonic names. A phrase may, for obvious reasons, pass into, and out of, this class (*e.g.* 'the Great War').

V

I want to conclude by considering, all too briefly, three further problems about referring uses.

(*a*) *Indefinite references.* Not all referring uses of singular expressions forestall the question 'What (who, which one) are you talking about?' There are some which either invite this question, or disclaim the intention or ability to answer it. Examples are such sentence-beginnings as 'A man told me that . . .', 'Someone told me that . . .' The orthodox (Russellian) doctrine is that such sentences are existential, but not uniquely existential. This seems wrong in several ways. It is ludicrous to suggest that part of what is asserted is that the class of men or persons is not empty. Certainly this is *implied* in the by now familiar sense of implication; but the implication is also as much an implication of the *uniqueness* of the particular object of reference as when I begin a sentence with such a phrase as 'the table'. The difference between the use of the definite and indefinite articles is, very roughly, as follows. We use 'the' either when a previous reference has been made, and when 'the' signalizes that the same reference is being made; or when, in the absence of a previous indefinite reference, the context (including the hearer's assumed knowledge) is expected to enable the hearer to tell *what* reference is being made. We use 'a' either when these conditions are not fulfilled, or when, although a definite reference *could* be made, we wish to keep dark the identity of the individual to whom, or to which, we are referring. This is the *arch* use of such a phrase as 'a certain person' or 'someone'; where it could be expanded, not into 'someone, but you wouldn't (or I don't) know who' but into 'someone, but I'm not telling you who'.

(*b*) *Identification statements.* By this label I intend statements like the following:

(i*a*) That is the man who swam the channel twice on one day.

(ii*a*) Napoleon was the man who ordered the execution of the Duc d'Enghien.

The puzzle about these statements is that their grammatical predicates do not seem to be used in a straightforwardly ascriptive way as are the grammatical predicates of the statements :

(i*b*) That man swam the channel twice in one day.
(ii*b*) Napoleon ordered the execution of the Duc d'Enghien.

But if, in order to avoid blurring the difference between (i*a*) and (i*b*) and (ii*a*) and (ii*b*), one says that the phrases which form the grammatical complements of (i*a*) and (ii*a*) are being used referringly, one becomes puzzled about what is being said in these sentences. We seem then to be referring to the same person twice over and either saying nothing about him and thus making no statement, or identifying him with himself and thus producing a trivial identity.

The bogy of triviality can be dismissed. This only arises for those who think of the object referred to by the use of an expression as its meaning, and thus think of the subject and complement of these sentences as meaning the same because they could be used to refer to the same person.

I think the differences between sentences in the (*a*) group and sentences in the (*b*) group can best be understood by considering the differences between the circumstances in which you would say (i*a*) and the circumstances in which you would say (i*b*). You would say (i*a*) instead of (i*b*) if you knew or believed that your hearer knew or believed that *someone* had swum the channel twice in one day. You say (i*a*) when you take your hearer to be in the position of one who can ask : 'Who swam the channel twice in one day ?' (And in asking this, he is not saying that anyone did, though his asking it implies — in the relevant sense — that someone did.) Such sentences are like answers to such questions. They are better called 'identification-statements' than 'identities'. Sentence (i*a*) does not assert more or less than sentence (i*b*). It is just that you say (i*a*) to a man whom you take to know certain things that you take to be unknown to the man to whom you say (i*b*).

This is, in the barest essentials, the solution to Russell's puzzle about 'denoting phrases' joined by 'is'; one of the puzzles which he claims for the Theory of Descriptions the merit of solving.

(*c*) *The logic of subjects and predicates.* Much of what I have said of the uniquely referring use of expressions can be extended, with suitable modifications, to the non-uniquely referring use of expressions; *i.e.* to some uses of expressions consisting of 'the', 'all the', 'all', 'some', 'some of the', etc. followed by a noun, qualified or unqualified, in the *plural*; to some uses of 'they', 'them', 'those', 'these'; and to conjunctions of names. Expressions of the first kind have a special interest. Roughly speaking, orthodox modern criticism, inspired by mathematical logic, of such traditional doctrines as that of the Square of Opposition and of some of the forms of the syllogism traditionally recognized as valid, rests on the familiar failure to recognize the special sense in which existential assertions may be implied by the referring use of expressions. The universal propositions of the fourfold schedule, it is said, must *either* be given a negatively existential interpretation (*e.g.* for A, 'there are no Xs which are not Ys') *or* they must be interpreted as conjunctions of negatively and positively existential statements of, *e.g.*, the form (for A) 'there are no Xs which are not Ys, and there are Xs'. The I and O forms are normally given a positively existential interpretation. It is then seen that, whichever of the above alternatives is selected, some of the traditional laws have to be abandoned. The dilemma, however, is a bogus one. If we interpret the propositions of the schedule as neither positively, nor negatively, nor positively *and* negatively, existential, but as sentences such that *the question of whether they are being used to make true or false assertions does not arise except when the existential condition is fulfilled for the subject term*, then all the traditional laws hold good together.   And this interpretation is far closer to the most common uses of expressions beginning with 'all' and 'some' than is any Russellian alternative.   For these expressions are most commonly used in the referring way.   A literal-minded and childless man asked whether all his children are asleep will certainly not answer 'Yes' on the ground that he has none;   but nor will he answer 'No' on this ground. Since he has no children, the question does not arise.   To say this is not to say that I may not use the sentence, 'All my children are asleep', with the intention of letting someone know that I have children, or of deceiving him into thinking that I have.   Nor is it any weakening of my thesis to concede that singular phrases of the form 'the so-and-so' may sometimes be used with a similar purpose.   Neither Aristotelian nor Russellian rules give the exact logic of any expression of ordinary language;   for ordinary language has no exact logic.

UNIVERSITY COLLEGE, OXFORD

Chapter III

THE PICTURE THEORY OF MEANING

BY E. DAITZ

How can words have meaning ? You may answer that a
word is, in a way, a picture, and that its meaning is what it
pictures; and if words are put together to make a sentence,
they can picture a more complex unit, the fact. Let us call
this the Picture Theory of Meaning. I hope to show why it
must be a wrong account of 'how words mean'. Some
philosophers hold the Picture Theory outright. Others,
although they do not say explicitly that names of things are
like pictures of things, or that sentences picture facts, yet
describe language in terms that properly describe not language but pictures. I shall mostly draw examples from
three sources : Russell, Wittgenstein's *Tractatus Logico-*
Philosophicus, and Wisdom's articles on 'Logical Constructions'.

For ease of statement and with no commitment to any
use beyond that introduced, pictures, maps, sentences, etc.,
will be said to be signs that signify. A sign will be composed of elements. What the picture, etc., depicts, the
signified, will also be said to be composed of elements.

A picture, for example, might have as its elements splodges
of paint; if what it signifies is a landscape, the signified might
have as elements stones, leaves, trees. It is possible to set
up a correspondence between elements of the sign and elements of the signified : the brown strokes correspond to the
tree trunks, the green dots to leaves. However, a picture is
not a jumble of variegated paint patches. To show trees in a
forest the browns and greens must be disposed on the canvas
in a particular arrangement, an arrangement similar to the
arrangement of the leaves and the tree trunks they represent.
This elicits three characteristics of the relation which

holds between picture and pictured. The elements of a picture represent elements in the pictured. The arrangement of the elements in the picture shows the arrangement of the elements in the pictured. To each element in the picture there corresponds an element in the pictured. There are further features of 'picture' which influence elucidations of 'word' or 'sentence' in picture terms.

There is no differentiation of function among the elements of a picture. One patch of paint does not do this, and another that. All elements of a picture bear the same relation to the elements of the pictured : that of 'representing'. Further, the terms between which the relation of picturing holds, the picture and the pictured, are both entities in the sense that, unlike dreams or the meanings of words, they are among the furniture of the world. When a picture stands in a relation to something which is not a thing, we no longer speak of it as picturing that thing. It illustrates a story; *The Old Wives' Tale* is not a thing and it is that which is illustrated. Or it is a graph of a temperature ; a record of nervous impulses in the brain ; a spatial interpretation of a symphony. Not only must both picture and pictured be entities, but they must also be entities in what — for want of a better word — I call the same *genre*. A picture is a visual pattern and can picture only what is visually accessible. A still-life of a duck cannot show the taste of the bird as it may show its markings. The sense in which a picture shows a tasty bird is the sense in which I see a tasty bird, that is, I see a bird which looks as if it would be succulent to the taste. I cannot *see* the taste of a bird any more than a picture can show it. As Wittgenstein says : '2.171 The picture can represent every reality whose form it has. The spatial picture, everything spatial, the coloured, everything coloured, etc.' Of course, picture and pictured cannot be in the identical *genre*. If they were, the one would be a replica, a duplicate, or a model of the other and not a picture of it. To be a picture something must be omitted, but what remains can show only features of the scene in the same *genre* as itself, *i.e.* certainly spatial and possibly coloured features.

It is now possible to summarize features we may expect in a description of language which uses the picture as a model. Elements of the sign will stand for, and be in one to one correspondence with, elements in the signified. The arrangement of elements in the sign will show the arrangement of the elements in the signified. There will be no diversity of rôle among the elements of the sign. Sign and signified will be entities in the same *genre*.

Look now at a description of language in picture terms. Wittgenstein says : '4.01 The proposition is a picture of reality. 4.0312 The possibility of propositions is based upon the principle of the representation of objects by signs. 3.21 To the configuration of the simple signs in the propositional sign corresponds the configuration of the objects in the state of affairs'. As in a picture, so in a proposition '4.0311 One name stands for one thing, and another for another thing, and they are connected together. And so the whole, like a living picture, presents the atomic fact'.

The *Tractatus* also satisfies the model's demand that sign and signified be in the same *genre*. It achieves this by equating the sign (the proposition) to the signified (the fact). '2.1 We make ourselves pictures of facts. 2.141 The picture is a fact.' Russell, in *Our Knowledge of the External World*, is constrained 'to preserve the parallelism in language as regards facts and propositions' (p. 63) and to talk of the one as he talks of the other for the same reason. In addition propositions and facts must become entities. '3.1431 The essential nature of the propositional sign becomes very clear when we imagine it made up of spatial objects (such as tables, chairs, books) instead of written signs.' Here Wittgenstein thinks of propositions and — since propositions coincide with facts — of facts as complexes of objects. So does Wisdom : 'It is true that the fact expressed by "This is red" is not merely two things *this* and *red*. It is these two stuck together and stuck together in a certain way' (*Mind*, 1931, p. 197). Again, Wisdom writes — note the italics and

initial capital substituted for the significantly omitted 'that'
— 'suppose I say "Some dogs are sleepy" and speak truly.
Then there will be one or two facts out in the big world of
this sort : *This is a dog and this is sleepy*, *That is a dog and
that is sleepy*, *Thet*[1] *is a dog and etc.*' (*Mind*, 1931, p. 473).
That on this model facts are things is here even plainer.

Different philosophers may make different use of the
picture model. They may pick on different features or stop
short where another might go on. Wittgenstein asserts a
correspondence between elements of the sign and elements
of the signified ('3.2 In propositions thoughts can be so expressed that to the objects of the thoughts correspond the
elements of the propositional sign') but does not go on to
assert that this correspondence is one to one. There are
elements in the sign, *e.g.* the logical constants, which do not
represent, that is, do not stand for objects. Nor, in consequence, does he assign the same rôle to all elements in the
proposition. Wisdom, on the other hand, adopts these two
features of the picture model. There must be an isomorphism
of elements in the proposition and the fact — this is what he
means by 'identity of form' ; and all elements in the proposition stand for elements in the fact. Wisdom says they are
all Demonstrative Symbols in Stebbing's sense — ('A
demonstrative phrase is like a bodily gesture, it points at
something for consideration.' *A Modern Introduction to
Logic*, p. 15) — that is, they all perform the same function.

At once, for views like these there are difficulties. Consider first those created by the notion that elements of the
sign stand for elements in the signified. Take the phrase
'The river' in 'The river is long'. For what could it stand ?
The river ? But then, since all words in the sentence stand
for an object, for what does 'long' stand ? The river too ?
But this is absurd. Shall we say then that 'The river' stands
for the river without its length, and 'long' stands for its
length ? This is to take the road that will end at the bare
particular. Or shall we say that 'The river' stands for the

[1] This is a new demonstrative invented by Wisdom *ad hoc*.—EDITOR.]

river with all its properties and 'long' stands for its length, *i.e.* one of its properties ? This makes all relations internal. Clearly, a 'stand for' account of the function of the words in a sentence will not do. Equally clearly, theories of meaning which say: The name means the object, even if they do not acknowledge it, use 'mean' with the logic of 'stand for'. And how can it apply at all to conditional sentences or negative sentences ? Does 'not' name an element in the world ? If it does, how odd an element ; if it doesn't, how do we describe the difference between 'This is red' and 'This is not red' ? 'This', confesses Wisdom (*Mind*, 1932, p. 461), 'is the sleeping dog negation and we hurry past. . . .'

Again, how can the view that the arrangement of elements in the sign shows the arrangement of elements in the signified account for statements, which, though they have a different arrangement of elements yet express the same fact ? May not 'This is red and round' and 'This is red and this is round' state the same fact ? Either it must be claimed that no two sentences can ever express the same fact — which is to deny a use to 'same fact' — or it must be admitted that the arrangement of elements in the sentence does not always show the arrangement of elements in the fact, that some sentences are better at doing this than others, *e.g.* that 'This is red and this is round' more nearly shows the arrangement of elements in the fact than the misleadingly telescoped 'This is red and round'. And then the suspicion arises that no ordinary sentence intimates really well the structure of the fact, that only some as yet undisclosed sentences could do this, perhaps; or is it that no *sentence* can be used to do this at all ?

Consider next difficulties created by the transformation of facts into things. There is a modicum of plausibility in 'The fact *Sophia hit me* is in the world'; there is no semblance of it in 'The fact *Something hit me* is in the world'. While the first fact is composed of *Sophia* and *me* in a certain relation, what would be the elements of the second fact ? *Something* and *me* ? But what sort of thing is *something* ? Sentences like 'Everything which is round is red', 'The thing which is round is red' pose the same problem as will any sentence not composed of names of objects and simple verbs. Clearly, a philosopher committed to treating facts as things must discard embarrassing elements like *something*, *everything*, *the thing which*, etc. Consider, for instance, the devices Wisdom resorted to. His first stratagem is to introduce the new relation of 'referring'. He separates the fact *expressed* by these embarrassing sentences from the facts to which they *refer*. The facts referred to are always of the satisfactory concrete sort. 'Suppose I say "Some dogs are sleepy" and speak truly. Then there will be one or two facts out in the big world of this sort : *This is a dog and this is sleepy. That is a dog and that is sleepy. Thet is a dog and etc.* What I refer to by my sentences are these facts. What I express by my sentence is *the* fact that there are such facts as these.'

This is unsatisfactory : the fact expressed still contains deplorable elements. Wisdom's second expedient is to jettison both the relation of 'expressing' and his self-devised 'referring'. He invents a new one — 'locating'. Sentences now simply locate facts. The difference between 'Sophia hit me' and 'Something hit me' is now describable as a difference in completeness of location. 'Sophia hit me' precisely locates the fact *Sophia hit me*. 'Something hit me' partially locates the facts *Sophia hit me, Amos hit me, Martha* . . . The facts are all composed of tangible elements with no difficult *somethings*, or *everythings* occurring in them. Thus we find old facts discarded, like the fact that someone hit me, and new facts invoked, like *Sophia hit me, Amos hit me, Martha* . . . We find that the intimate link between sentence and fact has been broken, and in its place a loose union between a sentence and countless other facts. Would one not have thought that 'Someone hit me', if related to any fact, would be related to the fact that someone hit me, and not to *Sophia hit me, Amos hit me, Martha* . . .?

Finally, consider one of the consequences of the assimilation of sentences to facts. '3.1432 We must not say "The complex sign '*aRb*' says '*a* stands in relation R to b'"' ; but we must say, "that 'a' stands in a certain relation to 'b' says that aRb".' Normally we should say that it was a fact *about* the sign 'aRb' that 'a' stands in a certain relation to 'b', not that the sign 'aRb' *is* that fact. This way of converting sentences into facts creates a difficulty : in conversion, an n-termed sentence becomes an $n+1$-termed fact. Consider 'Sophia hates Amos'. This becomes the fact '*Hates*' *is between* '*Sophia*' *and* '*Amos*', which has the consequence that it is impossible to gear the form of a sentence to the form of the fact. The sentence 'Sophia hates Amos' is not identical in form with, *i.e.* has not the same number of elements as, the fact *Sophia hates Amos*. For the sentence is the fact '*Hates*' *is between* '*Sophia*' *and* '*Amos*', *i.e.* it has four elements while *Sophia hates Amos* has only three. This view brings with it the consequence that all ordinary sentences have, for fact-stating purposes, one word too many!

All these difficulties strengthen the suspicion that pictures are, as a model for sentences, unfortunate. In some cases, *e.g.* negative sentences, there is no fit ; in other cases, *e.g.* sentences containing words like 'something' contriving is needed to achieve a fit, and in even the best cases the fit is uncomfortable — it is time to examine closely pictures and sentences. To bring out their logic I propose also to examine reflections and maps.

Reflections, pictures, and maps share a feature of fundamental importance. They are icons.[1] An icon is a sign which has at least one of the properties of that for which it is a sign, and signifies in virtue of such a property. In a drawing of a cat with her small kitten, more of the picture will be occupied by the cat than the kitten ; the relative dimensions of the cat and the kitten are repeated in the picture of the cat and the kitten. Reflections, pictures, and maps duplicate the spatial properties of that which they reflect, picture, or map.[2] Sentences, on the other hand, are

[1] I adapt this term from C. S. Peirce.
[2] This is inaccurate. It fails to take account of the effects of, *e.g.*, perspective or projection. So to take account would complicate but not, I think, alter the description.

not icons. In the sentence 'The cat is bigger than the kitten', 'cat' is in the same type as 'kitten'. To convey our meaning we have no need to write 'THE CAT is bigger than the kitten'.

The next difference to notice between icons and sentences is important. Icons show, sentences state. A reflection in water shows the trees on its bank, a picture shows a girl holding a cat, a map shows the course of a river. A sentence states that the tree is on the river bank, that the girl holds a cat, that the river flows from north to south.

Before continuing it may be worthwhile to examine briefly a sense of 'show' which in this context is confusing. It is a sense different from the sense in which *e.g.* a picture of a girl holding a cat has been said to show a girl holding a cat. In the new sense of 'show' a picture of a girl holding a cat may show something other than a girl holding a cat; it may, in this sense, show the influence of a school of painting or that the artist's technique has improved. This sense of 'show' is applicable to sentences too. A sentence may show care in construction or that its writer spells poorly. It seems to me clear that 'show' in this sense of 'reveals' is not of direct interest to us. From now on I ignore it to discuss 'show' only in the sense in which an icon, but not a sentence, may show.

To continue, then, with the comparison of showing and stating. Both relations are resoluble into two components. Showing consists in representing and arranging, stating in referring and describing. Here the similarity ends. It is possible to point at a reflection in a river saying 'Look at the tree in the water'. Similarly, of a picture we may say 'This' — pointing at a line in a drawing — 'is the tree trunk', or of a map 'Here's Oxford and there's Woodstock' — indicating two dots with the finger. But we cannot say as we indicate one of the words in a sentence 'This is a tree'. The fact that icons are like what they signify is acknowledged by our willingness to say that the icon *is* what it signifies.

There is no locution alternative to 'is' for the relation

between the elements of a reflection and the elements of what it reflects. Its elements are trees, clouds, leaves. We do not say that a reflection represents or stands for or denotes or refers to the scene it reflects. Perhaps this is so because it is a causal phenomenon and these relations all imply an agent who uses the sign to represent, stand for, denote, or refer to the signified. The image on a television or cinema screen is spoken about in a similar way. 'Look, there's Philip Harben' and not 'Look, that represents, or stands for, etc. Philip Harben'. Of a picture, on the other hand, in addition to saying that a curved stroke is the tree trunk, we may say that it represents the tree trunk. Similarly, of a map, the dot which is Oxford may also be said to stand for Oxford. Instead of writing : The elements of an icon stand for, represent, or are, elements in the signified, let us use the single relation of representing and say : The elements of an icon represent elements in the signified. Now, showing is not merely representing. The elements of an icon must be in a certain arrangement. The lines which represent the trunk and the speckles which represent the leaves will not make a picture of a tree unless (roughly) the lines and speckles are arranged so that the speckles are on top of the lines. Thus the arrangement of the elements in the icon must be similar to the arrangement of the elements in what it signifies.

Now contrast showing, which we have resolved into representing and arranging, with stating. The elements of a sentence, viz. its words, neither are, nor do they stand for, or represent what they signify. 'Tree' is not a tree in the way that a drawing of a tree is a tree, and nor does 'tree' represent a tree in the way that a drawing does. Words have meaning — unlike strokes and lines — and are used to refer to and characterize things (these are two of many uses chosen because we are concerned with sentences in their fact-stating function). 'The tree is bare' both refers to a tree and describes it as bare. In 'The tree is bare', 'The tree' refers to an object and 'is bare' describes that object. So to

F

apportion the function of 'The tree' and 'is bare' is not, of course, quite correct as Strawson pointed out in 'On Referring' (Chapter II above). 'The tree' is descriptive as well as referential, as we see if we contrast it with 'It' in 'It is bare'.

Although stating, like showing, resolves into two components, the relations between stating, referring, and describing are different from the relations between showing, representing, and arranging. To begin with, referring and describing are not the counterparts of representing and arranging. Rather do both referring and describing correspond to the one relation of representing. Some elements of a sentence refer, some describe, some do both; all the elements of an icon represent. Arranging is an ordering of elements all of which represent, but describing is not an ordering of elements all of which refer. Describing is on a par with referring in the way in which arranging is not with representing.

Next, showing bears a relation to representing different from the relation that stating bears to describing and referring. A sentence states, but its elements cannot state. An icon shows — and so do its elements. Compare the sentence 'My cat sits on his cushion' with a picture of a cat on a cushion. If from the drawing I erase the cushion I leave a picture of a cat. The removal of 'sits on his cushion' from the sentence leaves, not a sentence, but a phrase. In other words, elements which represent also show; but elements which refer or describe do not also state. Not only do all the elements of an icon signify in the same way, but the icon signifies the way all its elements do. In contrast, a sentence states, but does not, as its elements do, refer or describe.

Finally we must notice that showing is not first representing and then arranging. Representing is simultaneous with arranging. Stating, on the other hand, is first referring and then describing, or perhaps first describing and then referring. The order in a sentence *may* contribute to fixing its meaning, but difference in meaning may be achieved by means other than difference in word order by, *e.g.*, case inflexion. The order found in a spatial icon, however, must contribute to fixing its significance. The order of words in a sentence is a conventional order of presentation; the spatial ordering of the elements in a reflection, picture, or map is an iconic order of representation.

By now it is clear that it is a mistake to think that showing is composed of representation and arrangement in the way that stating is reference and description. We now see that not only is showing unlike stating, but also that representing and arranging are related to showing in a way unlike the way in which referring and describing are related to stating.

There are further differences between icons and sentences. If all the elements in the sign represent elements in the signified, it is possible to set up a correspondence between the elements of each. In the case of a reflection the correspondence is clearly one to one. As Wisdom put it : 'When a mirror mirrors a scene then for each coloured patch in the reflection, there is a coloured patch in the scene and *vice versa. . . .*' A reflection may be blurred as in rippled water, or distorted as in a concave mirror ; these are respectively a defect of clarity and a peculiarity in projection. It cannot, however, omit detail. To each element in the scene there must correspond an element in the reflection. This does not hold good of pictures. Though it is still the case that a correspondence can be set up between the elements of a picture and the elements of the pictured, the correspondence need not be one to one. A portrait may be faithful to the last detail, but it may not. It may be a sketch, or an outline drawing, or even a composition design, showing only broad masses and omitting detail completely. Similarly, a map may omit detail, and in so far as it does, it ceases to be in one to one correspondence with that of which it is a map. For example, a map of England may show every English river, or it may show instead merely the main rivers. Reflections, pictures, maps, form a series of decreasing iconicity, *i.e.* they differ in the number of features they must have in common with what they signify. Language, of its mode though

signification is conventional and not iconic, contains a few
iconic devices like 'creak', 'buzz', 'tinkle'. These are similar
in sound to the sounds they may be used to refer to. Even
though it is only the elements of a reflection, and not of a
picture or map, which must be isomorphic with the elements
of the scene, it is still in general true that the elements of
an icon can be set in correspondence — though not always
in one to one correspondence — with the elements of that of
which it is an icon. This is so because *all* the elements of
an icon represent. We saw above that the elements of a
sentence have no function analogous to representing. At
best, referring is its analogue — and not all words refer.
Since the elements of a sentence do not represent elements
in the signified, *a fortiori*, the elements of a sentence do not
correspond to elements in the signified.

The elements of icons and sentences differ in another
respect. The elements of a sentence are part of a vocabulary,
the elements of an icon are not. Whether we take as elements
of an icon lines, dots, and patches, or meaningful combinations of such lines, dots, and patches, the point still holds.
If the lines, etc. are themselves to be taken as elements, then,
as they have no constant significance, they cannot constitute
a vocabulary, as the items in a vocabulary must be usable
with the *sâme* meaning on different occasions. A 2 cm. line
could be used to represent the side of a fan, a mouth, etc.
If meaningful combinations of lines, dots, etc., *i.e.* such combinations as represent a recognizable object, are taken as
elements, the elements of an icon still cannot form a vocabulary as they cannot be used in many situations: being
themselves icons, they represent a specific object. A sketch
of a face, for example, has a specific shape and a specific
arrangement of features; it represents *that* face and no
other. As iconicity decreases so the possibility of a vocabulary
increases.

Maps, which are less iconic than pictures and reflections,
have the beginnings of a vocabulary. Dots stand for towns,
crosses for churches, etc., and the dots and crosses are used

with the same significance in different instances. Since the signs may stand for other things in another map the vocabulary is relative to each map. Each map needs, therefore, a legend to interpret its signs. It would be possible to have a standard set of symbols for map-making, so that no key — for this purpose — was necessary. In practice some cartographic symbols are standard and others vary from map to map. They still constitute a vocabulary whether they have a constant significance merely for a particular map, or whether they are general cartographic conventions.

However, not all the elements in a map are items in a rudimentary vocabulary. Lines standing for rivers and sea-fronts are not so for the reasons that the elements of a picture are not. A map stands midway between a picture and a language. Its more iconic elements are like picture elements ; its less iconic and therefore more conventional elements are like language elements. The fact that maps and languages have a vocabulary is connected with another difference. A conventional sign does not, like an icon, show what it signifies. There is nothing in the sign 'cat' to show that it signifies a cat, as there is in a drawing of a cat. We have to learn the meaning of 'cat' in a way we do not have to learn the meaning of a drawing. We learn to read (significant idiom) a map because it is to some extent conventional.

Consider now the question of entities. That sentences, unlike icons, do not signify *qua* entity can be brought out by comparing a sentence with an icon. Take a picture of a cushion between a cat and a mouse, and the sentence 'This adjoins that'. To speak of the sentence as the fact that 'Adjoins' is between 'this' and 'that' (3.1432 . . . That '*a*' stands in a certain relation to '*b*' says that aRb) is to regard it as three marks in ink in the way that a picture of a cushion between a cat and a mouse is three marks in ink. But a sentence does not signify because it is a pattern of marks — its physical appearance is irrelevant in the sense that there is no correlation between appearance and function, *e.g.* homonyms look alike but have different meanings, a sentence looks no different from its component words, yet signifies differently, and so on. It is just because the sentence, unlike the picture, does not signify *qua* collection of ink marks, that we do not talk about it as the sentence 'Adjoins' is between 'this' and 'that' (cf. the picture of the cushion between the cat and the mouse). Nor is what is stated, a fact, on a par with the scene reflected, person pictured, or country mapped. Facts are not things. Anyone who holds that they are must do violence to the concept of fact. By this I mean that they must misuse the term 'fact', for I take the question of whether a fact is a thing, or an event or a true statement, to be the question of whether the idioms appropriate to the one are appropriate to the other (see Ch. VII below). Though fact and thing idioms merge, *e.g.* da Gama discovered the Canaries, Poirot discovered the facts, facts and things may be overlooked, concealed, unearthed, etc., the merging is minute compared to the vast terrain of each which remains separate. Facts cannot be broken or identified, they neither exist nor do they not exist. Yet they seem so brute, so inescapable, surely they are out there in the world — just like the table? But the table is not a fact, nor is the table is brown, nor the table being brown. That the table is brown is (or rather may be) a fact — and there are no 'thats' in the world.

We must now consider one last difference of great importance between icons and sentences. As icons signify by being like what they signify, their range of signification is limited. The special restriction of a reflection to what is in spatial proximity to it is unconnected with its iconicity, and due solely to the fact that it is a causal phenomenon. Both reflections and pictures, however, can show only spatial and coloured relations, *i.e.* they can show only what is in (what I earlier called) the same *genre* as themselves. A song or a taste can be neither reflected nor pictured. Maps, being less iconic and more conventional, may show the spatial relationships of a greater variety of things than reflections or pictures, *e.g.* although we cannot picture the equator, we can

mark it on a map. A map's range of signification expands
in other directions too. As well as geographical maps,
there are political maps, rainfall maps, ethnological maps.
This increase in scope depends upon and is accompanied by
an increase in conventionality. Since language is wholly
conventional it has an unlimited range. It is restricted to
no *genre* spatial or otherwise. To show you how someone
looks I can paint a picture; to show you how she sounds I
must sing, not paint; in words I can tell you both how she
looks and how she sings. It is the strength of the icon that
it signifies with great specificity. It is its weakness that it
can signify only what is like itself. Language can describe anything bar the ineffable—and even this it characterizes as such.

It seems to me that this review of reflections, pictures,
maps, and sentences reveals two vastly different modes of
signification : the iconic and the conventional. Earlier we
summarized the demands of the picture model. We can
now see them as demands which can only be fulfilled by a
misdescription of language. They demand, in effect, that
language signify iconically. But since language does not
signify in virtue of properties it has in common with what is
signified — it is not an icon — any description of it which
describes it as iconic misdescribes it. It is clear that sentences do not show, but state, that arrangement, which is
an essential factor in iconic signification, need not occur in
conventional signification, that the elements of a sentence
do not stand for objects but (may be used to) refer to or
describe objects. And since the words in a sentence do not
stand for objects, they cannot be in correspondence, let alone
one to one correspondence, with objects. Nor can a language
fulfil the demand that the sign be in the same *genre* as the
signified since it does not signify in virtue of being itself like
what is signified and nor, in the case of language, can the
sign and the signified be treated as things. A sentence and
a picture differ in the very respects in which — if the one is
to be a model for the other — they would have to resemble
one another.

It now becomes clear too why, on the picture model, sentences always have a word too many. An icon needs no mark for what it shows by likeness. A drawing of one thing adjoining another needs a mark for one thing and a mark for the other, but no mark for the relation of adjoining. This it shows by the spatial placing of the marks for the two things. A sentence needs a mark where a picture does not : it cannot show that this adjoins that, but must *say* so. (Wittgenstein was wrong in saying : '4.1212 What *can* be shown *cannot* be said'.) Say we drop the mark for *adjoins* and write 'This that' in place of 'This adjoins that'. How would we indicate that this adjoins as opposed to surpasses or divides into that ? Again, words like 'a', 'the', 'which', 'all', 'some', 'three', do a job which, as opposed to iconic, is characteristically linguistic. Since a language has a vocabulary, *i.e.* is composed of signs which may be used on different occasions to talk about different things, some device is needed to show which thing is being talked about on any given occasion. To say merely 'Cats on cushions' would not tell whether it is the cats (my neighbour's and my own), all cats, some cats, or no cats, that are on cushions. The function of 'the', 'all', 'some', 'no', is not to destroy the non-existent correspondence which holds between a sentence and a fact but to help identify which cats are being spoken about. Indeed, any censure of a word on the ground that its occurrence in a sentence wrecks the isomorphism between language and reality must be mistaken — language does not try so to correspond, and nothing, therefore, can cause it to fail to do so.

Why are negative statements, conditional statements, disjunctive statements, etc. not describable in picture terms ? The reason is that they are the very statements which have no pictorial counterparts. I can say that a cat is black and I can picture a black cat. But whereas I can also tell you that it is not black, I cannot picture this. To say that a cat is not black is not to say of what colour it is ; but if I paint I must paint a cat of *some* colour. And how could we show in a picture that all cats are black, that *the* cat (as opposed to *a* cat) is black ? The sentences which do not yield to the picture model are just those which cover a region no picture could picture. Variations in tense — we can picture a black cat but how could we picture a cat that was or will be black ? — is another example. And were a picture theory to succeed in the fact-stating sphere, some other account would still be needed for commands, questions, prayers, promises, hopes, wishes, fears. If we consider how small a proportion of actual discourse is composed of simple sentences of the cat-on-the-mat type, we see what a small part of language this model could even purport to elucidate.

Of course, iconic and conventional signs are not wholly diverse. At the least they share the grammar of 'sign'. For instance, both sorts signify well or ill. A portrait can be faithful, true to the original, or show a face as other than it is ; a map can be accurate or inaccurate ; a sentence, when used informatively, true or false. All are further alike in that they can signify in various 'projections'. A concave mirror will in a regular manner distort what it reflects ; a picture may be cubist or pointillist in its form of representation ; maps can be in different projections, *e.g.* Mercator's ; and a tale can be told in the first person singular, or in an impersonal reporter's idiom, in Freudian terms, etc. As well as variation in projection there is variation in style. By this I mean that there may be differences not due to any regular transformation. Idiosyncratic omissions, high-lighting of one detail rather than another, occur in stories, and also in pictures, *e.g.* a caricature, and in maps, *e.g.* a diagram. Again, pictures, maps, sentences, are all alike in this : to know if they are faithful, adequate, true, whether they distort or not, something other than themselves must be examined, that which they purport to reflect, picture, map, or describe. It is also true that iconic signification slides into linguistic. Historically a large number of our conventional signs have come ultimately from pictographs. The prejudice that what has a common source has common properties may

lead us to think icons and linguistic signs more alike than
they are. Thus Wittgenstein could say : '4.016 In order to
understand the essence of the proposition, consider hiero-
glyphic writing, which pictures the facts it describes. And
from it came the alphabet without the essence of the representation being lost'. Picture languages embody the transi-
tion from iconic to conventional, having signs at once both
(hieroglyphs for instance). Such signs may be representa-
tional to a larger or smaller extent. The human figure with
protruding ribs that represents famine or the weeping eye
that stands for sorrow are stylized pictures, ideographs,
representing simple abstract ideas. If a drawing of an eye
comes to represent not only ideas suggested by eyes but also
all homonyms of 'eye', then a sign of purely phonetic value
has emerged, and the picture has become conventionalized.
All this fills in the fissure between iconic and conventional
signification.

None the less, although an icon and the elements in it
represent, neither the proposition nor its parts represent. A
picture has parts which are little pictures, that is, an icon
stands for something just as its elements do. But with a
sentence the case is different. Parts of a sentence are not
themselves sentences and though its elements may refer to
or describe something the sentence itself cannot. Put in
this way, it is clear that it is a possible description of the
search for a correlate of a sentence to parallel the correlates
of the words in a sentence, to say that it is an assimilation
of stating to showing. This is, among other things, to
imagine that just as the icon, like its elements, represents
something, so the sentence, like its elements, refers to something. We see too why the picture can be a model for words
as well as sentences. Since the elements of a picture are
themselves pictures one could think that words are pictures,
as well as that a sentence is a picture. Thus we might say
that 'the name like the picture is an imitation of the thing'
(Plato, *Cratylus* 430) or that 'The proposition is a picture of
reality' (*Tractatus* 4.12).

Consider the 'picture' elucidation of names. This may be put as 'The name means the object, the object is its meaning'. To say this is to use 'means' with the logic of 'stand for' or 'represent', *i.e.* to construe words on the iconic model. The attendant puzzle : 'If the word means *this* object, perhaps the one by which it is ostensively defined, how can it mean any other object ?' comes from trying to fit an essentially linguistic attribute into an iconic description. If an icon represents *this* object, it can represent no other. A painting of a red rose shows a rose of a determinate shade and a particular shape and the picture cannot picture a rose of any other colour or shape. An icon must always be specific. A language on the other hand has signs that can be used with the same meaning on different occasions. Thus to ask : 'How if the word means this object can it mean another ?' is first to assimilate words to icons and then to demand that an icon signify linguistically. This is to ask of a sign that it at once 'mean' the object (signify *specifically*) and have meaning (signify so that there are *general* directions for its use). The complaint that words are too indeterminate in their signification — which often accompanies the thesis that the name means the object — can be viewed as a complaint that words are not iconic enough in their signification. The ideal name would picture, say, a particular.

Although the Picture Theory brings with it puzzles that even its holders recognize as insoluble, it nevertheless seems to have the virtue of dealing adequately with two questions, which may, as a result of certain philosophical views, become problems : How is it that we immediately understand a sentence we have never heard before ? How can a false sentence have meaning ?

We *understand* a new combination of words for the same reason, we might say, that we comprehend a picture on seeing it for the first time. No explanation is necessary in either case : the picture 'speaks' for itself, it shows what it pictures ; the sentence speaks for itself, it 'shows' its sense.

The parallel is most clearly stated by Wittgenstein: '4.01 The proposition is a picture of reality. 4.02 This we see from the fact that we understand the sense of the propositional sign, without having had it explained to us. 4.021 The proposition is a picture of reality for I know the state of affairs presented by it, if I understand the proposition. And I understand the proposition without its sense having been explained to me. 4.022 The proposition *shows* its sense. 4.027 It is essential to propositions that they can communicate a new sense to us'. This seems to explain how it is that we can understand a new sentence, but does it really? A sentence does not show its meaning — consider the impenetrability of a sentence in an unmastered language. To understand a statement we must first have learnt the language in which it is made — but in the sense in which there are foreign languages there are no foreign pictures. Only if learning was unnecessary for languages too would Wittgenstein be right in saying '4.03 A proposition must communicate a new sense with old words. The proposition communicates to us a state of affairs, therefore it must be essentially connected with the state of affairs'. We do not understand a sentence on first hearing it because it is *essentially* connected with reality; for a sentence is *conventionally* connected with reality. '4.012 It is obvious that we perceive a proposition of the form *aRb* as a picture. Here the sign is obviously a likeness of the signified.' But a sentence, unlike a picture, is not a likeness of the signified, so that this must fail to explain how we find a new sense in old words. Indeed, the picture view itself creates the need for an 'explanation'. This is the puzzle, this time with sentences instead of names, of how if the sign means *this*, can it ever mean anything else? As before, the puzzle pivots on saying that the sign is an iconic sign and then wishing that it would function as a linguistic sign.

The Picture Theory appears also to explain how a *false* sentence can have meaning. We can come to be perplexed about the meaning of false sentences as a result of a view such as Russell's that 'the components of the fact which makes a proposition true or false . . . are the *meanings* of the symbols we must understand in order to understand the proposition' ('The Philosophy of Logical Atomism', *The Monist*, 1918–19). This view apparently accounts for the meaningfulness of true propositions, for in this case the fact 'corresponds in a way that makes the proposition true'. Suppose it is a fact that this is red and I say: 'This is red', then 'this' means *this* and 'red' means *red*. But what if I say: 'This is blue' when in fact this is red ? 'This' means *this* but what now does 'blue' mean ? What component in the fact that this is red *can* blue mean ? Either we must say that since *blue* is not a component of the fact — viz. this is red — which makes 'This is blue' false, 'blue' has no meaning, or we must say that 'blue' means *red* — in 'the false way'. Neither pleases. It seems better to press the model further and say that just as a picture shows what it pictures even when it does not picture any actual thing so a sentence shows what it means even when it does not mean any actual fact. '4.061 If one does not observe that propositions have a sense independent of the facts, one can easily believe that true and false are two relations between signs and things signified with equal rights. 2.22 The picture represents what it represents independently of its truth or falsehood, through the form of representation. 2.221 What the picture represents is its sense. 4.022 The proposition *shows* its sense.' Since, as was pointed out earlier, a proposition can show only what is *other* than its sense this account of the meaningfulness of false sentences is not correct. Nevertheless, by making meaning independent of truth or falsity it does come nearer a right description.[1]

Finally, let us notice it is not for nothing that philosophers thought 'there will always be a certain fundamental identity of structure between the fact and the symbol for it'. The truth in this is that a sentence 'S' cannot be used to state in any way inadequately the fact that S. 'S' may default in

[1] See Strawson, 'On Referring', Chapter II above.

the statement of a fact F only if 'S' is other than 'F'. 'S', for example, may state approximately the fact that F, where 'S' is an approximation to 'F', *e.g.* 'There are two thousand men on strike' says in round figures or is a less precise statement of 'There are 1763 men on strike'. Take another case. 'S' may state without detail the fact that F, where 'S' is a sentence giving less information than 'F', *e.g.* 'She walked up the hill' states a bare, a plain, an unvarnished fact compared with 'She walked slowly up the hill singing all the way'. A hesitation can of course appear whether 'S' states the fact that F in a less detailed way than 'F', or whether 'S' and 'F' state different facts. Does 'She walked up the hill with Roderick' add a detail to the fact that she walked up the hill or state a further fact about her? There seems to be a tendency to give the answer that 'S' adds a detail to 'F' if 'S' and 'F' are linguistically similar, and to give the opposite answer, to say 'F' states a new fact, if 'S' and 'F' are linguistically different. 'She walked up the hill with Roderick' adds a detail to the fact that she walked up the hill. 'Roderick was her escort' supplies a fact additional to the fact that she walked up the hill.

The important point for us is that the question whether 'S' states the fact that F loosely or approximately, in less or in great detail, cannot arise unless 'S' is different from 'F'. It makes no sense to ask whether 'The cat is on the mat' is an approximate, a plain, a full, or an adequate statement of the fact that the cat is on the mat. If 'S' is identical with 'F', *i.e.* when 'S' states the fact that S, then 'S' states altogether adequately the fact that S, is, if you like, in perfect correspondence with the fact it states. But if, in such a case, we put it this way, we must mean by correspondence no more than that it makes no sense to question the fitness of 'S' to state the fact that S. Sentences and facts cannot correspond in any way that suits the needs of a Correspondence Theory of Language.

Chapter IV

METAPHYSICS IN LOGIC [1]

BY G. J. WARNOCK

ONE is not accustomed in philosophy nowadays to the assumption that one is either a Platonist or a Nominalist. These venerable names, with their deceptive suggestion of clear and sharp opposition, are no longer regarded as profitable banners under which to attack philosophical problems and opponents, nor as party titles exhausting the possibilities of disagreement. However, disputes couched in exactly these terms are still keenly waged among mathematical logicians. It is said that there is, attached to the study of mathematical logic, a different and in some ways more important enquiry, called Ontology: and that leading questions in this enquiry are, for example; what abstract entities there are in addition to the concrete objects with which we are all familiar; or whether, on a more radical view, there may be no abstract entities at all. The central ontological question is, it seems, the question whether there are abstract entities. It is commonly supposed that there is no difference of principle (though certainly there are very many differences of some sort) between properties, relations, concepts, numbers, classes; that all of them are in some way reducible to classes, and so that the admission of these lets in all the rest. And accordingly as one does or does not make this admission, one is a Platonist or a Nominalist.

[1] This is an extensively revised version of a paper originally published in the *Proceedings of the Aristotelian Society* for 1950–51. That paper was very defective, being confused at many points, in some passages irrelevant, and written also in a rather disagreeable polemical tone. The present version, though still directed at the same targets, is milder, shorter, and, I hope, much clearer. I am most grateful to the editor for allowing me the opportunity to make these changes.

It is, as one would expect, exceedingly difficult to come to grips with this debate, since the doctrines between which one is to choose are so curiously worded. Do we believe that there is a 'reality behind linguistic forms'? Surely we do. But Professor Quine regards this as the thin end of the Platonic wedge,[1] which we must be prepared to extrude if we wish to 'renounce abstract entities'. Are we willing, or not, to make this renunciation? But we do not know what it is that we are invited to renounce. It would be both arrogant and rash to assume that these queer-looking disputes are quite without substance, but it does not appear at first sight that any sensible choice could be made between such alternatives.

Professor Quine has made numerous highly expert attempts to sharpen the ontological issue for us. However, in this paper I shall seek to show that the apparatus which he brings to bear does not clearly or naturally *apply* to some at least of the fields in which he has advocated its employment. I believe that some scrutiny of the logical symbolism and logicians' devices which he uses, and some comparison of these with certain features of ordinary language, will reveal that the logician's apparent sharpening of the issue involves in part the manufacturing of unnecessary problems, and in part a distortion of what may be quite serious problems ; and I shall suggest that this may come about through an insufficient sense of the perils involved in imposing the neat simplicities of logic upon the troublesome complexities of language. It is hardly necessary to say that I pick no quarrel with mathematical logic itself, but only with some of the peripheral uses to which its weapons are sometimes put. The particular weapon which is, as I shall suggest, importantly misused in the present case is the existential quantifier.

A preliminary distinction should be made at once. The central ontological question is, as I said above, the question whether there are abstract entities. But this question is in

[1] 'On Universals', *Journal of Symbolic Logic*, September 1947.

an important sense secondary to the question whether some given system of discourse *implies* that there are abstract entities. The initial problem is said to be that of detecting the 'ontological commitments' of a language or some department of a language; thereafter the different question can be raised what language, and hence what commitments, one is to adopt. It is not suggested that any strictly logical tests will serve to answer the latter question, which seems to be regarded as 'pragmatic'; it is, however, claimed that the question of ontological commitment falls within the purview of the logician. As Quine puts it, 'perhaps we can reach no absolute decision as to which words have designata and which have none, but at least we can say whether or not a given pattern of linguistic behaviour *construes* a word W as having a designatum'; [1] and one is held to be ontologically committed to the existence of such entities as must be designated by those expressions of one's language which one takes to be designating expressions. A nominalistic language will be such that all expressions in it which are taken to have designative uses designate only concrete objects; a platonistic language will be such that it contains expressions, construed as having designative uses, the designata of which must be abstract entities. The first problem, then, is that of deciding whether a given language or part of a language is platonistic or nominalistic; and if satisfaction were obtained on this point, it would be possible to proceed to the further question, which is the proper sort of language to use.

(1) 'WHAT IS THERE?'

Are there classes? Do numbers exist? Are there such things as abstract entities? Quine has on more than one occasion boiled down such typical ontologists' questions to the simple and uncompromising formula, 'What is there?'

It needs no argument to show that this way of posing

---

[1] 'Designation and Existence', *Journal of Philosophy*, 1939.

the question, perhaps never meant to be taken seriously, is unprofitable; it appears to invite a quite indefinite and possibly endless range and variety of answers. There is a pen in my hand; there is a pain in my ankle; there is a virtue in necessity; there is general confidence in the dollar. These are all correct expressions, and what they state may well be true. It cannot be supposed, however, that to add to such truths at random is the proper way to solve the ontological problem. We are really more interested in the question what *kinds* of things there are — are there abstract as well as concrete entities? — and even this question is, as has been pointed out, strictly secondary to the question what kinds of things we are committed to believing that there are. So let us try to approach this latter question more firmly.

(2) DESIGNATION

One method of approach to the problem begins with the unexceptionable assumption that, if a given expression designates something, then there is something which it designates; or more cautiously, that if an expression has a designative use, there is something which in that use it designates. If, for example, 'Tito' has a designative use, then there is such a person as Tito. It is taken for granted that there are concrete objects, such presumably as Tito, which may be designated; it is a question whether expressions which, if they had designative uses, would designate abstract entities, are in fact taken to have designative uses. If they are so taken, then we must hold that there are abstract entities; if not, not — or at any rate not unless they turn up in some other way.

We require, then, tests by which to decide what expressions are taken to have designative uses, and hence what we must hold that there is to be designated. Quine has more than once described two such tests, admitting that they are not absolutely conclusive. I shall seek to show that the case is worse than this.

The most important of these tests consists in an operation called 'existential generalization'. Suppose I say

(1) Leeds is a City

Then, since there is in fact a city of which 'Leeds' is the name, I am presumably entitled to state that there is something of which my statement is true. That is, I can safely assert

(1*a*) Something is a city. Or

(1*b*) There is something which is a city. Or even

(1*c*) There is an x such that x is a city.

If on the other hand I had said

(2) Valhalla is mythological,

I would certainly wish to convey that there is actually no such place; and it is assumed that I must object to the inference that there is something which is mythological. I must not allow

(2*a*) There is an x such that x is mythological,

since my point was that there is *not* a place called 'Valhalla'.

It is then argued that this difference between the logical behaviour of 'Leeds' and 'Valhalla' can be attributed to the fact that 'Leeds' is, and 'Valhalla' is not, taken to designate, name, or refer to an actual place. It might seem, then, that we have in this device a method of deciding in general whether or not a given expression is regarded as having a designative use, or (to put the point more insidiously) as designating *something*.

Suppose then that we try to apply this test of existential generalization to disputed cases — say to 'appendicitis', or '17', expressions which, it is held, must designate abstract entities if they designate anything at all. We might say, for instance,

(3) Appendicitis is painful. Or

(4) 17 is a prime number.

Now is there something of which each of these statements is true? Can we infer that something is painful, that something is a prime number?

But here we encounter a curious difficulty. How can we possibly decide whether or not to tolerate these inferences? The trouble is that

(3*a*) There is something which is painful, and
(4*a*) Something is a prime number,

are wholly odd and mystifying sentences, for which it is difficult to imagine plausible contexts of utterance. And for this reason it seems impossible to pronounce generally on the question of their admissibility.

But let us see what can be done. Suppose someone says, 'He is suffering from appendicitis'. I might, if I were uncertain about this diagnosis, reply, 'Perhaps he is; he is certainly suffering from something'; and it might turn out in the end to be appendicitis. Or suppose I have worked out a sum, and found the solution of it to be 17; but I forget this, and later when I try to re-work the sum I get stuck. In such a case I might well say, with an air of dogged bewilderment, 'Well, *something* was the right answer' — perhaps in order to insist that the sum does work out somehow, is not insoluble. There are thus some cases at least in which one might use 'something' where, if one had more or better evidence, or exact knowledge, one would instead have said 'appendicitis' or '17'; and so perhaps one would have no reason to object, though one might be extremely puzzled, if one were invited to reverse the usual procedure and to replace 'appendicitis' or '17' by 'something'. One decides, let us say, to accept existential generalization in these cases.

What does this prove? It is supposed to prove that one is thereby recognizing appendicitis and 17 as 'somethings', entities, and, furthermore, as abstract, Platonic entities. But surely it does not prove anything like this; for at this point one begins to encounter the invaluable non-simplicity of ordinary speech. The difficulty is that 'something' does not behave in the way required in the logician's argument. For if I inform a bored or inattentive listener that Valhalla is mythological, it would be perfectly in order for him, if questioned about our conversation, to say, 'He was telling me that something or other was mythological'; and this use of 'something' would not be taken as evidence that he thought there really was such a place, nor would his report be condemned as self-contradictory. And if I say, secretively, that I am imagining something, I do not thereby evince belief in the actual existence of what I imagine. If one were to use the queer-sounding sentences, 'There is something which is mythological', or 'There is something which I am imagining', one would certainly perplex one's hearers; but the use even of these odd sentences cannot be said to be flatly ruled out merely because the mythological does not, and the imagined may not, actually exist. Still less (indeed in no way) conclusive is the mere use of 'something', without 'there is', in sentences of a quite different construction.

It is in fact pretty obvious that one's readiness or reluctance to use 'something' in the cases mentioned has really no sort of connexion with the question whether or not one supposes that diseases, numbers, etc., are abstract entities, possible designata of abstract expressions. The word 'something' has an entirely different function. One is ordinarily disposed to use the word 'something' in cases where one does not know what in particular, or where for some reason one does not wish to specify; and there is no sharp restriction upon the sorts of expressions which in such cases one cannot or does not wish to use, so that one has recourse to the use of 'something'. Hesitation in admitting such sentences as (3a) and (4a) is indeed justified — not, however, because their admission would entail acceptance of any philosophical doctrine, but because it would be very hard to see when or why one might wish to say such things, or what one could possibly be getting at if one did.

The failure of existential generalization to do for us what is required can be explained, in part, briefly as follows. In manipulating the symbolism of logic, if I have the expression 'Fa', I am undoubtedly entitled to write down the expression '(Ǝx)Fx'; and in so far as the rules for the use of this expression are fixed, there is no uncertainty as to what is meant. But if I come across the expressions '17 is a prime number' or 'Valhalla is mythological', I cannot be sure that I am right if I say, 'Something is a prime number', nor can anyone else be sure that I am wrong if I say, 'Something is mythological'. For the former sentence is doubtfully admissible as English, the latter might be intelligible and true in suitable contexts. In any case it would be quite impossible to say, simply on the basis of someone's readiness to employ these sentences, that he was a Platonist or self-inconsistent; for in the ordinary language in which they purport to be expressed, they simply would not have the implications thus imputed to them.

But perhaps a yet more important consideration is this. The test of existential generalization is most simply employed as a device for revealing how names of actual persons, cities, etc., may be made to function differently in some contexts from story-tellers' names for mythical or fictitious persons and cities. But it is further supposed that the very same device can be applied at once to the job of detecting the existence or non-existence of abstract entities. This assumption appears to embody the supposition that the question whether there are or are not abstract entities is just like the question whether there is or is not a city called 'Leeds'; that, if there are no abstract entities, then appendicitis, etc., belong in the same list as Pegasus, Apollo, Mr. Pickwick; that, if '17' does not designate anything, it fails to do so in the same way as 'Cerberus' fails.

Now here again it is surely in point to draw a contrast between logic and language. If we have a form of discourse already reduced to the pattern of quantificational logic, then doubtless we can draw a simple distinction between expressions allowed to be 'substituends' for bound variables, and expressions debarred from such employment. But there is no warrant for the belief that expressions in ordinary language can be dichotomized in a similarly simple manner. It seems almost too obvious that no one device could force

'Pegasus', '23', 'intelligence', 'redness', and 'republican-ism' into a single bag. No doubt none of these designated a concrete object, but they fail to do so — if indeed they can be said even to fail — in ways that are utterly diverse. 'Pegasus' designates no concrete object, and it is true that there is no such thing as Pegasus ; 'republicanism' designates no concrete object, but that there is no such thing as re-publicanism is, of course, straightforwardly false; '23' does not designate a concrete object, but that there is no such thing as 23 is so queer a remark that, unless further explained, it must defy the assignment of any truth-value.

At this point a protest might also be entered against the alleged dichotomy between concrete objects and abstract entities. It is manifest that, unless this distinction is clear, we do not clearly know what Platonism or Nominalism is, and also that, unless it is exhaustive, we do not know that these are necessary alternatives. But consider such a list as the following : (1) 'gravitational field'; (2) 'the North Pole'; (3) 'the Heaviside layer'; (4) 'the Common Law'; (5) 'shadows'; (6) 'rainbows'; (7) 'the Third Republic'. Any of these expressions may occur in true or false state-ments not in fiction or myth. There is such a thing as the Common Law; there are such things as rainbows; there was such a thing as the Third Republic, etc. None of these things could be called a Universal; none has 'instances'; some require the definite article ; yet none would naturally be called 'concrete'; and it is at least uncertain which, if any, should be labelled 'particular'. What is referred to by (2) or by (3) has a definite position ; shadows and rainbows have dimensions; and the Third Republic had a definite duration. But shadows and rainbows, though visible, cannot be touched, heard, or smelt ; the Common Law cannot be seen, and also has no position, shape, or size ; the Heaviside layer can move, but cannot be seen or heard or felt to be moving. And so on. Again, it may very well be that in the symbolism of logic some clear distinction can be made corresponding to that alleged between the abstract and the concrete ; but that this is so, if it is so, settles nothing when we return to ordinary words. The distinctions here are perhaps not useless, but they are certainly neither precise nor exhaustive. It surely follows that — outside logic — no definite sense can be attached to the supposed assertions and denials of the Nominalist, just as no definite results could be obtained by the device of existential generalization.

The second test by which it has been hoped to identify expressions having designative uses is the converse of existential generalization, and is called 'application'. We have so far attempted to decide whether or not (say) 23 is an entity, or is thought to be so, by asking whether what is true of 23 is thereby true, or thought to be so, of an x, a something. It is now proposed that we take some formula which we know to be true of all x's, and ask whether it is thereby true of (say) appendicitis. Suppose we agree that, for all values of x, $x=x$; can we proceed to infer that appendicitis $=$appendicitis ?

This is not much help. In addition to the over-simplifications already noted, there is here the further defect that the conclusion to be drawn (or rejected) by application seems merely fantastic. Why should such an expression as 'appendicitis$=$appendicitis' ever be written down, uttered, asserted, or denied ? It says nothing whatever about anything ; it is not a mathematical equation ; it does not look like any sort of logicians' theorem. And if we were for any reason persuaded to allow this sort of expression, it would be hard indeed for the speaker of plain English to see why any version of it should be, or indeed how it could be, denied. 'Pegasus$=$Pegasus' looks odd, but not deniable ; there seems to be nothing wrong with 'pink$=$pink', nor yet with 'if$=$if'. If this is a test for designative use, then every expression designates.

Let me say again, at some risk of being tedious, what I think it is that goes wrong with the logico-ontologist's argument. It is supposed that because, in the symbolism of logic, certain distinctions can be clearly drawn and certain inferences made, the same should be true of discourse in general; that since we can be clear what sorts of logicians' expressions may be used, and how they may be used, in contexts of existential quantification, it should be possible similarly to discover the 'existential commitments' of ordinary talk. This is, however, not so. For the expressions supposed to correspond to the existential quantifier ('There is . . .', '. . . exists', 'Something . . .', 'There is something which . . .') are too diverse and intricate in their uses to yield the necessary results; and the supposed distinction between abstract and concrete entities is too wavering and non-inclusive. The Nominalist, launched with this inappropriate equipment upon the field of ordinary discourse, is obliged ('There is no such thing as appendicitis') to conduct his campaign in a manner so exceedingly awkward that doctors and other philosophical non-combatants must inevitably be assailed along with the Platonic army.

(3) Fragmentation of Sentences

I would next like to enter, consistently with my general thesis, a mild protest against another logicians' practice, doubtless innocent enough in many contexts, but liable to cause much perplexity in the present case. Consider the straightforward statement

(5) There is a prime number between 13 and 19.

This might indeed be called — though for reasons given below only with due caution — an existential statement, so that it should be a fair case for the use of the existential quantifier. But even here the conventions of logicians are fraught with some peril. For in their hands such a sentence is apt to become, by accepted translation of the symbolism,

(5a) There is something which is a prime number and is between 13 and 19.

It is important to notice that into this transformed version an 'and' has mysteriously entered, so that the whole sentence now appears to contain as a proper part the sentence, 'There is something which is a prime number', or 'There is a prime number'. But how is this surprising appearance generated ? It is of course an accepted rule of logic that from $(\exists x)(Fx.Gx)$ we may without qualms derive $(\exists x)Fx$; there is no doubt that the latter expression is well formed, or that it is entailed by the former. From this, however, it does not follow that the first half of (5) or (5a) is by itself an impeccable and intelligible sentence in English ; on the contrary, it is clearly not so. For if someone were to say, 'There is a prime number', and then stop, one would wait expectantly for the rest of his observation ; one would not suppose that he had already come to the end of it. One does not assert bare Being. 'Go on', one might say, 'what about it ?' And if he were merely to repeat, '*There is* a prime number', this being the whole of his contribution, one would be left in bewilderment. What can he be getting at ? Can he suppose that anyone has ever said that there is *not* a prime number ? And even if someone had ever said this, in what would the disagreement have consisted ? If one takes it for granted that the baffling fragment, 'There is a prime number' is really a proper part of a conjunctive sentence and so could stand alone, it may seem necessary — since it has no ordinary use — to invent some curious sense for it, to interpret it as meaning something odd — that there is an object called a prime number, an Entity, one of the things that *are*. Here indeed we seem to be treading Platonic ground ; but it is easy to see that by this path at least we would never have got there, if the original plain statement had not been broken in two. In general : Sentences of English cannot usually be taken to pieces in the way in which their corresponding formulae can be.

(4) EXISTENTIAL QUANTIFICATION

Let us now make a final and more head-on attack upon the logico-ontologist's apparatus. It is sometimes said, with a view to clarifying the issue, simply that we must admit into our accepted 'universe of entities' all those things which we allow to be values of the bound variables of quantification. We may discourse of classes, as Boole does, or of propositions, as in the propositional calculus, without thereby committing ourselves to Platonism ; for we can discourse in these ways without taking the fateful step of 'quantifying over' a class, or a proposition. If we take this crucial step, however, we fall into the ontological grip of the existential quantifier.

Let us begin at a point where all seems reasonably clear. We may, for example, wish to indicate that some algebraic formula holds for all values, or for at least one value, of the variable occurring in it ; and here 'values' has the familiar sense of 'numerical values'. Dealing with integers we might say, 'For all values of x, 2x is even', or 'For at least one value of x, x = 7 - 3'. And the first of these expressions states that whatever integer we choose, if we multiply it by 2 we have an even number ; the second that there is at least one integer equal to 7 minus 3.

But a statement of this latter kind has been thought to raise a peculiar difficulty. It might be described as an existential statement, and if so, do we not by making it commit ourselves to the important view that a certain number (in this case 4) *exists* ; and so, since a number is presumably an abstract entity, to the acceptance of Platonism ? Are we not thus trapped by the existential quantifier ?

To this there appear at once to be the following objections. First, the existential statement in question, whether true or false, can be shown to be true or false by purely mathematical operations. In fact every schoolboy knows quite well that it is true, even if he has never so much as heard of Plato, and there could be no serious argument about it. Further, even if one were to call for a full demonstration, one would be offered no contentious philosophical arguments, but only a bit of mathematics. The whole matter is entirely remote from the arena both of Platonic and of anti-Platonic philosophizing.

And in any case, second, the statement does not state that the number 4 exists, but only that there is an integer equal to 7 minus 3 — a very different matter. To say that there is a number of a certain sort is not at all the same as to *mention* a number and then assert that it exists. The question whether there is an integer equal to 7 minus 3 is closed, once we have said and if necessary shown that 4 is such a number. Whether the number 4 itself exists is, if there could be any such question at all, a quite different question — a different *sort* of question; and certainly we do not answer it in the affirmative merely by answering affirmatively the other question.

However, it seems, I suppose, tempting to argue that, if there is an integer equal to 7 minus 3, and 4 is such a number, then at least there must *be* such a number as 4. This I take to be odd, rather trivial, but presumably true. But even this does not either require or license us to say that the number 4 *exists*; for the phrases 'There is . . .', 'There is such a thing as . . .', and '. . . exists' are not, as they are so often assumed to be, synonymous and interchangeable.

Consider

(6) There are tigers in Africa.
(7) Tigers still exist.
(8) There are such things as tigers.

First, clearly (6) would sound odd and incomplete if we omitted from it the words 'in Africa'. It would then be, in fact, a mere fragment of a sentence, just as 'There is a prime number' was a fragment of a sentence. Sentence (7) is perfectly natural, in as much as it contains the word 'still', and thus would be understood as conveying the information that tigers are *not extinct*. 'Tigers exist' would be by comparison queer; it is not easy to see why anyone should want to say such a thing, though perhaps it might be intelligible enough in some suitable context. I think that (8) would usually be understood as a denial of the idea that tigers are fictitious or mythological beasts, employed to distinguish tigers from phoenixes and unicorns. It might have other uses, but this would be typical enough.

Now it is no doubt the case that the seriously made statement 'There are tigers in Africa' would not be true *unless* (*a*) tigers still existed, were not extinct, and (*b*) there were such things as tigers, non-fictitious, non-mythological. But it is equally clear that to say that there are tigers in Africa is not to *say* that tigers still exist, nor is it to *say* that there really are such animals. Of course there are connexions, but there are also marked differences, between these three statements; the situations, questions, counter-assertions, etc., which would naturally call for their utterance are quite distinct.

Consider next

(9) There are shadows on the moon.

There is no doubt that this is both intelligible and true. But in this case there seems to be no plausible counterpart to sentence (7). What could be meant by saying that shadows (or, the shadows) exist? There is no question of shadows being or not being extinct — of their still, or perhaps no longer, existing. Certainly we should not say that the shadows on the moon do *not* exist; this would be too much like saying that they are not really there (but are really seas, or due to defects of eyesight, etc.). But if we say that the shadows on the moon exist, or in general that shadows exist, might we not appear to be suggesting that shadows lie about on things as sheets do — that perhaps they could be taken up and erected for shelter? After all, a shadow is in many ways more like the absence of something than the presence of anything; in a way, there *is* nothing there when we say there's a shadow. And so, if someone were to ask whether shadows *exist*, we should not know what he had in mind, we should feel reluctant to answer either yes or no. We do not in fact use the word 'exist' in talk about shadows.

What then of 'There are such things as shadows'? The most plausible use that I can think of for this is an ironic one, calling attention to the obvious — addressed, for instance, to a painter who always leaves the shadows out of his pictures. Similarly, one might say 'There are such things as tigers' as an ironically phrased reason for not spending the night in the open. These remarks are clearly quite unlike the enigmatic 'Shadows exist', or 'Tigers exist'.

In this connexion numbers, classes, properties, etc. resemble shadows rather than tigers. We can say 'There is a number which, multiplied by 3, gives 21'; but we feel wholly baffled by the question whether this number *is*, whether it exists, whether numbers exist. No one surely supposes that numbers might be extinct, or that they figure only in legend and fiction; and every one knows that there is such a subject as arithmetic, that in this sense there are such things as numbers. Of course one does not wish to *deny* that numbers exist — one does not use the word 'exist' at all, in talk about numbers.

The expressions I have been considering are of course familiar ones, and it is really pretty obvious that they have different uses. However, employment of the existential quantifier is liable to blind the logician's eye to just such points as these. To this one device is given the job of symbolizing such phrases as 'There is . . .', 'There is such a thing as . . .', '. . . exists', and even 'Some . . .', 'At least one . . .', and 'There is something which . . .'. Because all these phrases are ordinarily dealt with by the use of the existential quantifier, it is easy to assume that they are interchangeable, all really the same; it may even be naïvely supposed that logic has somehow *proved* that they are really the same, and that one must be wrong if nevertheless one insists that they are different. (Too often the boot gets on the wrong foot in this way — as if a map-maker should complain that the mountains were inaccurate.) It is of course possible that *for some purposes* — perhaps for most of the purposes of logicians — the phrases in question are not relevantly different, and so that a single symbolic device may be more or less workable. If there is, say, a green book on my table, then it is at any rate *true*, for what it is worth, that there is something of which I could say 'It is a green book'; that there is at least one book which is green; that there is such a thing as a green book; even, perhaps, by stretching matters a little, that some books are green and that a green book exists. But for many *other* purposes the differences between these locutions will remain of vital importance. It will often be highly important to remember that where, for example, it is intelligible and true to say 'There is such a thing as x', to say that there is x or that x exists may be unintelligible, and even if not unintelligible will usually be different. Those who use expressions of the sorts supposed to correspond to the existential quantifier are not all saying the same kind of thing, nor can there be any single philosophical position to which they are committed by their readiness to use such expressions. The proper understanding of these expressions is not assisted, but on the contrary rendered almost impossible, by the lavish introduction of quantifiers. For thus the harmless will constantly be transformed into the peculiar; progress will be held up by unnecessary questions, needless scruples, and false dilemmas; and in the obscurity Plato's ghost will seem to be lurking.

I have been arguing in this paper that the efforts of the logician to clarify problems of ontology fail, since the devices employed all turn on notions of quantificational logic, particularly on the use of bound variables and the existential quantifier; and that this apparatus has little or no clear application to the ordinary words and idioms in which the problems are initially expressed. I need finally to defend this argument against the charge of irrelevance. Professor Quine has recently written[1] that 'the philosophical devotees of ordinary language are right in doubting the final adequacy of any criterion of the ontological presuppositions of ordinary language', since 'the idiomatic use of "there is" in ordinary

[1] *From a Logical Point of View*, p. 106.

language knows no bounds comparable to those that might reasonably be adhered to in scientific discourse painstakingly formulated in quantificational terms'. However, he observes that this is a minor affair, since the enquiry into ontological commitments is properly concerned, not with ordinary language at all, but with 'one or another real or imagined logical schematization of one or another part or all of science'. If so, it would of course follow that my argument, though within its own limits possibly sound, has been substantially beside the point. Now one way in which I might seek to ward off this charge would be by maintaining, first, that most of the last ten years' literature of ontology embodies no such awareness as Quine now expresses of the limitations of symbolism in application to ordinary language; and second, that there is also little evidence in that literature of any particular concern with science, except for one or two brief *statements that* some unspecified science is the subject ultimately in view. However, to adopt either of these courses would involve much rather acrimonious citation of texts, with much risk of distortion, misconstruction, and misunderstanding; it would be a mere exercise in *post mortem* polemics. In any case I think that it is more to the point to make a counter-charge of irrelevance. If it is true that ontology in its modern dress can get firmly to grips only with scientific discourse really or imaginedly schematized, then certainly it can have little relevance, if any, to philosophical problems about universals, concepts, etc. — abstract entities in general, the supposed subject-matter of the enquiry. For these problems arose from, can be posed, clarified, discussed, and (in their way) settled in, quite ordinary, unregenerate language; they can neither be confined to, nor settled in, language of any specially regimented pattern. If one cannot deal with philosophical problems of ontology upon the field of discourse in general, one cannot deal with them at all; one can only pass them by. This itself, if admitted, would be a useful conclusion to reach. At least it would be clear that there are problems which we cannot look to the logician to settle for us, and that the old problems of ontology remain among them.

Perhaps after all this is really to say no more than that they are philosophical and not logical problems. But in uttering this highly charged platitude, I suspect that one can only be pretending to have arrived at an absolutely uncontroversial terminus.

MAGDALEN COLLEGE, OXFORD

Chapter V

WHAT IS EXPLANATION?[1]

BY JOHN HOSPERS

I

WE are sometimes presented with a statement describing some observed fact, and when we ask 'Why?' we are presented with another statement which is said to constitute an explanation of the first. What is the relation between these two statements? What is it that makes the second statement an 'explanation' of the first? By virtue of what does it explain? Though everyone is constantly uttering statements which are supposed in one way or another to explain, few persons are at all clear about what it is that makes such statements explanations. Nor is the situation clarified when it is declared on the one hand that science explains everything and on the other hand that science never explains at all but only describes.

The question 'What is it to explain?' admits of no general answer, for the term 'to explain' covers many activities: one may explain how, and why, and whither, and whence, and how much, and many other things. Very frequently when we ask someone to explain what he has just said we are merely asking him to restate his assertion in clearer or simpler words.

In this essay I shall treat only explaining *why*. Even within this area there are some cases with which we shall not be concerned: one may explain why the angles of a Euclidean triangle must equal 180°, and this is quite dif-

[1] This is a revised version of a paper originally published in the *Journal of Philosophy*, June 1946. Grateful acknowledgment is due to the Editor for his suggestions in connexion with the revision of the paper for its present publication.

ferent from explaining why iron rusts. The latter is an
event or a process, and I shall be concerned solely with
explaining why in the special context of temporal events :
roughly, why did event x happen, or why do events of class
X happen? The illustration from geometry is, I should
prefer to say, an example of giving *reasons* rather than
explanations. Another example may further illustrate the
point : If you ask me to explain why I hold a certain belief,
I may reply by giving *reasons* for it — statements which I
take to be evidence for the belief in question. Now, if I am
rational, the fact that there is good evidence for p may
explain why I believe p — that is, the reason for my believing p may also constitute an explanation of why I believe
p. But this may not be so : the explanation of a person's
believing in a benevolent Deity may be that he wants a
father-substitute or that he needs a protector in a cold harsh
world ; but when asked to explain why he believes in a
benevolent Deity he may cite reasons, *e.g.* the Argument from
Design, which may have nothing to do with *why* he holds
the belief. We shall be concerned here, then, with the
explanation of events, not with reasons or evidences one
might cite in favour of propositions.

II

What, then, is it to explain why an event occurs ? (1) It
has sometimes been said that we have explained it if we have
stated its *purpose*. 'Why did you walk through the snow for
ten miles when you could have taken the bus ?' 'Because I
wanted to win a wager.' 'Why does that dog scratch at the
door ?' 'He's cold and he wants to get in.' When such
answers are given we are inclined to feel that our question
has been answered and that the event has been satisfactorily
explained ; and it has been explained with reference to a
purpose which some sentient being(s) had in attaining a
certain end. This is the most primitive conception of explanation. People like to feel that there is a purposive

explanation for everything: if not in terms of human or animal purposes, then of divine ones, or mysterious forces and powers. We tend to extend what holds true of some events to all events whatever; we know what conscious motivation is like from our own experience of it, and so we 'feel at home' with this kind of explanation.

We shall examine the scope and legitimacy of purposive explanation later in this paper. It is enough to remark here that if explanation must always be in terms of purpose, then the physical sciences do not explain anything. The properties of uranium, the rise of aeroplanes, the phenomena of magnetism are not explained in terms of any purposes at all; biologists even avoid talking about animal events such as the hen sitting on eggs in terms of purpose. However animistically the nature of explanation may at one time have been conceived, purposiveness is certainly no essential part of its meaning now. The stone is no longer held to fall because it wants to get to the centre of the earth.

(2) Another account of the nature of explanation is that an event has been explained when it has been shown to be an instance of some class of events which is already familiar to us. For example, when a person's behaviour seems strange to us, we are satisfied when it is 'explained' to us as being really impelled by the same sort of motives and desires as occur in us, and are therefore familiar to us. 'Why is he introducing the man he hates to the woman he loves?' 'Because he wants them to fall in love with each other' would not generally be accepted as an explanation, for this very reason. When we observe that a balloon ascends rather than descends, unlike most objects, and it is made clear to us that air has weight and that the gas inside the balloon weighs less than would an equal volume of air, we are satisfied; the phenomenon has been 'reduced' to something already familiar to us in everyday experience, such as a dense object sinking in water while a hollow one floats. The event is no longer unusual, strange, or unique; it has been shown to illustrate a principle with which we were already acquainted.

When we want to know why gases diffuse when released into a chamber from which the air has been pumped out, the explanation offered by the kinetic theory of gases is satisfactory to us because it asserts that molecules behave *like* particles with which we are already acquainted in our everyday experience.

Only those who have practised experimental physics know anything by actual experience about the laws of gases; they are not things which force themselves on our attention in common life, and even those who are most familiar with them never think of them out of working hours. On the other hand, the behaviour of moving solid bodies is familiar to everyone; everyone knows roughly what will happen when such bodies collide with each other or with a solid wall, though they may not know the exact dynamical laws involved in such reactions. In all our common life we are continually encountering moving bodies, and noticing their reactions; indeed, if the reader thinks about it, he will realize that whenever we are passively affected by it, a moving body is somehow involved in the transaction. Movement is just the most familiar thing in the world; it is through motion that everything and anything happens. And so by tracing a relation between the unfamiliar changes which gases undergo when their temperature or volume is altered, and the extremely familiar changes which accompany the motions and mutual reactions of solid bodies, we are rendering the former more intelligible ; we are explaining them. (Norman Campbell, *What Is Science?*, Dover, N.Y., p. 84.)

Professor Bridgman holds that all explanation is of this kind : ' I believe that examination will show that the essence of an explanation consists in reducing a situation to elements with which we are so familiar that we accept them as a matter of course, so that our curiosity rests' (P. W. Bridgman, *The Logic of Modern Physics*, p. 37).

And yet I am sure that such a view as this must be mistaken. In the *first* place, we may seek explanations for the most familiar events as well as of those unfamiliar to us. We may ask why stones fall as well as why aeroplanes rise, and be curious for an answer equally in both cases. True, our motivation for asking the latter question is probably greater because the kind of phenomenon in question is (or was) less familiar; most people would not think to ask it about stones because the falling of stones is familiar and usual — but the question can as legitimately be asked in the one case as in the other. In the *second* place, the explanation may not be familiar at all: it may be far less familiar than the event to be explained. The discoloration of a painted kitchen wall when gas heat is used may be a familiar phenomenon to the housewife — surely more familiar than its explanation in terms of the chemical combination of sulphur in the gas fumes with elements in the paint, producing a compound that is dark in colour. Yet this is the true explanation. If the explanation is not familiar, one is tempted to say, it ought to be, as long as it is true. Surely its familiarity is irrelevant to its validity as an explanation. Familiarity is, in any case, a subjective matter — what is familiar to you may not be familiar to me; and yet the explanation, if true, is as true for me as for you.

The only grain of truth in the view that explaining is rendering familiar seems to be this: the law that does the explaining may not be familiar, *but* the fact that the phenomenon in question, such as the flight of an aeroplane, *can* be subsumed under a law — the fact that the behaviour *is* lawlike and hence predictable — tends to make it less mysterious, less like a miracle, and thus in a sense more familiar. To show that the behaviour of something is lawlike is to show it to be a part of the order of nature, and in that sense familiar, although the particular law or laws stating the uniformity may be quite unfamiliar.

In what, then, *does* explanation consist? The answer, I think, is quite simple: (3) to explain an event is simply to bring it under a law;[1] and to explain a law is to bring it under another law. It does not matter whether the law is one about purposes or not, or whether it is familiar or not; what matters is that if the explanation is to be *true* (and we surely seek true explanations, not false ones), the law invoked must be true: indeed, this is already implied in the use of

[1] With qualifications to be discussed later.

the word 'law', which refers to a true, *i.e.* a really existing, uniformity of nature; if the uniformity turned out to be only imaginary, or having exceptions, we would no longer call it a law.

In saying that explanation is in terms of laws, I use the word 'law' in a wider sense than is sometimes employed : in the sense I mean, any uniformity of nature is a law. Thus, it is a law that iron rusts, and it is a law that iron is magnetic — although both of these are usually listed in textbooks as 'properties of iron' rather than as laws. In this sense, it seems to me that explaining why something occurs always involves a law. If we ask, 'Why don't the two liquids in the flask mix?' and someone answers, 'Don't you see, the one is transparent and the other is red?' this does not strike us as an explanation (*i.e.* as a true explanation) of the phenomenon, because we know of no law according to which red liquids will not mix with transparent ones. But when we are told that the red liquid is coloured water and that the transparent liquid is gasoline, we consider the phenomenon to be explained, for we hold it to be a law of nature that water and gasoline do not mix. In the sense in which I am using the word 'law', the non-mixture of water and gasoline is a law ; and *only* if a law is brought in do we have an explanation of the phenomenon.

Sometimes, I should add, all we have available is a 'statistical law' — a law not of the form 'All A is B' or 'Whenever A, then B', but, *e.g.*, '75 per cent of A is B'. Can such a 'law' constitute an explanation? I should be inclined to say that it is, although we would still want an explanation of why 25 per cent of A's are *not* B's. If water did not always boil at 212° F. but did so only 75 per cent of the time, we might explain the boiling of this kettle of water by saying that its temperature had reached 212°, though we would still want an explanation of why the kettle of water next to it, which had also reached 212°, did not boil. In other words, our statistical law would still not answer the question, 'Why this and not that?' and in order to answer *this* question, we would need a non-statistical law of the form, 'Under such-and-such conditions, water always boils at 212° F., but under such-and-such other conditions, it does not'. It would seem, then, that a statistical law has in turn to be explained by a non-statistical one, although of course we may not, at any given stage in the progress of science, know of any non-statistical law by which to explain the statistical one.

Another example: 'Why does Johnny have a cold?' 'Because Johnny has been playing with Roger, and Roger has a cold.' It is not a law that everyone who plays with someone who has a cold also gets a cold; the best we can do here is to state a percentage of cases in which this happens. So far as it goes, this is satisfactory; some uniformity is better than none. And yet, surely, we do not rest satisfied with this; we want to go on and ask why it sometimes happens but sometimes not. And the answer to this question would be a non-statistical law: 'People always get colds under such-and-such conditions'. Whether a statistical law can *always* be explained in terms of a non-statistical one depends not only on our powers of discovery but upon the nature of the universe. It is certainly no *a priori* truth that nature's uniformities are all of the 100 per cent variety instead of 75 per cent.

One further qualification: We have said that we explain particular events in terms of laws, and laws in terms of wider laws. But sometimes we give at least tentative explanations of them in terms not of laws but of general *hypotheses*: if a law is a well-established statement of how nature works, a statement about nature's workings that is not well established, or perhaps not even probable but only possible, cannot be a law. And yet we can use it to explain a law. But to whatever degree the hypothesis is uncertain, to that degree the explanation is jeopardized. An explanation cannot be known to be true if it involves a hypothesis which (by the definition of 'hypothesis') is *not* known to be true. Whether the explanation is a true explanation, then, depends on the fate of the hypothesis. (In the 'higher reaches' of most sciences, where the most general laws are involved, the only explanations possible are usually those in terms of very general hypotheses.)

III

So much for a general statement of what explanation consists of. I should like now to append some comments and to answer some questions to which the above account may give rise.

1. Thus far we have been content to answer the question 'Why does A do B ?' by saying 'Because all A's do B' But there are those who say that such an answer is no explanation at all. 'To say that all gases expand when heated', says Norman Campbell (*What Is Science?*, p. 80), 'is not to explain why hydrogen expands when heated ; it merely leads us to ask immediately why all gases expand. An explanation which leads immediately to another question of the same kind is no explanation at all.'

I want to insist that the answer given *is* an explanation of the occurrence in question ; to say 'Hydrogen is a gas, and all gases expand when heated' is a perfectly satisfactory answer to the question why hydrogen expands when heated. But it is *not*, of course, an answer to *another* question — Why do all gases expand when heated ? — and this is probably the question which the person meant to ask in the first place. These questions must not be confused with each other ; I believe Campbell's position is the result of this confusion. It is fatally easy to telescope (unconsciously) two questions into one, and then be dissatisfied with the answer. Distinguishing them, we get :

Question 1. Why does this gas expand when heated ?
Explanation. It is hydrogen, and hydrogen expands when heated.
Question 2. Why does hydrogen expand when heated ?

Explanation. Hydrogen is a gas, and all gases expand when heated.

Question 3. Why do all gases expand when heated?

Here we attempt to give an explanation in terms of the kinetic theory of gases. To criticize Answer 1 because it is not an answer to Question 2, or Answer 2 because it is not an answer to Question 3, is surely a confusion. I want to say that Answer 1 is a perfectly satisfactory explanation for the phenomenon referred to in Question 1, though of course not for those referred to in Questions 2 and 3. But there is a frequent tendency to telescope these questions and demand to Question 1 the answer to Question 3.

The situation may be illustrated in another way. If I ask, 'Why did the water-pipes in my basement burst last night?' someone may answer that it is because the basement got too cold, and another may answer that it is because water expands when it freezes, while yet another may say that we do not know the 'real explanation' unless we can state why water expands when it freezes. Here, again we must separate the questions:

Question 1. Why did the water-pipes break?
Explanation. They always do when the temperature falls to below 32°.

Question 2. Why do they break when the temperature falls . . . etc.?
Explanation. Because the water in them expands when it freezes, and the water on expanding breaks the pipes.

Question 3. Why does water expand when it freezes?
Explanation. Here we try to answer in terms of the structure of the water-molecule.

But to say that we have not explained (1) until we have explained (3) is grossly to underestimate the number of phenomena for which we do have perfectly satisfactory explanations. That is, we *do* have explanations for (1) and (2), and our having them is *not* contingent upon having an explanation for (3).

We could put our point in another way. *Logically* the answers given to each question in turn are satisfactory explanations; but *psychologically* they may not be equally satisfying, *depending on the previous knowledge of the questioner*. To the questioner who knew nothing about the relation of pipes bursting to temperature, the answer 'Because they got cold' (to the first question) would be psychologically quite satisfactory, but not to the person who already knew that it had something to do with temperature, for the question *he* meant to ask was (2) or (3). Again: If I ask why this wire conducts electricity, it is a perfectly good explanation to answer 'Because it is made of copper, and copper is a conductor of electricity'. Psychologically, however, this answer would not be equally satisfying to everyone ; it *would* be to the person who knew nothing of the properties of copper (or who did not know that this wire was copper), but it would *not* be to the person who already knew the properties of copper but was really enquiring as to why copper, unlike many other substances, is a conductor of electricity.

2. Can an event have *two* explanations ? Why not ? Let us suppose that we want to explain an event E, and that we have a law saying that every time conditions A are fulfilled, E happens, and another law saying that every time conditions B are fulfilled, E happens. A will then be a complete explanation for the occurrence of E, and B will also be a complete explanation. Whether any such state of affairs actually occurs in the world is, of course, another question. Most of the suggested double explanations of events are in fact parts of a single explanation. Thus, for example, if we are asked to explain why the burglar committed the robbery last night, the detective may explain it in terms of his expertness at picking locks, the butler may explain it in terms of the family being out of the room, the maid may say it was because the bedroom window was open,

the policeman may say it was because the night was foggy and visibility at a minimum, the sociologist may explain it in terms of the criminal's background of slum conditions, and the psychologist may explain it in terms of pseudo-aggressive impulses dating from a childhood period marked by intense family quarrels. All these explanations are probably correct enough as far as they go. It may well be that in the absence of any one of these factors the burglary would not have occurred. But these are, it would surely seem, parts and aspects of *one* complete explanation — and in explaining human actions the whole explanation may be inconceivably complex. Still, the possibility remains that in *some* cases there may be two separate and complete explanations for an occurrence; at least it cannot be ruled out *a priori*.

3. Must there be a *deductive* relation between the thing to be explained and the explanation, such that one can deduce the statement of the phenomenon to be explained from the explanation ?

> All copper conducts electricity.
> This wire is made of copper.
> Therefore, This wire conducts electricity.

Here the explanation yields the desired conclusion easily, and it is quite clear that what we have here is a genuine explanation. The question is, must all explanation conform to this model ? Have we failed to give an explanation if we have failed to deduce the explanandum from the explanation ?

Let us first note that in many cases, if this is required, the explanation would be bewilderingly complex, and the premises in the deduction extremely numerous. Consider the burglary example just cited. From the fact that the weather was foggy and that the man had tendencies to steal and that he had a poor background . . . etc., we cannot deduce the fact that he committed the theft. We cannot deduce it, indeed, from any set of premises known to be true. What we need for deducing it is a law, to the effect that if such-and-such conditions are fulfilled an act of this kind will always occur, and then a minor premise to the effect that these conditions were in fact fulfilled. The conditions would indeed have to be extremely numerous, and the statement of the law immensely complicated. Yet such a law is required if the desired conclusion is to be deduced.

We never in fact use a deductive model in cases like this one, and it is worthy of note that we do not deny ourselves the claim that we have explained the event because of this. What, therefore, are we to say of the deductive model as a *sine qua non* for all explanation? As I see it, we have two alternatives open to us :

(*a*) We can, in the light of such examples, scrap the deductive model entirely. We can say that often one can in fact deduce the explanandum from the explanation, but that this is not essential to explanation. We might add, as some do, that to perform the deduction is one way (the best way ?) to *justify* an explanation we have put forward, but that the giving of a true explanation is not dependent on this.

(*b*) We can still insist that a complete explanation does involve the deduction, but that what we often give is in fact less than a complete explanation. We list, as in the burglary example, a few salient facts and either take the remainder as too obvious to mention or do not know what they are. But such measures are concessions of failure. The fact is that the only way to be sure of our explanation is to deduce the phenomenon in question from premises which we know to be true.

I merely wish here to state these alternatives, not to decide between them. It is, surely, a matter of how liberally or how strictly we wish to use the term 'explanation'; and, though I incline toward the second alternative, I do not wish to champion without reserve a 'puristic' account of explanation which is not in fact followed by anyone — at least anyone in the psychological and social sciences — and which, it is sometimes declared, is in practice almost useless and boringly academic.

Thus far in enquiring about the need for a deductive relationship, we have considered only the explanation of particular events : we have deduced them from two premises, one stating a law and the other stating a particular condition : 'All copper conducts electricity ; this is copper, therefore this conducts electricity.' 'All water freezes at 32° F., the water in the pond went below 32° last night ; therefore the water in the pond froze.' And so on. But, as we saw earlier, we not only explain particular events ; we also explain *laws*. And the same question could be repeated here : is the deductive requirement necessary ? There is no doubt that in the 'neat, tidy' cases it is fulfilled : for example, Kepler's laws of planetary motion can be deduced from Newton's laws of motion together with the law of gravitation ; and thus the latter clearly explain the former. But is this strictly a requirement for *all* explanation of laws ? Again, some would say that it is — that anything short of this is not a full explanation. Others would say that it is not — that the deductive case is only the ideal one but that explanation does not require it. For example, a law can be explained in terms of a very general theory, from which the law cannot be strictly deduced, but which will nevertheless entitle the theory to be called an explanation. (The deductivist will reply that it is not *known* to be an explanation until the acid test, *i.e.* the deduction, is performed.)

4. In any case, whether deducibility is a necessary condition of explanation or not, it is not a sufficient condition. One can deduce that this watch will not work from the premises that watches will not work if gremlins get into them and that gremlins are in fact in this watch. Yet no one would accept this as an explanation for the misbehaviour of the watch. Similarly, one might deduce it from the premises that whatever God wills happens and that God has willed the misbehaviour of this watch. One can deduce anything if one selects one's premises carefully.

One might remark at this point that it is also necessary that the premises be *true*, and that this is the required addition. I would unhesitatingly agree that the premises must indeed be true — false statements cannot form parts of true explanations (indeed, if explanation is in terms of law, and a law is a true statement of a uniformity, *i.e.* one that actually occurs, then this proviso has already been implicit in our account of explanation). But suppose we make this proviso explicit — is it enough ? I do not believe so. It might be true that God wills everything that happens, but as long as we have no means of knowing this, we cannot use it as a premise in our explanation. That is, we cannot use it as an explanation unless the proposition is not only true, but is *known to be so*.

Suppose, then, that we accept this last revision — will it do the trick ? I hardly think so ; it still misses the main point. Let us imagine a deeply religious scientist who holds that everything that happens is the result of divine will ; he may yet reject the theological explanation as an account of *why* things happen as they do. The reason is surely fairly obvious : what the scientist wishes to discover is why this happened *rather than that*, and the theological explanation will not enable him to make this discrimination : *whatever* happens, one can deduce it from the premises that God willed it to happen and that whatever He wills happens.

What condition, then, remains to be supplied ? The condition seems to be a rather simple one, yet one which it is difficult to state precisely. What we have in mind is this : we want to eliminate the indiscriminate 'explanatory' power of the gremlin-hypothesis and the God-hypothesis, even though they slip through the deductive net, because they do not enable us to explain why this happens *rather than that*. 'What explains everything explains nothing.'

This *can* be put by saying that the explanation must have *predictive* value, but this is a bit misleading. For one thing, it places undue emphasis upon the future, whereas explanation of past is just as important as explanation of future ; we would have, then, to use a tenseless sense of 'predict'. For another thing, there are many explanations which seem to be true but whose predictive power is minimal or at any rate difficult to see : many biological phenomena can be explained in terms of laws of mutations, for example, but it is not clear what these laws enable us to *predict* — certainly not where or when a mutation will occur or what kind it will be when it does arise.

Perhaps what we want to say can be best expressed by the simple proviso that the explanation must explain *other* phenomena than those it is invoked to explain, and yet, unlike the God-hypothesis, not just everything indiscriminately : in other words, it should explain other events (whether past, present, or future makes no difference), but it should all the same be *capable of disproof* by empirical observations, whether or not any actual empirical observations ever disprove it, it must be capable of testing. Without this condition it would not be considered an explanation in any science.

In fact all this is implicit in our requirement that an explanation be in terms of law or laws. A law is a universal proposition about all events or processes in a certain class, and if it holds for A, a member of the class (a present event), it also holds for members B, C, and D (future events) ; thus by the very nature of a law, laws explain more than a single event. The testability of explanations is also implicit in the concept of law, for a law is an empirical statement of a uniformity of nature, and, being contingent, it is always subject to disconfirmation by observation. Still, it is well to make the implicit explicit to show why the deductive requirement is not enough and what more is required of an explanation.

5. In evaluating the extent to which proffered explanations yield us genuine empirical knowledge (*i.e.* are real empirical laws), much care is required, for in this field the verbal booby-traps in our way are numerous and intricate.

If someone asked, 'Why is this object spherical ?' and the reply were given, 'Because it's globular', everyone would recognize the answer to be trivial because it is analytic.

Many so-called explanations do not give much more information than this, although even very bad ones are not usually
quite as empty as this one. Even when one says that opium
produces sleep because of its dormitive power, we are at least
told that it is because of something within it that sleep is
produced, not by some outside factor such as the atmosphere.
When we ask why hydrogen combines with oxygen to form
water, and are told that it is because hydrogen has an *affinity*
for oxygen, again the reply is relatively empty : it tells us
only that under certain conditions hydrogen does combine
with oxygen but tells us nothing of why hydrogen rather
than some other substances does this ; but at least we know
from the answer that there *is* a law relating the combination
of elements to some set of conditions, though we do not yet
know that this law is. And if we ask why the mother cat
takes care of her kittens and fights to defend them, and are
told that it is because she has a *maternal instinct*, at least
we know that the activity is not a learned one — and this is
indeed something — although again the answer may not give
us the kind of thing we were asking for. Most explanations
in terms of instinct, tendency, affinity, power, and faculty
are of this next-to-worthless kind, conveying only a minimum
of information, and leading us to ask a why-question of the
explanation given.

Let us observe how easily the invention of a name may
make us assume that an explanation has been given. If it
is asked, 'Why is iron magnetic ?' and we answer, 'Because
iron, cobalt, and nickel are magnetic', no one would think
much of this as an explanation ; but the moment we give a
name to the behaviour of these metals, and call them, say,
'fero-affinitive', then when someone asks why iron is magnetic, we can say, 'Why, because it's a fero-affinitive metal,
that's why'. And yet no more has been said in the second
case than in the first. Similarly, if we had a name for the
tendency of seeds to sprout upwards to reach the surface
of the ground, people would be readier to say that their
tendency to rise could be *explained* by the presence of this

I

property.   Yet a name for what it does is a different thing from an explanation of why it does what it does.

Not all examples are as simple as this. When external influences tend to reduce or raise the bodily temperature of an organism, various bodily mechanisms come into play to return the temperature to normal. This is known as 'homeostasis'. So far, we simply have a name for the phenomenon, and if someone volunteered it as an *explanation* he would surely be mistaken. But now suppose a bird finds its nest partially destroyed and it sets about rebuilding it to the way it was before; we ask why, and are told, 'That's the bird's homeostatic tendency'. Now the name 'homeostasis' is no longer merely a label for the temperature-controlling mechanisms; it relates these mechanisms to a quite different thing, the bird's attempt to restore the *status quo*. In both examples there is an attempt to restore a state which has ceased to exist. Is 'homeostasis' now an explanation, or is it simply a description-in-a-nutshell, a *generalized* description, of what the organism does, without attempting to explain why?

Observe, incidentally, how easily all these so-called explanations slip through the deductive net. We can deduce the required conclusion easily: 'When organisms have homeostatic tendencies, they do so-and-so. This organism has homeostatic tendencies. Therefore, it does so-and-so.' The deductive requirement will let good and bad explanations alike slip through like water through a sieve. This shows us again that, whether necessary to explanation or not, the deducibility requirement is not sufficient.

But let us return : Is homeostasis an explanation of the organism's behaviour or not? Before we say, 'No, it isn't', let us reflect on this point : if appeal to homeostatis is simply a short way of saying that birds do this and people do that, is not the appeal to gravitation simply a short way of saying that apples do this and stars do that? And yet the Law of Gravitation is one of the most sacred of our explanatory principles. Perhaps, as Wisdom says, talking about gravitation is simply a way of saying that apples fall *and so on* ; but then is not homeostatis simply a way of saying that birds rebuild their nests *and so on*?

It is, of course, incorrect to say that apples fall because of gravitation, if we mean by this that gravitation is some animistic force or pull, just as it would be wrong to say that birds behave so-and-so because of homeostasis, if we mean it to be a separate force or magnetism within birds. If we are so tempted, it is both useful and important to say that each of the explanations referred to is simply a way of saying 'this happens *and so on*'. But it is, I should think, the *extent and range* of the 'and so on' that matters here. What gives the Principle of Gravitation its remarkable explanatory power is not its appeal to an occult force but its bringing together under one formula an enormous range of diverse and complex phenomena. Because of this range, and the exactitude with which it can be applied to widely separate phenomena, the Law of Gravitation is the classical case of a law having predictive power — and it is extremely doubtful whether homeostasis possesses or ever will possess this. We rest, then, once again with this second and all-important necessary condition of explanation (the first being, at least in common opinion, the deducibility requirement): its power to explain a wide range of phenomena *other* than those it was invoked to explain.

6. No mention has thus far been made of explanation in terms of *purpose*. And yet this is the oldest concept of explanation and still the one most frequently employed by primitive peoples. And there are contexts in which we still employ the concept of purpose in giving explanations — for example, when we say that my purpose in going to the store was to do some Christmas shopping, and that this is *why* I went.

The word 'purpose' is, of course, ambiguous. (*a*) Most frequently in ordinary usage a purpose is something of which I am conscious — a conscious intent to do something. The conscious intent is not the *whole* of the purpose : part of the criterion of whether it is my purpose to do X is whether I am disposed towards doing X, whether I take steps towards X and do X if I have the chance. (*b*) Some tendencies to act are not accompanied by any state of awareness ; and here psychologists speak of *un*conscious purposes. We need not stop here over the exact interpretation of this way of speaking ; let us simply say that one is said to have X as his unconscious purpose if he consistently acts, without intending it, so as to bring about X. (*c*) We speak of inanimate objects as having purposes — for example, the purpose of a hammer is to drive nails. This of course is not a purpose consciously envisaged by the hammer. All we mean here is that the mechanical object *reflects* the conscious purposes of its makers. *We* had a conscious purpose in making the hammer, and thus we speak elliptically of the hammer as having that purpose. Strictly speaking, of course, the purpose is ours and not the hammer's.

In all of these cases a purpose implies a purposer, or someone to have the purpose. We do sometimes use the word 'purpose' in another sense which carries no such implication, (*d*) when we say, 'What is the purpose of the heart ?' 'To pump blood through the body.' Here purpose simply means function — *i.e.* what does it *do* ? what part does it play in the bodily economy ? If the word 'purpose' is used here I would view it as a 'degenerate' usage — a misleading locution in which another word, 'function', would serve much better. It is true that someone, in asking the purpose of the heart, might have in mind a theological question, 'What purpose did God have in endowing us with this organ ?' but if this is meant, we are back again to purpose in sense 1, in which purpose implies a purposer and the word 'purpose' refers to conscious intent — the only difference now being that it is God's intent and not ours that is in question. But this, of course, is not what medical men generally have in mind when they ask purpose-questions about parts of organisms ; else every such medical question would be a disguised theological question.

Having disentangled these senses of 'purpose', let us

ask about the legitimacy of purposive explanations. Briefly I think it comes to this: explanations require laws, and if there are laws *about* purposes, there is no reason why they cannot figure in some explanations just as laws about falling bodies figure in other explanations. To the extent that laws about purposes have been established, they can be used as explanations like any other laws. Unfortunately the only laws (if any) that we are in a position to make about purposes are about human ones. Explanations in terms of divine purposes cannot be employed because no laws about divine purposes have ever been established. Even explanations of biological events in terms of animal purposes is frowned upon: we do not count it an explanation if it is said that the hen sits on her eggs *in order to* hatch chicks, because we have no indication that the hen does so with this purpose in mind; even if this is true, we do not know it, and therefore we cannot use it as a law in our explanation. In the human realm alone we know that purposes exist, and only there can we therefore employ them in explanations. We can even deduce conclusions from them, thus:

People act so as to fulfil their purposes, unless prevented by external circumstances.
My purpose was to go shopping, and I was not prevented . . . etc.
Therefore, I went shopping.

This way of putting it may sound rather silly, as the deductive model often does, but at any rate a deduction can be achieved from premises which are in all probability true.

The chief mistake which people are in the habit of making with regard to purposive explanation is probably that of wanting an answer to a why-question in terms of purpose when the conditions under which a purpose-answer is legitimate are not fulfilled. People extend their questioning unthinkingly from areas in which purposive explanation is in order into areas in which it is not. Thus: 'Why did he go to New York?' 'Well, in response to impulses from certain centres in his brain, some muscles in his arms and legs started moving towards the airport and . . .' 'No,

that's not what I mean. I mean, why did he go ? what did
he go for ? what purpose did he have in view ?' 'He went
in order to see some operas.' Contrast this with the following : 'Why did he die ?' 'Well, a bullet entered his lung,
puncturing some blood vessels, and the blood filled his lung
so that he couldn't breathe any more, and . . .' 'No, that's
not what I mean. I mean, *why* did he die ?' But here we
can no longer give an answer in terms of purpose — unless,
that is, our talk is rooted in a theological context and we are
willing to say that, just as the first person went to New
York because he wanted to see operas, so the second person
died because God had some purpose (intent) in seeing to it
that he was murdered. If this is what is meant, one could
try to answer the question in the theistic context of divine
purposes ; but if this context is rejected, the why-question
demanding an answer in terms of purpose is meaningless,
because an answer is being demanded when the only conditions under which the question is meaningful are not fulfilled.

This point is worth emphasizing because it is so often
ignored in practice. Having received answers to why-
questions when these questions were meaningful and explanations could be given, people continue to use why-
questions even when they no longer know what they are
asking for. One need not be surprised that no answer is
forthcoming to such questions. And in our discouragement
with such questions we are all too prone to make a mistake
ourselves and terminate an exasperating series of why-
questions with a remark such as, 'That's just something we
don't know,' as if it were like cases where something definite
is being asked but we do not yet know the laws which explain
the phenomena we are asking about. If something in the
case is not known, there must be something in the case
which we could fail to know. If we are to ask a meaningful
question, we must know what it is that we are asking for ;
only then can we recognize an answer as being one when
we do find it.

7. This leads us directly into an important question,

How far can explanation go ? We may explain an event in terms of a law, and this law in terms of other laws, and so on ? but must we not finally come to a stop ? The bursting of the pipes is explained by the expansion of water on freezing ; let us assume that water expands on freezing because the water-molecule has such-and-such a structure ; now why does the water-molecule have this structure ? Perhaps this can some day be explained by reference to electron-proton arrangements within the atom, and this in turn by reference to the disposition of more minute particles (if they can be called such) yet to be discovered ; but sooner or later must we not say, 'That's just the way things are — this is just an ultimate law about the universe. We can explain other things in terms of it, but it we cannot explain' ? Are there ultimate laws, laws which explain but cannot even in principle be explained ?

In practice we come rather quickly to laws which cannot be explained further. Laws about atomic structure are typical of such laws. Laws of psycho-physical correlation are another example. *Why* do I have a certain colour-sensation which I call red, indescribable but qualitatively different from all others, when light within a certain range of wave-length impinges upon my retina, and another indescribably different sensation which I call yellow when rays of another wave-length strike the retina ? That this wave-length is correlated with this visual experience seems to be sheer 'brute fact' — a law [1] which cannot be explained in terms of anything more ultimate than itself.

At the same time, we should be careful in dismissing any uniformity we cannot explain as a 'brute fact' or 'basic law'. Many things, such as why this element has this melting-point and these spectral lines, were once considered basic and unexplainable properties of the element, but have since been explained in terms of the intra-molecular structure

---

[1] A law which would, to be sure, have to be qualified to take care of abnormal cases, *e.g.* colour-blindness, jaundice, etc. The genesis of colour-sensations is complex and does not depend *merely* upon the kind of light-rays entering the eye.

of the element. No matter how much at a loss we may be for an explanation, we can always ask and speculate. If it had been accepted as a basic law that water starts to expand when it gets below 39° F., we would never have gone on to discover anything about the structure of the water-molecule. Fruitful scientific procedure depends on assuming that no given law is basic; if scientists did not continue always to ask the question 'Why?' the process of scientific enquiry would stop dead in its tracks.

Thus, if there *are* basic laws, it seems that we cannot know of any given law that it is one. We can know that it is *not*, by explaining it in terms of other laws; but how could we know that it *is*? Discovering basic laws is epistemologically similar to discovering uncaused events: if there are uncaused events, we can never know that there are, for all we can safely say is that we have not yet found causes for them.

One further point about basic or ultimate laws: If a law is really a basic one, any request for an explanation of it is self-contradictory. To explain a law is to place it in a context or network of wider and more inclusive laws; a basic law is by definition one of which this cannot be done; therefore to ask of an admittedly basic law that it be explained is implicitly to deny that it is basic and thus to deny the very premise of the argument. It is a request for explanation in a situation where by one's own admission no more explaining can be done.

Like so many others, this point may seem logically compelling but psychologically unsatisfying. Having heard the above argument, one may still feel inclined to ask, 'Why are the basic uniformities of the universe the way they are, and not some other way? Why should we have just *these* laws rather than other ones? I want an *explanation* of why they are as they are.' I must confess here, as an autobiographical remark, that I cannot help sharing this feeling: I want to ask why the laws of nature, being contingent, are as they are, even though I cannot conceive of what an explanation of this would be like, and even though by my own argument above the request for such an explanation is self-contradictory.[1] The fact is, as we saw above, that why-questions have had answers so many times that we tend automatically to ask them here even when they can have no answers because we have ripped them out of the only context in which they have meaning — like the situation of the child who, being told what is above the table and above the ceiling of his room and above the house and above the earth, now asks what is above the universe. The question has now gone outside the context of meaningful discourse, and so has the request for the explanation of a basic law. We should remember : to explain is to explain *in terms of something*, and if *ex hypothesi* there is no longer any something for it to be explained in terms of, then the request for an explanation is self-contradictory : it demands on the one hand that you explain X in terms of a Y while insisting simultaneously that there is no Y.

8. One sometimes encounters the complaint that science does not really explain but only describes. 'Science doesn't tell us *why* things happen,' it is said, 'it only tells us *how* things happen.' Now it does often happen that the exact intention of the user of a why-question is not very clear — as we have already seen. But in the way in which the term 'why' is most commonly used, science *does* explain why : for example, the bursting of the pipes, the formation of ice at the top of ponds rather than at the bottom, and many other phenomena, are explained by reference to the law that water expands when it freezes. (If someone says we have *not* explained why the pipes burst, then what does he mean by 'why' ? What sort of thing is he asking for ? What *would* answer his question ? Let him state in other terms what it is that he is asking for.)

'But is not explanation after all merely description ?' It

---

[1] Explanation in terms of divine purposes again will not help : if we are told that the laws of nature are as they are because God willed it so, we can ask why He should have willed it so ; and if here again an answer is given, we can once again ask a why-question of this answer.

is all very well to say that when we explain something we actually describe — *e.g.* stating laws of nature is describing how nature works. But this does not preclude the fact that we *are* explaining. When the question is asked why pressing the button turns on the light, we explain by describing just what goes on — currents, open and closed circuits, conduction of electricity by wires, dynamos in the power plant, and so on. But have we not in so doing explained the phenomenon about which we were asking? We have explained *by* describing, if you will; but certainly we have explained. To say that because we are describing we cannot be explaining would be like saying that because an object is red it cannot also be coloured.

9. A similar complaint is sometimes voiced against scientific explanation, that it 'explains things *away*'. Explaining something is interpreted as equivalent to explaining it away. Now the precise meaning of the phrase 'explaining away' is one which I have never been able to discover. What is one supposed to be doing when he explains something away? Surely not to declare that it does not exist! Explanation deprives us of no facts we had before. To 'explain colour' in terms of light-waves is not, of course (as should have been obvious), to take away the fact of colour-experiences. 'Thinking is nothing but the occurrence of certain neural impulses' should be changed into '*When* thinking takes place (and that it does is just as incontrovertible a fact as the neurons are), there are neural impulses.'

In the special context of beliefs, perhaps 'explaining away' may mean impugning the truth of one's conclusions. If so, there are again no grounds for fear. To 'explain away' someone's politically reactionary tendencies by saying, 'He's old, and people always get conservative when they get old', does not for a moment take away whatever truth the person's opinions may have; at most, it only exposes part of the causal genesis of his having them. And if the views of this person were 'explained away' by these biographical observations, the views of his opponent would be equally vulnerable:

'You needn't pay any attention to that young upstart, they're all hot communists when they're young' Reference to biography may, together with laws of human nature (if any are known in this area), explain why a person held a certain belief at a certain time, but the truth or falsity of the belief is quite unaffected by this and, of course, is tested on different grounds entirely. The idea that reference to a person's mental or physical condition could 'explain away' the truth of a belief is one of the most flagrant blunders of the materialistically minded laity of our day.

UNIVERSITY OF MINNESOTA

Chapter VI

SOME QUESTIONS CONCERNING VALIDITY

BY J. O. URMSON

THE programme of this paper is as follows. First of all I shall outline a method of argument which is often used in the work of modern philosophers, and which I take to be a perfectly legitimate type of argument in its proper place and when used for its proper purpose. This method of argument I shall call the appeal to the standard example or to the paradigm case. By it the philosophical doubt whether something is really an X is exposed as being in some way improper or absurd by means of a demonstration that the thing in question is a standard case by reference to which the expression 'X' has to be understood, or a doubt whether anything is X is exposed by showing that certain things are standard cases of what the term in question is designed to describe. In the second place I shall show how this sort of argument has been applied by some philosophers to the problems of the validity of deductive, inductive, and ethical argument, here, as later, with special reference to the latter two. As a first rough approximation one can say that the argument from standard examples has here been used to show that at least some arguments in each field must be valid since they are standard examples of validity in their sphere, by reference to which validity in that sphere must be elucidated, so that to query their validity must be absurd and improper. Thirdly, and finally, I shall try to show that because of the evaluative element in the meaning of 'valid' the argument from standard cases cannot be applied to these fields without considerable modification, and that after such necessary modification the argument does not prove all that many who have used it have wished to prove, though it is not entirely without weight. In particular, when thus modified the argument leads to a better formulation of the problems which it fails to solve. This is no mean achievement in such difficult fields.

(1) THE NATURE OF THE ARGUMENT FROM STANDARD EXAMPLES

Suppose that someone looking at what we would regard normally as a typically red object expressed a doubt whether it was really red. He might indeed express doubts whether it was really red because he thought that the light was unusual, or that his eyes were bad, or something of that sort. But suppose that he expresses doubt for none of these reasons but doubts whether the term 'red' can properly apply to this sort of thing. We would then be at a loss and probably ask him what on earth he meant by red if he was unwilling to call this red, or say that by 'red' we meant being of just some such colour as this — 'If we do not call *this* red then what would we?' Thus, using a simple form of the argument from standard examples, we can make him see that there is something absurd in his question, since there is no better way of showing what the word 'red' means than by pointing to things of this colour.

Now a slightly more sophisticated example to show what is here meant by the argument from standard examples. In his popular book, *The Nature of the Physical World*, in an attempt to bring out in a vivid fashion the difference between the scientific and everyday description of such things as desks, Eddington said in effect that desks were not really solid. Miss Stebbing, in her book *Philosophy and the Physicists*, used the argument from standard examples to show that this way of putting things involved illegitimate mystification; this she did by simply pointing out that if one asked what we ordinarily mean by *solid* we immediately realize that we mean something like 'of the consistency of such things as desks'. Thus she showed conclusively that

the novelty of scientific theory does not consist, as had been ·
unfortunately suggested, in showing the inappropriateness of
ordinary descriptive language.

Two comparatively trivial uses of the argument from
standard examples have been given to illustrate its character.
Obviously to give more subtle examples would require much
space, and at present we are concerned only with what the
argument is, not with showing that it is valuable or important.
But as for the rest of this paper I shall be attacking what I
consider to be illegitimate uses of the argument it would be
as well to say now that, usually in conjunction with other
techniques, this type of argument can be used to clear up
a number of vexatious philosophical problems. In particular, it can be used time and time again to show that
problems have traditionally been incorrectly formulated;
and every philosopher knows how important correct formulation of problems is.

It is to be hoped that enough has been said to show the
general character of the argument from standard cases. A
full discussion is not possible in the space available.

(2) THE ARGUMENT FROM STANDARD EXAMPLES AS APPLIED TO VALIDITY

I shall now set out the use of this argument to solve some
major problems about validity ; in the first instance this must
be done as persuasively as is consistent with extreme brevity.
As I think that these uses of the argument are, in part, illegitimate, our argumentation will at this stage embody error :
but we cannot expose error until we have it before us, pre-
ferably in an attractive guise. We shall first apply the argument to deductive reasoning, since it is instructive to compare
its use here with other uses ; we shall then apply it to inductive and ethical reasoning, which are for us now the
central issues. The reader is asked to bear in mind throughout this section that I am putting a case, not expressing my
own opinions.

(a) *Deductive reasoning*

Logicians, in so far as they have been concerned to understand the nature of reasoning and not to produce abstract calculi or 'languages', have not been producing arbitrary fiats for us to obey when they have put forward principles of valid inference. Nor again, do these principles present themselves as truths independent of actual reasoning. The logician is attempting to make explicit principles of validity already implicit in our judgments of the validity or invalidity of actual arguments. Thus it is not the case that the validity of the syllogistic arguments is determined by their conformity to the rules of the syllogism ; it would be more correct to say that suggested rules of the syllogism are to be accepted only if they recognize as valid what we would in any case recognize as valid, and nothing else. Rules of inference and principles of validity have to be abstracted from standard examples of valid arguments ; a suggested rule is refuted if it makes valid a standard example of an invalid argument, or *vice versa*. This being so, it is simply meaningless to ask whether the standard examples of valid deduction are really valid, or to ask whether any deductive arguments are valid. The meaning of 'valid' with regard to deductive argument is determined by these standard examples — they are the ultimate standard and court of appeal. To ask whether a tricky argument is or is not valid is in the end to ask whether it is like the standard examples of valid arguments or not, though our direct appeal may be to principles.

(b) *Inductive reasoning*

Perhaps no one has wished to query the validity of straightforward deduction, so that our last paragraph may have seemed to stress the obvious. But we may argue similarly with regard to inductive reasoning ; and the general validity of inductive reasoning has indeed been questioned ; this is the celebrated problem of induction. Now sometimes when the general validity of induction has been questioned the doubters have indeed had an independent criterion by which to judge it ; they have relied on the principles of valid deduction. But this is clearly an error. For inductive arguments are supposed to be inductive, not deductive, whereas if they answered to the criteria of deductive reasoning they would be deductive. A perfectly good cat would get low marks at a dog show, and be none the worse for that. But if we abandon the irrelevant criteria of deductive validity, how are we able to condemn all inductive reasoning as invalid ? Whence come our principles of judgment ? Do we not come near to the evident absurdity of saying that all men are abnormal, all perception illusory ? When we in fact regard an inductive argument as invalid it is because it differs importantly from those which we regard as valid ; a contrast is intended.

Here then, it appears, as in the case of deductive reasoning, we must start from the standard examples of valid and invalid argument and elicit from them our principles of inductive validity. It is not required that the scientific reasoning of a Newton or a Pasteur should conform to text-book canons but that text-book canons should be based on a study of them. Except by reference to such examples no meaning can be attached to the term 'valid' in the sphere of inductive argument. If the validity of such examples is denied, by what standards is it being judged ? If the irrelevant standards of deduction have not been dragged in, then surely there are no standards available. These examples set the standard.

That is how the argument runs with regard to induction. The problem whether any inductive arguments are valid is held up as absurd, and with it the traditional problem of induction.[1]

(c) Ethical reasoning

It is clear that we can use an exactly similar technique to prove that it is absurd to doubt generally the validity of

[1] To check my exposition of this argument readers may be referred to a few expositions of it. It is given *in extenso* in 'Bertrand Russell's Doubts about Induction', by Paul Edwards, *Mind*, 1949 (reprinted in *Logic and Language*, Vol. I). For shorter versions see, *e.g.* the last chapter of *An Introduction to Logical Theory*, by P. F. Strawson, and A. J. Ayer's introduction to *British Empirical Philosophers*, pp. 26-7.

ethical reasoning. Some writers on ethics have suggested that it is impossible to distinguish valid and invalid arguments about moral matters — C. L. Stevenson maintained this quite recently in his *Ethics and Language*. But it appears that just as inductive argument has been condemned for failing to conform to the standards of deductive reasoning, so ethical reasoning is condemned for not conforming to the standards of either deductive or inductive reasoning. But why should it ? Yet if we do not use such irrelevant standards of criticism we can surely not condemn ethical reasoning in general in this way. For our conception of what is valid and what is invalid in ethical reasoning must be derived from a study of ethical reasoning — we have here, as in other spheres, standard examples of valid and invalid argument. 'Valid' and 'invalid' must be used to mark a distinction within moral reasoning. It is no more possible for all ethical arguments to be invalid than for all men to be small men. We learn how to use the expression 'valid argument' with regard to ethics by hearing it applied to some arguments and not to others. Our task as philosophers is to make explicit the principles which we already implicitly have for distinguishing valid from invalid arguments. To query whether any ethical argument is valid is to ask a pseudo-question, not to raise a serious philosophical problem. As Mr. S. N. Hampshire said in *Mind*, 1949, p. 471, 'If the procedure of practical deliberation does not conform, either in its intermediate steps or in the form of its conclusions, with any forms of argument acknowledged as respectable in logical text-books, this is a deficiency of the logical text-books'.

(3) CRITICAL EXAMINATION OF THE FOREGOING ARGUMENTS

So far we have been concerned to present a reasonably plausible version of the argument from standard examples as applied to the question of the general validity of certain types of argument. I shall now try to show

K

(*a*) that the arguments that we have just considered only appear to be proper examples of the argument from standard cases because they have been mis-stated ;

(*b*) that when recast in a more correct form they are indeed the prolegomena to some very important philosophical investigations, but by no means dispose of the major philosophical problems, as many who have used them have thought they would. It will, however, be shown that they do require a change in the traditional formulation of these problems.

(a) *The arguments we have been considering are mis-stated*

If we ask, absurdly, whether such things as desks are solid, then the reply can be given that the meaning of 'solid' is determined by its application to just such things. As an explanation of what we mean by 'solid' it would not be wrong to say 'of the consistency of such things as desks'. Now if the argument from examples is to be applied to validity its main contention will be, put in its most succinct form, that 'valid' means 'like these standard examples in certain essential respects' and that 'invalid' means 'like these other standard examples in certain essential respects'. Which arguments are suitable standard cases and what respects are relevant will of course depend on whether we are considering deductive, inductive, or ethical arguments. But this is a mistaken contention, not merely in detail but in principle, and for a very simple reason. The reason is that to call an argument valid is not merely to classify it logically, as when we say it is a syllogism or *modus ponens* ; it is at least in part to evaluate or appraise it ; it is to signify approval of it. Similarly to call an argument invalid is to condemn or reject it. Therefore while it is plausible to say that 'solid' means the same as 'of the consistency of certain standard objects such as desks', it cannot be said that 'valid' means the same as 'of the same logical character as certain standard arguments such as a syllogism in Barbara' : in the former case we are legitimately equating the meaning of two classificatory expressions, in the second we are illegitimately equating the meaning of a classificatory expression, pure and simple, with an expression which is, at least in part, evaluative in its meaning.

I take it that once stated it is obvious that 'valid' is an evaluative expression. To speak of a good argument is in most contexts equivalent to speaking of a valid argument, for example; it would be ridiculous if, when asked to produce an argument to support a position which I had taken up, I were to enquire whether valid or invalid arguments would be preferred. It seems that any detailed argument on this point would be otiose. What we can more importantly do is to consider how the arguments under review can be restated when amended in the light of the point just made and then to ask of them how much they prove in the more correct form.

As a preliminary to the restatement of the argument we must first say something in general about the logic of evaluative terms. Shortness of space compels me to put this portion of my argument very dogmatically, for which fact an apology is undoubtedly .due to the reader. For my arguments in support of my views I must refer the reader elsewhere.[1]

Some evaluative expressions claim only to indicate a personal preference, as, for example, when we say that we like something. One is not compelled to give reasons for liking something, and, if one does, one's reasons are at the worst odd, not improper. But some evaluative expressions clearly claim a more general validity. If instead of saying that we like something we say that it is good then reasons are demanded, are counted as good or bad reasons, and may be argumentatively countered by reasons against. In general it would seem that the straightforward use of such terms as 'good' in a given field presupposes a set of agreed standards of goodness in that field amongst those who use it ; giving reasons for or against a thing being good is to show that it conforms to these standards. Thus in a given circle the standards for goodness in apples may be a certain taste, size, shape, keeping qualities, absence of worm-holes, etc. ; then to give reasons for saying

[1] 'On Grading' in *Mind*, 1950 (reprinted in *Logic and Language*, Vol. II).

that an apple is good is to show that it has these characters. If I sell as good apples which fall far short of the accepted standards I am liable to get into trouble ; if I do not know what standards are being used when they speak of good apples, then in a good sense I do not fully understand them. There is thus a close logical connexion between an evaluative expression and the accepted standards for its appropriate use ; but this cannot be identity of meaning, for no evaluation can be identical in meaning with a description. Here the analytic-synthetic distinction breaks down.

It is surely clear that 'valid' is one of those evaluative terms which, like 'good', claim to show more than a personal preference. It is more specialized than 'good' in its application, as are 'brave' and 'intelligent' ; it is used only to evaluate arguments and then only from a certain point of view — an invalid argument might indeed be preferable for the persuasion of stupid people, and as a valid argument may have false premises validity never can involve total satisfactoriness. But it seems that in its logical character validity resembles goodness very closely, and when the context is clear we often use 'valid' and 'good' indifferently. If there is this resemblance, then we may expect there to be factual criteria or standards for its use, whether implicit or explicit, and these criteria will have a close logical connexion not amounting to identity of meaning with the evaluative term itself. Let us see if we can reformulate our arguments from standard examples in a way which does justice to this logical situation.

If amongst a certain group of people the evaluative distinction between valid and invalid arguments is recognized, whether the arguments in question be deductive, inductive, or ethical, then we shall expect to find criteria of validity which are generally accepted by the group. Otherwise they will not be able to use the distinction but only at the best to argue about how to use it. If we want to know what these standards are, we can only find out what these standards or criteria are if we examine what are agreed to be valid and invalid arguments and elicit the criteria from them. Even if a list of theoretically agreed standards is already available we shall still have to check this list against actual practice if we want to know what the standards actually are ; the argument from standard examples must teach us that this is the final court of appeal on the question what the standards are, if it teaches us nothing else. So, as a reformulation of the argument from standard examples, we can at least say this : if we can elicit from the usage of a group a set of criteria for the validity of a certain kind of argument, then it is pointless to ask whether *for that group* there is any distinction between valid and invalid arguments of the kind in question, or to say that there is no such distinction for them ; for we already know what the distinction is. But, we can now add, we ourselves are a group which makes such distinctions, so that it is pointless to ask whether we have, or to deny that we have, criteria for the validity and invalidity of all these kinds of argument. Even if we have not yet been able to make these criteria explicit, none the less the fact that we do succeed in all these fields in using the words 'valid' and 'invalid' in an intelligible way, the fact that there are standard cases of validity which outside his study no one would deny, shows that the doubt when expressed in the study is absurd or at least incorrectly formulated.

(b) *What does this argument in fact show ?*

Now that we have reformulated the arguments with which we are concerned, or rather indicated a general way of re-formulating them without elaborating each in turn, what value can we attach to them ? Will they convince the philo-sophical sceptic ?

When we have elicited the standards for counting an apple good which are current in a group — taste, size, absence of worm-holes, etc., we can no longer ask whether it is possible for that group to distinguish good and bad apples. But we can perfectly properly ask why they use these standards and whether we ourselves have any good reason for using them — a question which in the case of apples is not very difficult to answer. We may note, too, that the question may be asked in two quite different spirits. We may ask in a spirit of genuine doubt whether we should accept these standards, and whether there are any good reasons for doing so, or we may be quite happy in the employment of these standards but ask why we employ them in a spirit of philosophical enquiry.

It is surely clear that in the same way when we have elicited our standards of validity we shall still be faced with the further question : granted that this is the way in which we distinguish between valid and invalid arguments in this field, what good reason have we for evaluating arguments in this way ? Once again, the question can be asked in a spirit of genuine doubt or as a philosophical enquiry. It is an unfortunate fact that philosophers have continually cast their question in the form of scepticism, when it is quite clear that in fact they have no thought of abandoning the distinction. Now it is a fact of usage that when someone is sceptical of standards he often formulates his query, not in the form 'Are there good reasons for using these criteria of goodness ?', but in the form 'Are these things *really* good ?' And so we get the question 'Are these arguments really valid ?' One cannot say that this is incorrect, as those who employ the argument from standard examples often say, but one can deplore it.

We have the first order question whether, say, an apple is good, and the second order question why we count such apples good. It appears that we have the same two questions with regard to the validity of arguments. We can ask of a particular argument whether it is good (valid), to which the answer will sometimes be that it is a paradigm of good arguments. But we can also ask why we count such arguments good, and there seems to be nothing improper in asking such a question, however much we may deplore the pseudo-sceptical form in which it is often phrased. Professor Ayer has said :[1] '. . . in the case of any belief about a matter of fact what counts as good evidence is inductive evidence. So to raise the general question whether inductive evidence is good, is to

[1] *British Empirical Philosophers*, pp. 26-7.

ask whether what counts as good evidence really is good evidence; and I do not think that this question is significant'. This may be correct, so long as we are clear that being inductive is a criterion of, not what is meant by, good evidence. But the question still remains why we count inductive evidence as good evidence; probably those who ask the question which Ayer regards as meaningless have in fact been asking this significant question in a misleading way.

Our arguments show, then, that there is something very misleading about the formulation of some traditional problems, and many philosophers have been misled by such formulations. It is wrong to ask whether inductive or ethical arguments are ever valid. But it would appear to be possible to reformulate these questions to run : 'Why do we count as valid those arguments, inductive or ethical, which we do count as valid ?' When so reformulated the questions are quite proper. It is therefore a mistake to think that the arguments we have considered dispose of these basic problems, for they remain.

It is worth noticing that the serious muddles which have arisen elsewhere have not risen in the case of deductive argument. It is true that some authors have spoken as though 'valid' were here a logical term of the same type as 'disjunctive', but this has not often caused trouble. In the case of deductive argument the higher order question has never, or hardly ever, been formulated in the misleading way : 'Are deductive arguments ever valid', but in the form 'Why are they counted valid ?', and in a spirit of philosophical enquiry. We may not be entirely satisfied with any answer to this question which has been given, but most discussion of the topic has been sane, and some of it has surely advanced the frontiers of knowledge. It is the ridiculous way in which the higher order question has been put that has prevented similar sanity with regard to ethics and induction.

The argument from standard examples does not then do what it was intended to do in the field of validity, at least by some who have used it. But it does compel us to reformulate

the traditional problems in a healthier way. This is no matter
of pedantry ; in philosophy the correct formulation of problems is half the battle. To move from the question 'Are any
inductive arguments valid ?' to the question 'What good
reasons can be given for rating arguments of a certain type
higher than arguments of another type ?' is to make a real
advance, before any answer is found. Above all, we get away
from bogus doubt into methodical philosophical research.
Above all, these arguments compel us to take seriously the
need for a careful analysis of the nature of the inductive,
ethical, and other types of argument that we actually use.
We cannot ask for the reasons for the use of the criteria of
validity that we do use without an actual examination of these
criteria. In the past there has been too much *a priori* argument about the 'possibility of induction' based on equally *a
priori* notions of what inductive arguments were actually
like. It is a merit of those philosophers whose arguments we
have been considering that they have seen the need for a careful examination of the forms of our arguments, even if it has
often been a defect that they have not seen that further
enquiries remain.

My main contention has been that the attempt to discuss
the question of validity by means of an argument from
standard examples is misconceived, leading to the attempted
dismissal of genuine philosophical questions. There is indeed
no important philosophical question 'Why do we call things
of the consistency of desks solid ?' If we assimilate the
logical character of validity to that of solidity we are tempted
not to notice, or to dismiss as absurd, the question 'Why do
we count arguments of this and that sort as valid ?' The
evaluative character of 'valid' is here overlooked. Thus ex-
aggerated claims have been made for the force of these arguments. Such problems as the central 'problem of induction'
have been thought to vanish into thin air. But I have also
wished to claim that these arguments have not been simply
misconceived. There are two problems : what are the criteria
for validity of arguments in a given field, and why do we

employ these criteria. As a result of these arguments we reach a better formulation of the second problem, and the need for a thorough examination of the first becomes apparent. If it is wrong to deny the existence of the second problem, it is at least as wrong to fail to notice the autonomy of the first.

QUEEN'S COLLEGE, UNIVERSITY OF ST. ANDREWS

Chapter VII

THE NATURE OF FACTS[1]

BY PETER HERBST

To be sincerely interested in a problem and to be interested in the solution of a problem are one and the same. If one approaches a problem with mental reservations, one shows thereby that one is not interested in solving the problem, but only in toying with it, or making use of it for purposes not connected with its solution, or in providing an apology for one given solution. The explanation of the interest in language shown by the philosophers who have contributed to this book, and by the many other like-minded philosophers, is that they think that certain sorts of linguistic study are relevant to philosophy. In this chapter I have set myself the task of showing how linguistic considerations bear on two questions which have been singled out as peculiarly philosophical and not at all linguistic, namely, 'How many kinds of fact are there?' and 'To what facts do certain (given) forms of expression refer?' About half the chapter will be concerned with drawing distinctions which bear on the question 'What is a fact?' (as distinct from, e.g., a theory). The remainder will be concerned with questions arising out of the notion that facts are what factual statements refer to.

I

How many kinds of fact are there? We cannot answer this question univocally. If it were asked 'How many kinds

[1] In its original form as an article this chapter had a particular polemical target. The present first paragraph has been inserted to replace a much more polemical and particular introduction, the last two paragraphs of the original have been omitted entirely to avoid this polemical particularity, and a large number of minor corrections and alterations have been made to the remainder.

of animal are there?' we might enumerate: 'Fish, birds, insects, mammals, reptiles . . .' or, counting on a different principle: 'Sharks and trout and hake and cod . . .' or restrict ourselves to two kinds, rational animals and non-rational animals. What is the relevance of this? It is part of what some call a 'linguistic study', an attempt to suggest and support an answer to the question 'How does the phrase "kind of" function?' It functions in such a way that for questions of the form 'How many kinds of x are there?' to be answered univocally, it must *at least* be specifiable for purposes of any given question what is to constitute a difference in kind. Furthermore, if it were asked 'How many kinds of motor-car are there?' and if it were to be understood that each brand of motor-car is to count as one kind, the question would still not be univocally answerable. The reason is that it is not clear what is to be included amongst motor-cars. For if only four-wheeled motor-carriages are to be considered, the number will be smaller than if six-wheeled and eight-wheeled vehicles, trucks, buses, and semi-trailers are to be considered also.

How, then, shall we get clear about what to include or what to exclude from amongst facts? It seems to me that in order to answer this question we must examine the use of such phrases as 'a question of fact', 'a matter of fact', 'the realm of fact', etc. Let us begin with a characteristic use of the phrase 'as a matter of fact'. Two people are talking about a child and one of them says, 'As a matter of fact, he is an orphan'. If the question whether the child is an orphan had come up for dispute, this man might have said, 'Well, I know it for a fact'. Such a remark has the effect or is intended to have the effect of cutting the argument short. Nevertheless the speaker can be asked to justify his air of authority or the assured manner with which he speaks. The challenge may take the form of 'How do you know?' or 'Why are you so sure?' His claim is made good if he can satisfy us that he is in a position to know or that he has satisfactory reasons. He may say that since he is on the board of governors of the orphanage he *ought to know*, or refer us to the parish register (or a guaranteed copy of the parish register), or again he may offer a (conclusive) set of reasons drawn from circumstantial evidence, etc.

If a man cannot justify a claim to know something for a fact and has no excuse for his inability to justify his claim, then he can reasonably be expected to withdraw it. For instance : it would be quite improper for a man to claim to know for a fact that the Emperor Barbarossa died in his bed (he was drowned) if he is unable to point to any new evidence bearing on Barbarossa's death. If he wishes to be entitled to say (on occasions on which history is being talked about seriously) 'As a matter of fact, Barbarossa died in his bed', then he must be able to present such evidence or advance such arguments as would place the question beyond reasonable dispute. If he cannot do that, then he must moderate his claim. To state something as a fact is to state it authoritatively (as one who is in a position to say), to vouch for it, or to state it without reservations or safeguards. And if I have established something with my own eyes, at leisure and in broad daylight, or if I have established it from what appeared to be conclusive reasons, then reservations and safeguards are idle. I can of course always add phrases like 'unless my eyes deceived me' or 'unless I am mistaken', but if I *always* add them, I do not safeguard myself. If they come to be used merely as a matter of convention they cease to operate as safeguards. We do not necessarily hold people dear whom we address as 'Dear Sir'. Also a man might say, 'My wife will soon be better, *God willing*', and we gather from this that there is cause for anxiety. But if we find that he adds '*God willing*' to *all* statements referring to the future, then we may conclude that our concern was misplaced.

Matters of fact contrast with matters of opinion. If any person wishes to make a statement or assertion for which he is in no position to vouch (as eye-witnesses are in a position to vouch) and for which he has no conclusive reasons or evidence, then he cannot preface his statement or assertion with the words 'as a matter of fact . . .', and he cannot claim that what he says is a palpable fact. If the evidence is more or less one way but insufficient, we will most likely speak of a conjecture or guess ; if the evidence could also be construed so as to support a plausible alternative conclusion, then we will say that he has stated an opinion. If one man lacks evidence which another man has, then the same utterance, as from the lips of the former, may apprise us of his conjectures or opinions, while as from the lips of the latter it ranks as a statement of fact. If there are any matters on which no one (nowadays) can speak with authority or possess such evidence as would enable him to claim to know the facts, then these matters are matters of opinion or matters for speculation or conjecture. *But to say of any matter that it is a matter of opinion or a matter for speculation or conjecture is not to say that questions concerning it are not questions of fact.* It is only to say that they are questions to which no one can justifiably give the answer with the authority of a witness or without qualification or apology.

You may recall questions of the type : 'How many ichthyosauruses were born during a given year so-and-so many thousand years ago ?' and argue that they cannot be questions of fact since they are utterly unanswerable. It is indeed unlikely that anyone can collect the evidence from which so specific a question can be answered after so long a time. It is also true that no contemporary human observer could have answered it at the time since there were no human observers then. The response — if not the answer — to such questions is 'God knows'. This is not a way of saying that the question is not a question of fact (does not God know all the facts ?). It is a way of saying that no evidence to answer this question can now be obtained and presumably also that it has always been impossible and will always be impossible within the limits of our experience for any human being to obtain this evidence. From this it does not, however, follow (as some have thought) that it is the sort of question which is unanswerable in principle. God's advantage over the rest of us lies only in His being the sole survivor from those days, Who then, without exerting Himself, was able to see all the ichthyosauruses there were all at one glance. It is clear then that we must distinguish between questions which are un-answerable in principle and which no conceivable observer could answer, and questions which are unanswerable only from lack of a sufficient number of sufficiently advantageously placed observers and computers. (God is formally equivalent to an infinite number of infinitely efficient observers and computers.)

Questions of fact stand opposed to questions of mathema-tics and formal logic, questions of language, questions of law, questions of right and wrong and good and bad, questions of philosophy and *e.g.* art-criticism, also questions of taste and questions of attitude, etc., etc. The manner of this opposition is more or less different for each case and it is not my task to give an exhaustive account of it here. Suffice it to say, for instance, that the opposition between questions of art-criticism and questions of fact is sharper than that between questions of mathematics and questions of fact. For in the matter of characterizing or appraising pictures we can neither claim to be in the position of witnesses, nor yet adduce irrebuttable demonstrative arguments so as to compel the assent of all rational creatures. Questions of criticism are not decided from the testimony of privileged observers; observation, measurement, and experiment have no part in answering them. Reasons for an appraisal of a picture are weighed against one another, but which is the weightier is not estab-lished with the aid of a beam balance. Thus questions of criticism are non-factual, but also such that no one can claim to know the answer 'as a matter of fact'. Things are very different in elementary mathematics. In an addition sum nothing remains to be discussed when the sum has been done. Nobody will be taken seriously if he claims to be able to upset the result with an entirely new set of arguments. If you carry out the appropriate mathematical operation (ad-

THE NATURE OF FACTS

dition) you obtain the answer, and if you have carried it out correctly then your answer is the right answer. If two people do an addition sum and get different answers, then one of them at least has made a slip or a mistake. It would be absurd to say of them that they were of different opinions.

I would like to say that (characteristic) factual questions are empirical questions. If, as I have suggested, it must always make sense in factual questions for there to be or to have been a (more or less infinitely observant) observer or witness to obtain the answer, then for all factual questions what somebody saw, heard, or felt, the outcome of some experiment, or what he measured or counted, etc., must always be relevant. But perhaps to speak only of observers or witnesses is misleading. Counting, exploring, inspecting front, back, and sides, feeling for something with one's hands, prodding, tapping (for sound), and sniffing (to see if one sneezes) are all empirical procedures, and there are many more. We must also take care not to exclude psychological factual statements in the first person singular, e.g. 'Whenever I sit in a cramped position I get pins and needles'. We do not observe, witness, or inspect our sensations or feelings, we have them. But questions concerning whether and when we have certain sensations and feelings are factual questions. If I have a pain, it is for me to say; concerning my pain I may speak with authority (though it certainly is not the authority of a witness). For simplicity's sake I will classify psychological assertions in the first person singular with the reports of witnesses and observers. But I do not wish to be taken thereby to have assented to the classical doctrines of introspection, intuition, and inner sense.

We may be tempted to think that all questions to which an answer may be returned with authority or justifiable assurance are factual questions. An examination of the use of such phrases as 'as a matter of fact . . .', 'he knows the fact that . . .', or 'are you aware of the fact that . . .?' inclines us to this conclusion. However, there are reasons why it should be rejected. There is a class of questions, drawn especially from mathematics and formal logic, to which answers may be returned with complete assurance (on matters which are certainly not matters of opinion) but which are nevertheless not questions of fact.   True, an examiner (who is reading a faulty examination paper) may be irked into exclaiming, 'This candidate does not seen to be aware of the fact that quadratic equations have more than one solution', nevertheless the candidate's ignorance is not on a point of fact.   The candidate cannot, for instance, complain 'nobody told me' without standing condemned out of his own mouth : this not a matter which he ought to have to be told.   He has to be told who discovered America or read it in a book, and he has to be told about the spots on the surface of the sun or look at the sun himself, but he need not be told about quadratic equations, and there is nowhere for him to look. It is always in principle possible for there to be or to have been an observer who is or was in a position to answer a (characteristically) factual question directly.   His authority does not lie in his being an *expert* in the sort of questions to which an answer is required, rather it rests in his being or having been in a position to observe.   An eye-witness has privileged access over other people to what he witnesses. They must reconstruct what happened from the reports of eye-witnesses, while *he just saw what happened.*   There are no people who can 'just tell us' about mathematics.   There are no mathematical truths to which anyone has privileged access.   Those who speak with authority on mathematics are the experts,[1] not the eye-witnesses.

There are some questions connected with the law to which the answer is arguable, but others to which the answer is beyond dispute.   Both kinds of question are legal questions

---

[1] In non-theoretical subjects such as geography or descriptive anatomy the experts are people who have all the facts at their fingers' tips, or else can lay their hand on all the facts in the reference books.   Tea-tasters and people with an absolute sense of pitch are also sometimes referred to as expert.   Their expertness consists in that they have more refined powers of discrimination than most other people, which in general they acquire by training.   In the present context I do not mean by an expert either a walking encyclopaedia or a person with refined powers of discrimination.

and not factual questions, though a lawyer who retails the contents of the statute-book to a layman may well avail himself of the idiom 'as a matter of fact the law says . . .'. It is true that law students sometimes complain that they have to learn such a lot of facts. What they mean is that they have to memorize things. But historians also have to commit much detail to memory and nevertheless there are no legal facts on an analogy with historical facts. For historical documents, records, and archives record something — not only events, but also intentions, hopes, fears, plans, projects, decisions, threats, and admonitions. But historical documents are often (especially taken one by one) unreliable guides to the past. They contain *inter alia* inaccuracies, misleading references, fantasies, wish-fulfilments, and deliberate misrepresentations, and often they fail to make it clear whether they contain reports or conjectures. They participate in the shortcomings of witnesses with the additional disadvantage that they cannot be cross-examined. But the statute-book does not witness to anything (unless it be the Will of Parliament); thus it is absurd to ask whether its testimony is reliable or objective. The law is (at least in part) what the statute-book records. The statute-book may specify that obstructing an officer of the Crown in the execution of his duty is an offence, but not because a parliamentary fact-finding commission has investigated whether this kind of conduct actually is generally punishable, but because the Sovereign on the advice of Parliament has decreed that it *shall be* punishable. The facts which law students have to learn are not recorded in the statute-book. What they have to learn is the fact that the contents of the statute-book are what they are.

There is a corresponding temptation to say that all empirical questions must be factual. This, however, would be a mistake : there are also theoretical questions which are empirical. Factual statements are opposed to theoretical statements. But for purposes of drawing this distinction it must not be thought that the statement of any theory whatsoever will count as a theoretical statement. All sorts of

L

things are referred to as theories which might, with greater incisiveness, be characterized as interpretations placed upon the facts or as speculations as to the facts or as conjectures. Even amongst characteristic theories there is sufficient difference in logical type to make generalizations hazardous. I will give one example of a theory which, so far from being opposed to fact, establishes a fact by being itself established.

It has long been known that a certain river loses water in one of its reaches. A geologist notices that certain springs a hundred miles away are exceptionally vigorous judged by the size of the catchment area. He considers the structure of the intervening rock-strata and arrives at the theory (or sets up the hypothesis) that there is a series of subterranean caves connecting river and springs. He tests his theory by adding potassium permanganate to the water of the river and waits for the springs to turn pink. If this succeeds he may take soundings or decide to look for an alternative entrance to the caves and explore them in detail. Now what sort of a theory is this? The theory states that a river and some springs are connected by subterranean caves. But if it is true, then there are such caves, and then it is a fact that there are such caves. Such a theory as this may be called a theory while it is *unconfirmed*, but after it is confirmed nobody wishes to speak of a theory any longer. What the theory asserts is a fact.

The example which we have just considered is drawn from the applied sciences. Now let us turn to theoretical science. The atomic theory, the molecular theory of gases, the anti-body theory of immunity, and the wave and quantum theories of radiation may serve as examples of general theories of the theoretical sciences. It seems to me that such theories as these do not assert facts. To interpret them as if they asserted facts is a sign of a certain naïveté. The student who upon being told that there are particles which have neither mass nor charge wishes to get hold of one of these with a view to weighing it on a beam balance is like a child who, upon being told that there is a country in which (non-luminous)

things are visible in the dark, wishes to go there to see for
himself. Theoretical statements contain mention of or make
reference to theoretical concepts. Examples of theoretical
concepts are atom, energy, quantum, entropy, and field.
Theoretical statements offer an explanation of the facts, but
not in terms of more facts. They cannot be understood
except with the aid of a set of rules for their interpretation
(though they are frequently naïvely misunderstood). One
cannot know what is meant by statements about forces in
classical mechanics unless one has been trained to interpret
them in the light of Newton's laws of motion, and of these
it has frequently been said that they do not only state truths
and falsehoods, but that, at least in part, they elucidate a
set of concepts to be employed in the interpretation and
explanation of dynamic phenomena. Of a fact we can always
in principle have more or less direct knowledge. I may
discover that a certain person is a convicted felon through a
study of old newspaper files though others know this even
without newspapers. I may come to suspect the existence of
certain subterranean caves from geological speculations and
to confirm it with soundings and potassium permanganate-
coloured water, but if I had been drilling a hole I might
have come across them directly. If I cannot now check up
directly on facts about the past this does not mean that people
in the past could not have checked up on those very same
facts directly, and if I personally cannot by observation check
up on some fact about all Americans, this is only because
there are so many of them. But supposing somebody offered
me a long, complicated and theoretical argument about there
being particles without charge (neutrinos), if I say to him
'Never mind the argument, let's go and have a look at one
of them' then it is not so much that my request is impracti-
cable, or makes excessive demands on the observer, or comes
too late, *it is absurd in principle and would never be made by
one who had properly understood the theory*. This also
explains why no one can offer theoretical statements with
the same air of authority with which some people can report

the facts.   Nobody can just tell us about the neutrino.
Nobody can travel to the land of the neutrino or meet it face
to face.   The theory about the neutrino is not like a person
who has been good enough to introduce us to a well-known
recluse with whom we subsequently come to be on intimate terms on our own account.   We cannot, so to speak,
after getting to know the neutrino drop the fellow who
introduced us.

Lastly, a few words about the difference between the
realm of fact and the realm of fiction.   Statements about what
Napoleon did or said, if true, state facts ; they are statements
within the realm of fact.   On the other hand, statements
about what Mr. Pickwick did or said do not tell us any facts
about a contemporary of Charles Dickens by the name of
Pickwick.   There never was a gentleman by the name of
Pickwick, or if there was, he was not meant.   Also there
never was any specific gentleman answering to the description
of Mr. Pickwick, or if there was, he was not meant either.
What Boswell says about Johnson is mostly true, but no
doubt sometimes false, according as Johnson did or said the
things attributed to him by Boswell.   But what Dickens says
about Pickwick is (in a straightforward sense) neither true
nor false, since there never was a character of whose life
Pickwick Papers purports to be the record.   Nevertheless
what you and I say about Pickwick may be true or false,
since what we say about Pickwick will presumably be about
the character created by Dickens, and what is true or false
about this character can be seen in Dickens's book.   There
are, I would like to say, some quasi-factual questions about
Mr. Pickwick, for instance the question whether he was ever
sued for breach of promise (this gets a mention in the book) ;
but there are some questions about Mr. Pickwick which, had
they been about Johnson, would have been factual questions,
but which in the nature of the case must *in principle* remain
a matter for speculation, for instance whether Mr. Pickwick
used to be chastised by his mother when he was little (this gets
no mention in the book).   Finally there are some questions

about Mr. Pickwick which in the nature of the case must be matters of opinion, such as whether he is a representative portrait of English middle-class gentlemen of his period, and moral questions, such as whether Mr. Pickwick behaved well in a certain situation.

It makes no sense to speak of a fictional question on an analogy with factual questions or questions of theory. We speak of a realm of fiction because every conceivable kind of question that can arise about an actual person can also be asked about a character in a book. True, many questions which would be sensible had they been asked about actual people are pointless if they are asked about a fictitious character, and the method of verifying an answer is generally different. We are apt to think of the scene created by the novelist as fundamentally like our own (only richer, more intense), and we half think of ourselves as viewing it through the window of the book, and half think of the writer as having viewed it and then recorded it for our benefit. But if we think of it thus, then we will wish to know how accurately he has 'recorded' this other world, and the answer must be, 'How can he have recorded it accurately or inaccurately, seeing that he created it?'

II

So far we have considered questions which we may or may not wish to describe as linguistic; the point of considering them was to help us to determine the range of the concept 'fact'. But I expect to be told that I have after all confined myself to an analysis of the use of factual expressions and have avoided saying anything about the facts to which they refer. The argument in favour of this contention may be that facts are distinct from factual utterances or statements, since the former are the standard of the truth or falsity of the latter. Some utterances state facts, others serve to remind people of facts, to ask factual questions or to appeal to facts in an argument; it might therefore be said that what they all have in common is that they refer to facts. Now just as it is possible to ask whom a given proper name names, and after what manner it refers to him whom it names, so it might be asked to what fact a given factual utterance refers and after what manner it refers to it. Information concerning the nature of one term of a relation cannot (according to this argument) be gathered from an analysis of the other term, hence the structure and use of factual expressions cannot be expected to yield information concerning the nature of facts.

Against this the argument must be that there is no such thing as first informing a person of a fact and then telling him which fact it is of which he has been informed. If I tell somebody plainly that his house is on fire, he cannot very well ask with which fact I had intended to acquaint him ; if he does, I shall be tempted to think that he is deaf. How should I do any better than I have already done ? I have told him — his house is on fire. But allowing for the possibility that perhaps he took me to be joking I may add the words, ' I'm in earnest'. If he *doubts my words*, I can do no better than take him to the spot and show him his burning house. But in so doing I do not *confront* him with the fact of which I had previously *informed* him, but I merely put him into the position of seeing for himself that what I had said to him was true. What he will see will be a burning house. True enough, he may say that he sees *that* the house is burning, but this will not be an additional sight. He who sees that a house is burning will naturally see a burning house, but this will not mean that he sees two things, first the fact that the house is burning and then the burning house, but only that he sees the one thing which entitles him to say both that he sees a burning house and also that he sees a house and that it is burning.

One to whom I address statements of fact may not understand my words, he may be in doubt about what interpretation to place on my words, ignorant of some matter referred to in my words, or not know how to construe my words — *e.g.*

seriously or as a joke. Above all, he may suspect me of lying, or wonder whether I might not be mistaken. But his doubts will not be like the doubts of the recipient of a cryptic telegram reading 'Contact Smith' who would like to know which Smith to contact. They will be more like the doubts of an engine-driver who finds a signal green which for his train is normally red. His difficulty is not that he does not know what a green light signifies, it is that he suspects that something may have happened to the signalman or that the signalling mechanism may have broken down.

We must look into this matter more closely. If one thinks of a statement as a sentence, one may incline to the view that the element of indefiniteness which characterizes so many sentences ensures that we may sensibly ask about the reference of any given statement. One calls to mind that factual statements may *inter alia* contain proper names. Thus if somebody says, 'John loves Mary', it is not evident from his words which John loves which Mary, and thus it is not clear to which amatory bond his statement refers. Against this we must bear in mind the possibility that nobody by the name of John loves any Mary and ask ourselves whether in these circumstances the statement that John loves Mary lacks a reference which it would otherwise have had, or whether it now refers to a potential fact or to an unrealized fact or to any other denizen of those spooky parts.

Intending to make a certain statement is one thing— succeeding in making a statement which conveys what one intends to state is quite another. Suppose that someone has been assaulted by robbers and means to make a statement to the police. What the police require from him is not just a statement, but a precise, unambiguous, accurate statement. If his statement is confused, muddy, contradictory or sketchy, full of veiled allusions, insufficiently specific references, or couched in incomprehensible language, then it is an unsatisfactory statement, and in the limiting case it is not a statement at all. Unsatisfactory statements are not proper ways of referring to an indefinite set of facts, they are improper ways

of making statements.   They may be variously interpreted
and variously treated according as they are interpreted, but
for those who make them there can be no question of inter-
preting them.   It is clear that if we found a slip of paper with
the words 'Foo was here' in the street, we would not treat
these words as a factual statement until we found the writer
of the words and elicited from him who was meant by 'Foo'
and what locality the reflexive 'here' referred to.   It is not
then a question of what the unsatisfactory statement states,
for by being unsatisfactory it fails to state.   The question is
what he who made the unsatisfactory statement meant to state.
But in explaining this, he *replaces* his unsatisfactory statement with another statement which, to fulfil its purpose must
be more intelligible than the original statement.

Thus if somebody says, 'John loves Mary, do you agree ?',
I am bound to side-step his question if I do not know who is
supposed to be loving whom.   How could I agree to his words
or fail to agree to them if I do not know what I am supposed
to agree to ?   Still, it might be objected that the speaker
might never have meant to state that any specific John loves
any specific Mary, but merely that somewhere somebody
named John loves somebody named Mary (in which he could
hardly be wrong).   If that is what he meant, then he was
right, provided that *any* lover is called John whose love's
name is Mary.   But this is not to say that there is any question
about what the statement states.   It merely means that the
conditions under which this factual statement is true are
wider than they would have been had the statement been
about a specific couple of lovers.   It is of course quite true
that the non-specific factual statement that somebody called
John loves somebody called Mary can be supported by any
of a number of specific facts, for instance that John Robinson
loves Mary Brown.   But it would be misleading to express
this by saying that it refers to this fact.   If I say that some
musicians turn politician, I may have had Paderewski in
mind, I may even be said to have alluded to him, but that is
not to say that my statement refers to the fact that Paderewski

turned politician. And if I say pointedly that some people overhear unpleasant truths about themselves, I may allude to Mrs. X, but that is not to say that my statement refers to the fact that Mrs. X has had this unpleasant experience. Some factual statements are only true if any of a class of factual statements are true; others (factual hypotheses or statements with a complex verification) are only true if quite a lot of other factual statements are true, and others still (inductions by complete enumeration) are only true if each several member of a given class of particular factual statements is true. But to say of any given fact that it makes some general factual statement true is not to say that the general factual statement refers to it, and to say of a fact that it enters into the verification of a factual statement is again not to say that this statement refers to it. In factual statements we make reference to whatever their referential terms (if any) refer to. In statements about John Robinson we refer to John Robinson, in statements about the solar eclipse of such-and-such a date we refer to a certain natural phenomenon. There are plenty of facts about John Robinson and about the eclipse, but they themselves are not facts.

The name 'John Robinson' (occurring in statements, whether or not they are true or false) has in each case a reference which it is possible to apprehend, misapprehend, or to fail to apprehend. This reference can be got right or wrong. If factual statements referred to facts there would presumably also be such a thing as *pointing out* the fact to which they referred. There would then be such a thing as warding people off mistakes and guiding them in the right direction — as we do when we say to a child, 'No, I don't mean that one, I mean the one over there by the table'. We can explain the reference. But in the case of facts no such question arises. There is no reference to facts that we can misapprehend, there is no reference to facts that we can apprehend correctly, there is no reference to facts at all.

Mr. Strawson has said : Facts 'are what statements (when true) state ; they are not what statements are about. They are not like things or happenings on the face of the globe, witnessed or heard or seen, broken or overturned, interrupted or prolonged, kicked, destroyed, mended or noisy'.[1]   In the language of ontology : facts are not part of the furniture of the world.   Hence the question, 'How many kinds of fact are there ?' or the question, 'To what sort of fact do certain (given) usages refer ?' are profoundly misleading.   The question, 'How many kinds of fact are there ?' should not be construed as 'How many things, beings, entities are there for factual statements to refer to ?' but as 'What manner of variety is there amongst sentences, statements, reports, utterances and suppositions which may be called factual ?'   Factual questions are empirical ; we decide whether something is a fact by using our eyes and ears, gathering evidence, counting, measuring, and by the rest of the established procedures of empirical investigation.   But that is not to say that facts are amongst the things we see or count or measure.   The question 'What is a fact ?' is utterly unanswerable and plunges us straight into a metaphysical miasma if we construe it as 'What sort of thing is a fact ?'   A fact is no sort of a thing, *a fact is what a true factual statement states*.[2]   Hence the question can only be answered via those other less mystifying and therefore less profound-seeming questions : 'What is a statement of fact, what is a question of fact, what is a matter of fact or a factual issue ?'   He who has heard a factual statement uttered with a serious mien and understood what was said, *ipso facto* understands that he is invited to consider what the statement states to be a fact ; if he does not understand this he must have mistaken the statement for a joke, a story, a linguistic exercise, or a philosophical example.   Of course he cannot know merely from understanding the statement whether it is true.   But if he has satisfied himself in the

---

[1] P. F. Strawson, contribution to symposium on 'Truth', *P.A.S.*, Suppl. Vol. XXIV, p. 136.

[2] This is no reason for thinking — as Mr. Strawson seems to think — that if there were no language there could be no facts either.   If a factual statement comes to be made for the first time, the fact which it states is not made along with it.   See pp. 153-4.

usual manner that it is true, then he is in a position to say
that the statement states a fact. *That which entitles us to say
that a factual statement is true and that which entitles us to
say that a factual statement states a fact, are one and the same.*

We stand in danger of a series of further misunderstandings. For it may be thought that if facts are removed from
amongst the furniture of the world, they must have been allo-
cated to the realm, of the spirit, or worse still, to the limbo of
language. It is natural to ask how a theory or indeed a whole
system of knowledge about the physical universe can be
based on facts, if the facts themselves are outside the physical
universe. Must we admit as a consequence of what has just
been said that the empirical sciences and, *e.g.* the reports of
intelligence officers are really about words or meanings and
not, as they appear to be, about things and people? This
would be just the sort of wild speculative leap which the
minute philosophers of recent years have been trying to avoid.
I think that there is no need to allocate facts to any specific
metaphysical category, neither to 'the world', nor to 'the
mind', nor yet to 'language'. Let us consider some arguments to decide whether facts belong to the logical order of
'meanings' as might appear plausible in certain circumstances.

There is a certain temptation to think that what my
statements state must be their meaning. Failing to apprehend
my meaning is tantamount to failing to understand what
I have said or stated. Statements convey something from
the speaker to his audience and the success or failure of
the speaker in conveying this is determined by whether the
audience apprehends his meaning. I make a statement —
you do not know what I mean — I tell you. Or might we
not say that I speak or write to you and that my sentences
tell you what I mean? If my meaning is evident from my
sentences then must not my sentences proclaim their meaning ?
Must they not state their meaning? Then perhaps, if it is
true that true factual statements state facts, we may be led to
suppose that facts are a kind of meaning, surely a surprising
conclusion.

There is no harm in saying that sentences proclaim their meaning. It is an epigrammatic way of putting it, but useful for differentiating the meaning of well-formed sentences from, *e.g.*, the meaning of the laying on of hands. For in order to know the meaning of a symbolic act you need to be told, or you must infer its meaning ; watching it being performed by itself is not enough. But sentences do not have to have their meaning written underneath. How indeed could it be written underneath except in more sentences ; If you understand English and I speak English and if I express myself properly then my words convey my meaning to you. Only if I do not express myself clearly or properly will there be occasion to ask me, 'What do you mean ?' You will not, however, expect to be presented with what my words were tokens for (now in the flesh, so to speak) but you will be satisfied if I tell you what I mean in other, more carefully chosen words. My meaning is not as it were a precipitate left behind when my words have fled. My mind does not act as a filter which allows words to pass but keeps meanings behind. If I say what I mean, or at worst, if I explain what I mean, I have *ipso facto* acquainted you with my meaning. My meaning does not lurk behind my words, *my words convey it*.

The words of my statements state that S is P, nevertheless my explanations of my obscure statements state what my obscure statements failed to convey. And if my words state *their* meaning it is in the sense explained above, that is : they proclaim it. But then this is to say no more than that they fit within the framework of our common language. For *all* my words are intended thus to proclaim their meaning, unless indeed I am making up nonsense-sentences for philosophical exercises or indulging in free expression or experimenting with suggestive word-painting for the magazine *Angry Penguins*. But not all my words are formed to make up statements. Some serve to ask questions, others to put forward suppositions, etc. Clearly then if *statements* state something, it cannot be what *all* well-formed sentences proclaim.

We must take care not to speak of facts as if they were material things; similarly we must not speak of them as if they were airy-fairy nothings. On the contrary, they are said to be solid, palpable, hard and stubborn. We also speak of probing facts. The fancies, the lies and the inventions melt away before our probing finger, but the facts resist. The metaphor arises because it is natural to think of the stubbornness of facts on an analogy with the recalcitrance of matter. Hard substances like steel are more recalcitrant than soft substances like putty. It is not only a matter of getting hurt when one bumps into them, but also that one cannot shape them at will, divide them up into bits, disintegrate them or mingle them with other matter. If one thinks of facts on an analogy with steel one will think of them as not easily destroyed or altered. But it makes no sense to speak of them either as easy or as difficult to destroy or alter or disintegrate or adulterate or to bring into being or to abolish or to keep for a long time. It is indeed possible to speak of new facts, but new facts ·are newly discovered facts, or facts newly brought to light. Facts about new things, e.g. a new motor-car, are not said to be new facts. We may perhaps be tempted to say that if a new thing has come into being, then in consequence of this a set of facts about this new thing has come into being also. But if a thing comes into being (in the ordinary sense of that phrase) then a time at which it would be true to say that that thing does not exist and false to say that it does exist is superseded by a time at which it is true to say that it does exist and false to say that it does not exist. Therefore if it makes sense to say of something that it can come into being, then it must at all times make sense to assert or deny that this thing exists. But in the case of the facts about the new Morris the time at which we can speak of there being such facts does not supersede a time at which we would merely have been mistaken in asserting that there were such facts, rather it supersedes the time at which no question concerning such facts could have arisen. If facts were independent existences like motor-cars, then it would have to be possible for the facts about the new Morris to have existed before the new Morris was built, or to have lagged behind after it was built. But this is absurd. The sort of sentences which are formally adequate for use in statements about the new Morris could not have been used in *factual* statements before the new Morris was built. They might have been used by Lord Nuffield to outline his conception, or by the Morris engineers to detail their plans, but not to state facts about a motor-car that did not as yet exist. It is highly misleading to say that if a new thing comes into existence facts about it come into being along with it. It is better to say what comes into being is a new subject for factual statements to be about.

One may be tempted to think that one can at least terminate the fact that Mr. Churchill is Prime Minister and create the fact that Mr. Attlee is (will be ?) Prime Minister by voting Labour at the next election. But those who contend that Churchill is Prime Minister now (*i.e.* at the time of writing this) are not refuted if Mr. Attlee gets back, and those who contend that Mr. Churchill will be Prime Minister for ever and ever have no claim to be stating a fact. Facts can be denied, forgotten, ignored, overlooked, glossed over or treated as if they were some foolish person's opinion, but they cannot suffer the fate of kingdoms, furniture or philosophical systems. Needless to say, facts also cannot be refuted. It makes no sense to speak of a false fact, the candidates for disgrace are contentions, statements and reports.

If after all this it is still felt that at any rate some facts must have a footing in spatio-temporal reality, let us remember that there are several terms which have this footing, and at the same time enter closely into the conceptual grammar of 'facts'. The most likely are 'events' (here taken to cover 'happenings', 'occurrences', 'beginning of . . .', 'end of . . .', 'change in . . .', etc.) and 'states of affairs'. The questions 'where ?' and 'when ?' are both relevant to either term. Events and states of affairs can be described, brought about or prevented, witnessed and observed, and people can be involved in them. States of affairs can be modified, altered, transformed, and terminated. In all these respects events and states of affairs differ from facts. They are part of the world, though if we accept the above criteria for hardness they are in this respect inferior.

The connexion between events or states of affairs and facts is as follows : The killing of Brutus by Caesar is an event. The statement, 'Brutus killed Caesar', states that this event took place. The statement is, however, a factual statement and we have every reason to think that it is true. What the statement states is therefore a fact unless we are mistaken in thinking that it is true. The fact in question is that Brutus killed Caesar. If Brutus had not killed Caesar then it would be false to say that this event, to wit the killing of Caesar by Brutus, ever took place. By the same token it would be false to say that Brutus killed Caesar. The factual statement 'Brutus killed Caesar' would then be false and would not be stating a fact. The sentence 'Brutus killed Caesar' and the barbarism 'the killing of Caesar by Brutus took place' both state the same thing. There are not two facts, one that Brutus killed Caesar and another that the event, to wit the killing, took place. There is only one fact. The barbarism rubs in what should be obvious enough to anyone who understands the factual statement, namely that if Brutus killed Caesar this was an event.

The feeling that unless factual statements refer to referents, they cannot be more than phantasms of the mind, can be dispelled. The notion that unless facts persist in space through time, they are airy-fairy rests on a misunderstanding.

I do not think that the spatio-temporal view of facts should be abandoned because it leads to difficulties in the case of general facts, but because it leads to absurdities in the case of *all* facts. Perhaps I should add in order to avoid misunderstandings that I can see no objection to saying that facts have a natural setting or context. Thus the fact that Brutus killed Caesar is undoubtedly *about* Brutus and *about*

Caesar too (it enters into the biographies of Caesar and Brutus) and in addition it may be said to be a fact *of* Roman history.

I think that characteristic questions of philosophy (questions which are at any rate not *about* language) cannot properly be attempted if certain considerations which spring from the analysis of language are ignored. I have tried to show that questions of the form, 'How many kinds of x are there?' are not univocally answerable unless it is specifiable what is to count as one kind, and that even so it is necessary to settle disputes about what is to qualify for the count. My procedure has roughly been to investigate what sort of things are *properly* termed facts. If something is properly called a fact then it follows that we have every reason to believe it to be a fact. And if I stop short of saying that if something is properly called a fact then it *is* a fact, this is not because it might turn out not to be a candidate for being a fact, but only because it is conceivable that evidence might come to light to show that our confidence in it had been misplaced. If we are mistaken about the manner of Caesar's death then the factual statement 'Brutus killed Caesar' might be said not to be true-in-virtue-of-a-fact, but not because it would be true in virtue of something else, but because it would not be true at all.

University College of the Gold Coast

Chapter VIII

PROBABILITY[1]

BY S. E. TOULMIN

So terrified was he of being caught, by chance, in a false statement, that as a small boy he acquired the habit of adding 'perhaps' to everything he said. 'Is that you, Harry?' Mama might call from the drawing-room. 'Yes, Mama — perhaps.' 'Are you going upstairs?' 'Yes, perhaps.' 'Will you see if I've left my bag in the bedroom?' 'Yes, Mama, perhaps — p'r'haps — paps!'
ELEANOR FARJEON, *A Nursery in the Nineties*, p. 252.

THIS subject is one in which the prolegomena are as neglected as they are important. Anyone who sets out to expound it as traditionally handled finds so much that is expected of him, so much that is beguiling to discuss — philosophical theories of considerable subtlety, a mathematical calculus of great formal elegance, and fascinating side-issues, like the legitimacy of talking about 'infinite sets' — that it is tempting to cut short the preliminary stating of the problem in order to get on to 'the real business in hand'.

Even Mr. William Kneale is open to criticism on this count; and this, despite the fact that his *Probability and Induction*[2] has deservedly become, from the day of publication, a standard work on the subject. The same difficulties arise over his book as over so many others. It is unclear what, in simple terms, are the questions which he is answering; and it is particularly hard to connect his statement of them with the sorts of everyday, practical situation in which words like 'probably', 'likely' and 'chance' are used. For Kneale writes almost exclusively in terms of such abstract nouns as 'probability', 'knowledge' and 'belief'. He appears

---

[1 Ideally this chapter should be read in conjunction with the same author's 'Critical Notice' of Rudolf Carnap's *The Logical Foundations of Probability*, in *Mind*, 1953; which it was impossible to reprint here.—EDITOR.]

[2] Referred to hereafter as *P & I*.

to accept as straightforward (and indeed states his problems in terms of) notions which to me are patent metaphors — even his initial description of probability, as 'the substitute with which we try to make good the shortcomings of our knowledge, the extent of which is less than we could wish',[1] being a metaphor taken from the trade in commodities.

Clearly this would not matter, if he gave a thorough account of the way in which his theoretical discussion is to be related to more familiar things : it would then be a legitimate and effective literary device.   But he does not.   And, if we reconstruct one for ourselves, we shall discover two things :

(i) that an abstract account of probability, knowledge and belief, such as Kneale gives, must fail in a number of essential respects to provide a satisfactory analysis of such phrases as 'I shall probably come', 'It seemed unlikely', 'They believe' and 'He didn't know' ; and

(ii) that the puzzles about probability at present fashionable are given their point by just this sort of over-reliance on abstract nouns : in fact, that it is to a great extent by asking the questions, 'What *is* Probability?   What are probability-statements *about*?   What do they *express*?' prematurely and in too general a form, that we set the discussion of the subject off along the traditional, well-oiled, well-worn rails, and hide from ourselves both the original source of the problems, and the reasons for their perennial insolubility.

1. I KNOW, I PROMISE, PROBABLY

Let us examine first what we all learn first, the adverb 'probably' : its force can best be brought out with the help of some elementary examples.

(1) 'There comes a moment in the life of a well-brought-up small boy when he finds himself in a quandary.   For the last week he has come every day after tea to play with the little girl who lives in the next street, and he has begun to

[1] Cf. *P & I*, p. 1.

value her esteem. Now bed-time is near, Mother has come to fetch him away, and his companion says, with bright eyes, "You *will* come to-morrow, won't you?" Ordinarily he would have answered "Yes" without a qualm, for every other evening he has fully intended to come next day, and known of nothing to stand in his way. But . . . but there was some talk at home of a visit to the Zoo to-morrow; and what if that, and tea in a tea-shop afterwards, and the crowds in the Tube, meant that they were late getting home, and that he was to fail, after saying "Yes"? . . . How difficult life is! If he says "Yes" and then cannot come, she will be entitled to feel that he has let her down. If he says "No", and then is back in time after all, she will not be expecting him, and he won't be able, decently, to come ; and so he will have deprived himself, by his own word, of his chief pleasure. What is he to say? He turns to his mother for help. She, understanding the dilemma, smiles and presents him with a way out : "Tell her that you'll *probably* come, darling. Explain that you can't *promise*, since it depends on what time we get home, but say that you'll come if you possibly can." Blissfully thankful for the relief, he turns back and utters the magic word : "Probably".'

The important difference to notice here is that between saying 'I shall come' and saying 'I shall probably come'. This difference is similar in character (though opposite in sense) to that which Professor Austin discusses, between saying 'S is P' or 'I shall do A', and saying 'I know that S is P' or 'I promise that I shall do A'. On this subject, let me quote Austin :

When I say 'S is P', I imply at least that I believe it, and, if I have been strictly brought up, that I am (quite) sure of it : when I say 'I shall do A', I imply at least that I hope to do it, and, if I have been strictly brought up that I (fully) intend to. If I only believe that S is P, I can add 'But of course I may (very well) be wrong :' if I only hope to do A, I can add 'But of course I may (very well) not'. When I only believe or only hope, it is recognized that further evidence or further circumstances are liable to make me change my mind. If I say 'S is P' when I don't even believe it,

I am lying: if I say it when I believe it but am not sure of it, I may be misleading but I am not exactly lying. If I say 'I shall do A' when I have not even any hope, not the slightest intention, of doing it, then I am deliberately deceiving; if I say it when I do not fully intend to, I am misleading but I am not deliberately deceiving in the same way.

But now, when I say 'I promise', a new plunge is taken: I have not merely announced my intention, but, by using this formula (performing this ritual), I have bound myself to others, and staked my reputation, in a new way. Similarly, saying 'I know' is taking a new plunge. But it is *not* saying 'I have performed a specially striking feat of cognition, superior, in the same scale as believing and being sure, even to being merely quite sure': for there *is* nothing in that scale superior to being quite sure. Just as promising is not something superior, in the same scale as hoping and intending, even to merely fully intending: for there *is* nothing in that scale superior to fully intending. When I say 'I know', I *give others my word*: I *give others my authority for saying* that 'S is P'.[1]

Our small boy's difficulty can be put as follows. If, in reply to his companion's appeal ('You *will* come to-morrow, won't you?'), he says 'Yes, I'll come', he *commits himself*. For to say 'Yes, I'll come' is to say you'll come, and this, while not being as solemn and portentous as a promise, is in some ways all but one. ('I didn't promise': 'Maybe not, but you *as good as* promised.') By saying 'Yes, I'll come', he not only leads her to expect him (*i.e.* to anticipate, to make preparations for, his arrival). He also ensures that coming to-morrow will be something that is *expected of* him: he gives her reason to reproach him if he does not turn up though not of course reason to reproach him in such strong terms as she would be entitled to use if he were to fail after having promised (*i.e.* after having said, in earnest, 'I promise that I'll come'). To say 'Yes', when there was any reason to suppose that he might be prevented from coming, would therefore be laying up trouble for himself.

[1] J. L. Austin, 'Other Minds' in *P.A.S.* Supp., Vol. XX (reprinted in *Logic and Language*, Vol. II), pp. 170-1 (pp. 143-4). What I have to say in the present Section owes a great deal to this paper, hereafter referred to as *J.L.A.*, and especially to pp. 170-5 (pp. 142-7).

The point of the word 'probably', as here used, is to avoid just this trouble. By saying 'I know that S is P' or 'I promise to do A', I expressly commit myself, in a way in which I also do (though to a lesser degree and only by implication) if I say 'S is P' or 'I shall do A'. By saying 'S is probably P' or 'I shall probably do A', I expressly *avoid* unreservedly committing myself. I insure myself thereby against some of the consequences of failure. My utterance is thereby guarded — that is, 'secured by stipulation from abuse or misunderstanding'.[1] But the insurance is not unlimited; the nature of the stipulation must, in normal cases, be made quite clear ('It depends on what time we get home'), and the protection afforded by the use of the word 'probably' extends in the first place only to those contingencies which have been expressly stipulated. To say 'I'll probably come, but it depends on what time we get back from the Zoo', and then not to go in spite of being back in plenty of time, would be (while not deliberate deceit) at any rate 'taking advantage'; as misleading as saying unreservedly 'I'll come', and then not going. You are again committed, and therefore again responsible: to attempt to excuse yourself by saying, 'But I only told you I'd *probably* come', is a piece of bad faith.

Nor of course is anyone, who uses the word 'probably' in this way correctly, permitted to fail either always or often, even though he may have 'covered' himself expressly every time. By saying 'probably' you make yourself answerable for fulfilment, if not on all, at least on a reasonable proportion of occasions: it is not enough that you have an excuse for every failure. Only in some specialized cases is this requirement tacitly suspended ('When a woman says "Perhaps" she means "Yes": when a diplomat says "Perhaps", he means "No"').

Finally, and in the nature of the case, certain forms of words are prohibited. To follow Austin again: 'You are prohibited from saying "I know it is so, but I may be wrong", just as you are prohibited from saying "I promise I will, but

[1] *Pocket Oxford Dictionary, v.s.* 'guard'.

I may fail". If you are aware you may be mistaken (have some concrete reason to suppose that you may be mistaken in this case), you oughtn't to say you know, just as, if you are aware you may break your word, you have no business to promise.'[1] In the same way, and for the same reasons, you are prohibited from saying, 'I'll probably come, but I shan't be able to'; for to say this is to take away with the last half of your utterance what you gave with the first. If you know that you will not be able to go, you have no right to say anything which commits you in any way to going.

(2) 'A complex disturbance at present over Iceland is moving in an easterly direction. Cloudy conditions now affecting Northern Ireland will spread to N.W. England during the day, probably extending to the rest of the country in the course of the evening and night.'

In our first example, we saw how the word 'probably' comes to be used as a means of giving guarded and restricted promises. Philosophers, however, have been concerned less with this use of the word than with its use in scientific statements, and especially (in view of the traditional connexion between the problems of 'probability' and 'induction') with its use in predictions : it is important therefore to illustrate the everyday use of the word 'probably' in such a context. I have chosen, for this purpose, a typical extract from a weather forecast.

All the features characteristic of our previous example are to be found here also. The Meteorological Office's forecasters are prepared to commit themselves *unreservedly* to the first of their predictions (that the cloudy conditions will spread to N.W. England during the day), but they are not prepared to do this in the case of the second (that the clouds will extend to the rest of the country during the evening and night) ; and they know that, the M.O. being the M.O., we have to go by what they say. If they unreservedly forecast cloud later to-day and the skies remain clear, they can justifiably be rounded on by the housewife who has put off her heavy wash on account

[1] *J.L.A.*, p. 170 (pp. 142-3).

of their prediction. (If they say '. . . will certainly spread
. .' or 'We know that cloudy conditions will spread . . .',
there will in case of failure be even more cause for complaint; but notice that, as it is the M.O.'s business to know,
as they are the 'authorities' on the subject, we tend to take for
granted in this case the introductory formula 'We know
. . .'.) In the present state of their science, however, they
cannot safely, cannot without asking for trouble, that is,
commit themselves to predictions of what will happen for
more than a limited time ahead : what then are they to say
about the coming night ?

Here again the word 'probably' comes into its own. Just
as it finds a place as a means of giving guarded and restricted
promises, so it can be used when we have to utter guarded
and restricted predictions — predictions to which, for some
concrete reason or other, we are not prepared positively to
commit ourselves. Once again, however, the use of the word
'probably' insures one against only *some* of the consequences
of failure. If the forecasters say '. . . probably extending
. . .', they cover themselves only within those limits which
have to be recognized as reasonable in the present state of
meteorology. If clouds do not turn up over the rest of the
country sooner or later, we are entitled to ask *why*. And if
in reply to this enquiry they refuse to offer any explanation
(such as they might give by saying, 'The anti-cyclone over
Northern France persisted for longer than is usual under such
circumstances'), but try to excuse themselves with the words
'After all, we only said the clouds would *probably* extend',
then they are 'hedging', 'taking refuge', 'quibbling', and we
are entitled to suspect that their prediction, even though
guarded and restricted, was an improper one, *i.e.* one made
on inadequate grounds. The importance of having 'adequate
grounds' if one is to claim that '*p*' or 'Probably *p*', still
more that you 'know that *p*', will become clear later on.[1]

Further, if you use the word 'probably' in predictions
correctly, you are not permitted to 'prove mistaken' either

[1] See especially Section 3, below.

always or often, even though you may be expressly 'covered' every time. In predictions as in promises, by saying 'probably' you make yourself answerable for fulfilment on a reasonable proportion of occasions : it is not enough that you have an 'explanation' of every failure. In predictions, too, certain forms of words must be ruled out. 'The cloud will probably extend to the rest of the country, but it won't' is no more permissible than 'I'll probably come, but I shan't be able to', 'I promise I will, but I may fail', or 'I know it is so, but I may be mistaken'. For a 'guarded prediction', though distinct from a positive prediction, is properly understood as giving the hearer reason to expect (hope for, prepare for, etc.) that which is forecast (even though he is not encouraged to 'bank on it'), and to utter such a prediction is incompatible with the flat denial of the prediction.[1]

Notice particularly a distinction which we shall have occasion to take up again later : that 'giving someone reason to expect something' is different from saying 'I expect it' (even 'with reason'). Thus, the M.O. forecasters are not *saying* (as some philosophers have suggested) that they are quite certain that the clouds will reach N.W. England to-day, but only fairly confident that they will extend to the rest of the country before the night is out ; though they are of course implying this (giving one to understand this), since it is their business as weather forecasters not to say '. . . will spread . . .' unless they are sure, nor to say '. . . probably extending . . .' unless they are reasonably confident.[2] It is the weather they are talking about, not their own expectations. 'Saying "I know"', as Austin points out, 'is *not* saying "I have performed a specially striking feat of cognition, superior, in the same scale as believing and being sure, even to being merely quite sure": for there *is* nothing in that scale superior to being quite sure. . . . When I say "I know", I *give others my word*: I *give others my authority for saying* that "S is

---

[1] Cf. 'Moore's Paradox', that though one can properly say '*He believes* that it will rain, but it won't', one cannot say '*I believe* that it will rain, but it won't'.

[2] Cf. *J.L.A.*, p. 170 (p. 143).

P".'[1] So also, saying 'S is probably P' is not saying 'I am fairly confident but less than certain, that S is P', for 'probably' does not belong in this series of words either. When I say 'S is probably P', I *commit myself guardedly* (tentatively, with reservations) to the view that S is P, and (likewise guardedly) *lend my authority* to that view.

2. 'IMPROBABLE BUT TRUE'

In the light of these examples, let me return to the difficulties which I found in connecting the statements about 'probability' in Kneale's book with the kinds of everyday use we make of the family of words, 'probably', 'probable', 'probability', 'likely', 'chance', and so on.

The first difficulty consisted in seeing, in concrete terms, what it was that Kneale was claiming when he used the abstract noun 'probability', or his own neologisms, 'probabilify' and 'probabilification'[2] instead of more familiar locutions. This difficulty is not the most serious, and could be overcome, at least in part, by careful attention to the context. Certainly many of the things he expresses in terms of 'probability' could be put in more concrete terms. For instance, in saying 'Probability often enables us to act rationally when without it we should be reduced to helplessness' (*P & I*, p. 1), he presumably has in mind this kind of fact : that to say of a man that he knows 'that it will probably rain this afternoon' implies that he knows enough to be well advised to expect and prepare for rain this afternoon, though not enough to be seriously surprised if it 'holds off' for once ; whereas to say that he does not even know that implies that he has nothing very definite to go on when it comes to predicting and preparing for the afternoon's weather (to describe him as 'reduced to helplessness' is too strong). What we are to make of 'probabilification', however, I am less sure.[3]

[1] *J.L.A.*, p. 171 (p. 144).   [2] *P & I*, pp. 11 ff.   [3] See Section 6, below.

The second difficulty was, however, more serious, and I cannot see how it is to be overcome. For in several places in his introductory chapter he not only misrepresents the familiar usages which he himself claims to be analysing and explaining, but in each instance *insists* on doing so, specifically claiming as good sense (despite appearances) something which to my mind is a solecism — and a solecism for philosophically important reasons.

Let me quote three instances :

(i) Probability is relative to evidence ; and even what is known to be false may be described quite reasonably as probable in relation to a certain selection of evidence. We admit this in writing history. If a general, having made his dispositions in the light of the evidence at his disposal, was then defeated, we do not necessarily say that he was a bad general, *i.e.*, that he had a poor judgment about probabilities in military affairs. We may say that he did what was most sensible in the circumstances, because in relation to the evidence which he could and did obtain it was probable that he would win with those dispositions. Similarly what is known to have happened may be extremely improbable in relation to everything we know except that fact. "Improbable but true" is not a contradiction in terms. On the contrary, we assert just this whenever we say of a fact that it is strange or surprising.[1]

On this passage I have four comments to make.

(*a*) What is known *by me* to be false may be described quite reasonably as 'probable' *by others*, having regard to the evidence at their disposal : by me it can, at most, be described as '*having seemed probable* until it was discovered to be false'.

(*b*) If we say that the general did what was most sensible in the circumstances, we do so because in relation to the evidence which he could and did obtain it *must have seemed* probable (was perfectly reasonable to suppose) that he would win with those dispositions. The form of words 'It *was* probable that he would win . . .' can in this context be understood only as a report, in *oratio obliqua*, of what the general may (reasonably) have thought *at the time*.

[1] *P & I*, pp. 9-10.

(*c*) What is (now) known to have happened may (before we discovered that it had) have *seemed extremely improbable*, having regard to everything we knew ; and it may yet seem so, with reason, to one who knows now only what we knew then. But while *he* may properly, though mistakenly, speak of it as 'improbable', *we* who know what actually happened may not.

(*d*) No one person is permitted, in one and the same breath, to call the same thing both 'improbable' and 'true', for the reasons we examined in the previous section : the form of words 'Improbable but true' is therefore ruled out.[1] (Whether or no we are to say that it is a 'contradiction' is another question, and one that might get us into deep water, though I think a strong case could be made out for calling it one.) We can, however, describe a tale as '*improbable-sounding* but true', and in the course of a conversation one person might describe something as 'improbable' until the other person assured him that it was true — after that, the sceptic would be limited to saying, 'It still *seems* to me most improbable', or more baldly, 'I don't believe it' : there is no place then for the words 'It *is* improbable'.

(ii) If I say 'It is probably raining', I am not asserting in any way that it is raining, and the discovery that no rain was falling would not refute my statement, although it might render it useless.[2]

I am not clear what Kneale would accept, or refuse to accept, as 'asserting' something 'in any way' ; nor what he means by his distinction between 'rendering a statement useless' and 'refuting it'. But I am perfectly certain that, if I say 'It is probably raining' and it turns out not to be, then (*a*) I was mistaken, (*b*) I cannot now repeat the claim, and

---

[1] Except of course as a deliberate 'shocker'. One can imagine a newspaper columnist's trading on the queerness of this form of words, as the title of a column similar to Ripley's *Believe It or Not*. No doubt it is this possibility which Kneale refers to in his last sentence, but in such a context the phrase 'Improbable but true' is effective just because it is a contraction of '*seems* improbable but *is* true', rather than of 'is improbable but is true'.

[2] *P & I*, p. 4.

(*c*) I can properly be called upon to say 'what made me think it might be raining'. (Answer, for instance : 'It sounded as though it was from the noise outside, but I realize now that what I took to be rain was only the wind in the trees'.) Does this not amount to 'refutation' ?

(iii) We know now that the stories which Marco Polo told on his return to Venice were true, however improbable they may have been for his contemporaries.

This is an example which Kneale quotes on page 1 of his book, and on which he places a good deal of weight : it is, he says, 'worth special notice, because it shows that what is improbable may nevertheless be true'.[1] Yet to my mind it contains a vital ambiguity ; and we cannot place any weight on it at all until this is resolved. For are we to understand the words 'however improbable they may have been for his contemporaries' as being in direct or in indirect speech ? If the latter, if they report in *oratio obliqua* the reaction *at the time* of Marco Polo's fellow-countrymen, then the example may be perfectly well expressed, but it does not in any way show 'that what is improbable may nevertheless be true' (*i.e.*, that what is properly described as 'improbable' may *by the same person* and *in the same breath* be properly described as 'true'). If, on the other hand, it is intended to be in direct speech, as it must be if it is to prove what Kneale claims that it proves, then it is expressed very loosely. However improbable the stories which Marco Polo told on his return to Venice may have *seemed* to his contemporaries, we know now that they were (substantially) true : we therefore have no business to describe them as ever having 'been improbable', since for us to do this tends in some measure to lend our authority to a view which we know to be false.

In each of these passages, Kneale skates over one or both of two closely related distinctions, which are implicit in our ordinary manner of speaking about 'probability' and essential to the meaning of the notion. The first of these is the dis-

[1] *P & I*, p. 2.

tinction between : saying that something 'is' or 'was' probable or improbable (*e.g.*, 'This man's stories of a flourishing Empire far away to the East *are wildly improbable*', or 'The idea that theirs was by far the richest Empire in the world had become so ingrained in the Venetians that tales of one yet richer *were not likely* to be believed') ; and saying that it 'seems' or 'seemed' probable or improbable ('Though substantially true, Marco Polo's stories of a flourishing Empire far away to the East *seemed* to the Venetians of his time wildly improbable'). The second concerns the differences in the backing required for claims that something is probable or improbable, when these claims are made by different people or at different times : at several places in the passages I have quoted, it is left unstated *by whom* or *on what occasion* the claim that 'probably so-and-so' is made, although it makes a vital difference to the grammar and sense how one fills in the blanks.

Neglected though they have been, these two distinctions are of central importance for the subject of 'probability', and they are more subtle than is usually recognized. We must spend a little time getting them straight, before we can hope to see clearly the nature of the problems with which philosophers of 'probability' concern themselves.

3. Improper Claims and Mistaken Claims

We can throw into relief these features of 'probability' ('probably', 'it seemed probable', etc.) by setting them alongside the corresponding features of 'knowledge' ('I know', 'He knew', 'I didn't know', 'He thought he knew', etc.).

The chief distinction which we must examine for these purposes is that between saying of someone 'He claimed to know so-and-so, but he didn't', and saying 'He thought he knew, but he was mistaken'. Suppose, for purposes of illustration, that I am trying to grow gentians on my rock-garden, and that they are not doing at all well. A plausible neighbour insists on giving me his advice, telling me what in his view is the cause of the trouble, and what must be done to remedy it. I follow his advice, and afterwards the plants are in a worse condition than ever. There are at this stage two subtly, but completely different things which I can say about him and his advice : I can say 'He thought he knew what would put matters right, but he was mistaken' or I can say 'He claimed to know what would put matters right, but he didn't'.

To see the differences between these two sorts of criticism, consider what kinds of thing would be proper responses to the challenge, 'Why (on what grounds) do you say that ?' If I say 'He thought he knew what would put matters right, but he was mistaken', and I am asked *why* I say that, there is only one thing to do in reply — namely, to point to the drooping gentians. He prescribed a certain course of treatment, and it was a failure : that settles the matter. But if I say instead, 'He claimed to know what would put matters right, but he didn't', the complaint is quite a different one. If asked why I say so, I shall reply (*e.g.*) :

(*a*) 'He has no real experience of gardening',

(*b*) 'He may be an expert gardener in his own line, but he doesn't understand Alpines',

(*c*) 'He only looked at the plants : with gentians you have to start by testing the soil',

(*d*) 'He may say he tested the soil, but he tested it for the wrong things', etc.,

ending up, in each case, '. . . so he *didn't* know (was in no position to know) what would put matters right'. I am now attacking, not the prescription itself, but one of two wholly other things : either the man's *credentials*, as in (*a*) and (*b*), or his *grounds* for prescribing what he did, as in (*c*) and(*d*). Indeed, the condition of the gentians is actually irrelevant, except as an indication of these other things : one might say 'He didn't know . . .' even in a case where his prescription was in fact successful ('It was only a lucky guess'). And equally, when I claim that he was 'mistaken', the quality of his credentials and reasoning are irrelevant : 'He thought he knew what would put matters right, and no one could be better qualified or in a better position to say, but he was mistaken nevertheless'.

To put this briefly : the phrase 'He didn't know' serves to attack the claim *as originally made*, whereas the phrase 'He was mistaken' serves to correct it *in the light of subsequent events*. In practice, we recognize a clear distinction between an 'improper' claim to know something, and a claim which subsequently turns out to be 'mistaken'. Criticism designed to attack (discredit, cancel out) a claim to know or to have known something, as opposed to 'correcting (modifying, revising) it in the light of events', must proceed in the first place by attacking, not the conclusion claimed as known, but the argument leading up to it or the qualifications of the man making the claim. Showing that a claim to know something proved (in the event) a mistaken one may do nothing at all towards showing that it was at the time an improper claim to make.

The distinction between 'It *seemed* probable (but it turned out otherwise)' and 'It *was* probable (though we failed to realize it)' is a parallel one. An insurance company may be prepared to ask only a small premium from a man of thirty whom they understand from their inspecting doctor to have chronic heart trouble, in exchange for an annuity policy maturing at age eighty ; for they will argue, reasonably enough, that he is very unlikely to live that long. But what if he does ? What are they to say on his eightieth birthday, as the chief accountant adds his signature to the first of several substantial annual cheques ?

This depends on the circumstances : notice particularly two possibilities. It may be (firstly) that advances in medical science, unforeseen and unforeseeable at the time when the policy was issued, have in the course of the intervening fifty years revolutionized the treatment of this type of heart disease, and so (as we might in fact say) 'increased the man's chances of living to eighty'. In this case, the directors of the company can, without casting any aspersions on the data and computations originally employed in fixing the premium, admit to having 'under-estimated his chances of living so long', saying, 'It seemed to us at that time, for the best possible reasons, extremely improbable that he would live that long ; but in the event our estimate has proved mistaken'. Looking back over the recent records of the company, they may now produce a revised estimate, the estimate they would originally have made 'could we have known then all that we now know about the progress of medicine in the intervening years' — and this they will refer to as the chance he 'actually' had, at the age of thirty, of living to eighty, as opposed to that which at the time it 'seemed' that he had. (This case is like the ones in which we say 'He thought he knew, but he was mistaken', the cases in which we revise and correct a past claim, without seeking to criticize its propriety.)

Alternatively, that which was responsible for the discrepancy between their expectation and the event may have been, not so much the advance of medicine, as some fault in the original data or computation. On looking into the matter, they may be led to say:

(a) 'He bribed the doctor to say he had chronic heart disease, when he hadn't',

(b) 'The doctor's report referred to another man of the same name, and got on to his file by mistake',

(c) 'His was an exceptional, sub-acute form of the disease, which it is hard to tell from the normal one',
(or, in other similar cases,

(d) 'The clerk looked at the wrong page of figures when working out his chances',

(e) 'Our figures for farm-workers were based on too small a sample', etc.).

In these circumstances, the directors will have to say that the company failed to recognize at the time just how large his chances of survival were : 'His chances of living to eighty were really quite good ; but, being misled by the doctor (the clerk, the records), we failed to recognize this'. (The present case is like those in which we say 'He claimed to know, but he didn't' : the propriety of the original claim is being attacked, and the fact that it also proved mistaken in the event is only incidental.)

To sum up : over claims that something is 'probable' as over claims to 'know' something, we recognize in practice the difference between attacking a claim as originally made, and correcting it in the light of subsequent events. Once again we distinguish between a claim which was 'improper' at the time it was made and one which subsequently turned out to have been 'mistaken'. And as before, criticism directed against the claim itself must attack the backing of the claim, or the qualifications of the man who made it : showing that in the event it proved mistaken may do nothing towards showing that it was at the time an improper claim to make.

So much for the moment about the two parallel distinctions :

(a) between saying 'It *was* probable, though we failed to recognize it', and saying 'It *seemed* probable, though it turned out otherwise', and

(b) between saying 'He claimed to know, but he didn't', and saying 'He thought he knew, but he was mistaken'.

Before we go on to discuss the philosophical importance of these distinctions, we must take a look at the closely related ones, between the kinds of grounds which are required as backing, either for a claim to know something, or for a claim that something is or was probable, when this claim is made and considered *on different occasions*.

When my neighbour makes his claim to 'know what will set my gentians right', he must, if his claim is to be a proper one, be sure of three things : that he has enough experience, of flowers in general and of Alpines in particular, to be in a position to speak ; that he has made all the observations and performed all the tests which can reasonably be demanded of him ; and that the judgment he bases on these observations is a considered one. Provided that these conditions are

N

fulfilled, he has done what we are entitled to require to ensure that his judgment is a *trustworthy* one, one which provides a *fit basis for action*. He is then entitled to make the claim 'I know . . .' and, unless we mistrust his judgment, we can equally properly 'take his word for it' and say 'He knows. . .' (Notice the "gerundive" forms 'trust*worthy*' and '*fit* basis': the fact that it is natural to use these here is important.)

The same kinds of consideration apply to the insurance company's claim that their prospective client 'is very unlikely to live to eighty'. They are required to be sure that their records are sufficiently comprehensive to provide a reliable guide, that the data about the client on which their estimate is based are complete and correct, and that the computation is done without slips. Given these things, we can accept their claim as a 'proper' one, for they too have ensured that, in the present state of knowledge, their estimate is a *trustworthy* one.

Whether a prediction ('*p*') is uttered 'with all your authority' ('I know that *p*') or 'with reservations' ('Probably *p*'), the situation is the same. If you have shown that there is *now* no concrete reason to suppose that this particular prediction will prove mistaken, when so many others like it have stood the test of time, all that can *now* be required of you before making the claim, 'I know that *p*' or 'Probably *p*', has been done. And if anyone is ever to attack the *propriety* of your prediction, or say with justice 'He claimed to know, but he didn't' or 'He failed to see how small the chances were', it is this claim which he will have to discredit.

This is a perfectly practical claim, and it must not be confused with another, and clearly futile one — the claim that your prediction can remain, despite the passage of time, beyond all reach of possible future amendment; that you can see to it now that there will never be any question of asking, in the light of future events, whether after all you were not *mistaken*. For, as time passes, the question whether the prediction *remains* a trustworthy one can always be reopened. Between the time of the prediction and the event itself, fresh considerations may become relevant (new discoveries about gentians, new treatments for heart trouble) and the backing which must be called for, if the predictions are to be repeated, may in consequence become more stringent. And further, after the event itself has taken place, one can check what actually happened. So, however proper the original claim to 'know' may have been when uttered, the retrospective question 'Was he right?' can always be reconsidered in the light of events, and the answer may in course of time have to be modified.

All this seems natural enough, if one comes to it without irrelevant preconceptions. After all, if it is the *trustworthiness* of a prediction that we are considering, the standards of criticism which are appropriate (the grounds which it is reasonable to demand in support of it) must be expected to depend on the circumstances in which it is being judged, as well as on those in which it was originally uttered. At the time a prediction is uttered, it does not even make sense to include 'eye-witness accounts of the event itself' among the evidence demanded in support of it : if this did make sense, it would be wrong to call the utterance a 'prediction'. But if we ask ourselves after the event whether the claim actually provided a fit and proper basis for action, it is only reasonable for us to demand that it should in fact have been fulfilled.

The moral ? — If we are to keep clear in our minds about knowledge and probability, we must remember always to take into account the occasion on which a claim is being judged, as well as that on which it was uttered. It is idle to hope that what is true of claims of the forms, 'I know', 'He knows', and 'It *is* probable', will necessarily be true of claims of the forms, 'I knew', 'He knew', and 'It *was* probable' ; or that what is true of such claims when considered before the event will necessarily be true of them when reconsidered in the light of events. Claims of this kind cannot be considered and judged *sub specie aeternitatis*, 'from outside time' as it were : any idea that they can is a superstition which may play havoc with the most careful arguments. And it is just those vital differences which one is led to overlook, just this superstition which is fostered, if one discusses 'probability', 'knowledge', and 'belief' in terms of these abstract nouns, instead of considering the verbs and adverbs through which we learn their meaning.

4. THE LABYRINTH OF 'PROBABILITY'

There can be no doubt, therefore, of the philosophical relevance of the distinctions to which I drew attention in Section 2, and tried to map out in the last Section (distinctions which are firmly rooted in our everyday language, but which Kneale goes out of his way to ignore). The questions we must now ask are, first, what the special importance of these distinctions is for the philosophy of 'probability'; and secondly, whether the direction of Kneale's linguistic eccentricities throws any light on the things he says about 'probability' and 'probabilification'.

I think it is possible, in outline at any rate, to see how the attention of philosophers has come to be focused on the wrong questions — and not just on 'the wrong ones', but on *wrong 'uns*. For, in recent philosophical discussions about 'probability', the chief bogy has been subjectivism; the object of the philosophers' quest has therefore been a Definition of the notion in 'objective' terms; [1] and the questions from which discussion has begun have been questions like 'What *is* Probability ?', 'What are "probability-statements" *about* ?', 'What is the true *analysis* of "probability-statements" ?', and 'What do they *express* ?' (Kneale evidently feels that, though the subjectivist's position is grossly paradoxical, his case is *prima facie* a strong one, for he makes its refutation his first business; [2] and he has no doubts about the proper starting-point:

If, as seems natural, we start by contrasting probability statements with statements in which we express knowledge, the question immediately arises: 'What then do we express by probability statements ?') [3]

---

[1] Cf. *P & I*, pp. 6, 8, 12-13.   [2] *P & I*, pp. 3-9.   [3] *P & I*, p. 3.

And indeed, when this kind of question is asked, we are at first at a loss, not knowing quite what to point to, quite where to look. Let us see why this happens.

If you ask me what the weather is going to do and, taking a look at the sky, I reply 'There will be rain this evening', there is no philosophical difficulty when it comes to answering the question, what my statement is about (refers to, etc.). The common-sense answer, 'the evening's weather', is acceptable to all, and if I turn out to have been right (spoken truly, predicted correctly) this seems very happily 'accounted for' by saying that what I referred to 'was a fact' — indeed was 'a fact', a perfectly definite 'fact' about the evening's weather : namely, it's raining this evening. But if I reply instead 'There will *probably* be rain this evening', philosophy and common sense tend to part company. Although the common-sense answer to the question what I am talking about remains 'the evening's weather', philosophers feel scruples about accepting this as an answer. For if we try to get at a more specific (*too* specific) answer to the question, what are we to pick on ? By using the word 'probably', I explicitly *avoid* tying myself down positively to any particular prediction (*e.g.* that it *will* rain this evening) and so, it seems, to any particular 'fact'; even if it does not rain, I may find some let-out ('The clouds were piling up all the evening, but didn't actually discharge till they got a bit further inland : still, it was touch-and-go the whole time') ; and we are therefore unable to point to anything (any one 'thing') about the evening's weather such that, if it happens, I spoke truly and, if it does not happen, I was wrong. This discovery makes us feel that the 'link with the future', which we think of — though to our jeopardy — as present in the case of a positive prediction, has in the case of the guarded prediction been irreparably severed ; and we are uncomfortable about saying any longer that my statement 'refers to' ('is about', 'is concerned with') the evening's weather, still more about saying that it 'expresses a future fact', for we dread the ruthless question, '*What* fact ?'

Having reached this point, we are wide open to the subjectivist's attack. He has noticed one 'thing' (perhaps the only one) which is present whenever the word 'probably', or one of its derivatives, is used correctly : everyone who says and means 'Probably *p*' does *believe confidently* that *p*. In advancing his doctrine that in all such cases the real topic of conversation is the speaker's 'strong belief that *p*', he can therefore challenge us to point to anything else : 'If what we mean by "probability" isn't *that*, what is it ?'

This question puts us in a quandary. Obviously there is something extremely queer about the subjectivist's doctrine. 'Degrees of belief' cannot be all that matter, for over most issues belief of one degree is more reasonable (is more justified, ought rather to be held) than belief of another : 'When a man sees a black cat on his way to a casino and says "I shall probably win to-day : give me your money to place on your behalf", we decline the invitation if we are prudent, even although we believe the man to be honest'.[1] Whatever 'probability' is (we want to say) it must therefore be more "objective" than the subjectivist can allow : 'The essential point is that the thinking which leads to the formation of rational opinion, like any other thinking worth the name, *discovers* something independent of thought. We think as we ought to think when we think of things as they are *in reality* ; and there is no other sense in which it can be said that we ought to think so and so.'[2] Instead of suspecting the propriety of the questions, what *exactly* my statement was about (as opposed, of course, to the common-sense answer), and what *exactly* it is that we mean by this word 'probability', we press onwards into the murk : it seems vital to find an answer of some kind to these questions for, if we fail to do so, shall we not be letting the case go to the subjectivist by default ?

When we begin looking around to see what exactly it is that we mean by 'probability', what exactly it is that probability-statements are 'about', *simply in virtue of being* 'probability-statements', a number of candidates present

[1] *P & I*, p. 7.   [2] *P & I*, p. 11.

themselves. 'The frequency with which events of the kind we are considering happen in such circumstances': if we bear in mind what goes on in Life Insurance offices, this seems to have strong claims. 'The proportion which the event under consideration represents of the number of alternative possible happenings': when we remember the calculations we did at school (about dice, packs of playing-cards, and bags full of coloured balls) this in its turn seems an attractive suggestion. And the philosophy of probability, as traditionally presented, is largely a matter of canvassing and criticizing the qualifications of these and other candidates. For once, however, let us refrain from plunging any deeper into the labyrinth : if we return the way we came, we can find reasons for believing that our present dilemma (which gives the search for the 'real' subject-matter of probability-statements its appearance of importance) is one of our own making.

These reasons are of two kinds. (1) The abstract noun 'probability' — despite what we learnt at our kindergartens about nouns being 'words that stand for things' — not merely *has no* tangible counterpart (referent, *designatum*, or what you will), not merely *does not* name a thing (of whatever kind), but is a word of such a type that it is nonsense even to *talk* about it as 'denoting' ('standing for', 'naming') anything. There are therefore insuperable objections to *any* candidate for the disputed title ; and in consequence, over the question what probability-statements are about, common sense has the better of philosophy. There can be probability-statements about the evening's weather, about my expectation of life, about the performance of a race-horse, the correctness of a scientific theory, the identity of a murderer . . . in fact, any subject concerning which one can commit oneself (with reservations) to an opinion ; quite apart from the guarded promises, cautious evaluations, etc., in which the word 'probability' can equally properly appear : *e.g.* 'Andrea Mantegna was, in all probability, the most distinguished painter of the Paduan School'. There *is* no special 'thing' which all probability-statements must be about, simply in virtue of the fact that they *are* 'probability-statements'.

(2) By refusing not only to produce any 'thing' as the universal answer to this question, but even to countenance the production of other answers, we do not in fact leave the subjectivist in possession of the field ; for the 'thing' which he puts up as a candidate is in as bad a case as all the others. It is true that the subjectivist *misses the point* of 'probability-statements', that they are (in some sense) more 'objective' than he will allow, but the 'objectivity' which he fails to provide is not of the kind which philosophers have sought ; and the discovery of a tangible *designatum* for the word 'probability', quite apart from being a delusory quest, would in no way help to fill the gap.

I must take these two points in order for, if I understand his introductory argument aright, Kneale has recognized some of the force of the first point, but has missed the second.

5. PROBABILITY AND EXPECTATION

Consider then, first, in what kinds of context the abstract noun 'probability' enters our language. Sometimes the Meteorological Office, instead of saying 'Cloud will *probably* extend to the rest of the country during the night', may say 'Cloud will *in all probability* extend. . . .' By choosing this form of words, instead of the shorter 'probably', they are understood to weaken the force of the implicit reservation (namely, that the indications are not so clear that one can safely make a positive prediction), so making it necessary for themselves to produce a more elaborate explanation if the cloud fails to turn up as predicted. Promises and predictions of the form 'In all probability, *p*', as opposed to 'Probably *p*', must be fulfilled not only on a reasonable proportion of occasions, but on *nearly all*: if we have to fall back at all often on excuses or explanations, we can be told to 'be more careful before committing ourselves'. Apart from this, however, there is little difference between the two forms : the phrase 'in all probability' serves *as a whole* a purpose of the same kind as the single word 'probably'. Likewise with 'The balance of probabilities suggests that cloud will extend . . .', and 'The probability that cloud will extend . . . is high'. In each case, the word 'probability' gets its meaning as a part of a phrase which serves *as a whole* a similar purpose to 'probably'. In each case, also, the metaphorical turn of phrase, with its suggestion (*e.g.*) that the question is so open that a pair of weighing-scales would be needed in order to find the answer, is taken simply as weakening or strengthening the force of the implicit reservations, so making the assertion either more or less positive, and failure correspondingly less or more excusable. Whatever else it does, it certainly does not imply in any way the existence of a thing or stuff called 'probability' which can literally be weighed in a balance.

If we consider only phrases like 'in all probability' and 'the balance of probabilities', there seems little point in talking about 'probability' and 'probabilities' in isolation. And if the word 'probability' never appeared, except in phrases which were obviously either unities or metaphors, there might be less temptation than there is to ask what it stands for. But the situation is more complicated. Sentences like 'The probability of their coming is negligible' remind us of other sentences, such as 'The injuries he sustained are negligible'; and we are therefore inclined to talk as though 'probabilities' could be talked about in isolation quite as sensibly as 'injuries'.

This resemblance is, of course, misleading. If we say 'The injuries he sustained are negligible', we mean that *the injuries themselves* can safely be neglected; and if asked how we know, or on what grounds we say this, we can appeal to experience, explaining that *experience has shown* that injuries of this type will always heal themselves without complications. If, on the other hand, we say 'The probability of their coming is negligible' we mean something of a different kind. What may safely be neglected in this case is not 'the probability of their coming' for, when compared with 'It is

safe to neglect his injuries', the sentence 'It is safe to neglect
"the probability of their coming"' is hardly even grammatical
English : rather, it is the *preparations against* their coming
which may safely be neglected — and this is surely what we
are meant to understand. The sentence 'The probability of
their coming is negligible' is in practice less like 'The injuries
he sustained are negligible' than it is like 'The *danger from*
his injuries is negligible'. Both sentences must be understood
by reference to their practical implications, namely, that his
injuries are such that complications *need not be* feared, or that
under the circumstances their coming is something that *need
not be* expected (feared, prepared for, etc.) : and 'danger',
like 'probability', is a word which is most at home in whole
phrases — *e.g.*, *danger of* complications (death by drowning,
bankruptcy), *from* injuries (a mad bull, high-tension cables),
to life and limb (peace, navigation). Nor, when we are talking
about 'probabilities' as opposed to 'injuries', is an appeal to
experience either needed or even meaningful. We can talk
of experience teaching us that there is no need to dress superficial grazes, or to expect shade temperatures of 105° F. or
more in England ; but we cannot speak of 'experience
teaching us' that there is no need to expect the extremely
unlikely, nor of 'experience teaching us' that things having
high probabilities are more to be expected than those with
low ones. And, correspondingly, one can ask why, under
what circumstances, or how we know that there is no need to
dress superficial grazes ; but not 'why', 'under what circumstances', or 'how we know that' there is no need to expect the
extremely unlikely. Such questions do not arise about truisms.

This last fact provides us with a test with which we can
rule out at once a large proportion of the suggested definitions
of 'probability' : if a definition is to be acceptable, it must
share at least this characteristic with the word 'probability'.
Any analysis of 'probability' which neglects this requirement
commits a fallacy closely akin to what, in ethics, G. E. Moore
called 'the Naturalistic Fallacy'. For, just as it becomes
clear that 'right' cannot be *defined* in terms of (say) promise-

keeping when one sees that the questions, 'But *is* promise-keeping right ?' and 'But *ought* one to keep one's promises ?', are at any rate not trivial ; so it becomes clear that 'probability.' cannot be *defined* in terms of (say) frequencies or proportions of alternatives, when one notices that it is certainly not frivolous to ask whether, or why, or over what range of cases, observed frequencies (or proportions of alternatives) do *in fact* provide the proper backing for claims about 'probabilities' (*i.e.*, about what is to be expected, reckoned with, etc.). To attempt to define the 'probability' of an event in terms of such things is to confuse it with the *grounds for* regarding the event as 'probable', *i.e.*, with the *grounds for* expecting it. And, whatever we do or do not mean by 'probability', whether or no the word can properly stand on its own, these two things are certainly distinct. As with so many of those abstract nouns formed from "gerundive" adjectives which have traditionally puzzled philosophers (like 'goodness', 'truth', 'beauty', 'rightness', 'value', 'validity', and so on) the search for a tangible, 'natural', non-gerundive counterpart for the word 'probability', once begun, is bound to be endless : whatever fresh candidate is proposed, Moore's fatal questions can be asked about that also.

To say that 'probability' cannot be defined in terms of frequencies or proportions of alternatives is not to say that the rôle of these things in the practical discussion of 'probabilities' is not an important one, and one which needs clarification. Rather the reverse ; for it shows that they are to be regarded, not as rival claimants to a tinsel crown — each claiming to be the real *designatum* of the word 'probability' — but as different types of grounds, either of which can, in appropriate contexts and circumstances, properly be appealed to as backing for a claim that something 'is probable' or 'has a probability of this or that magnitude'. And this at once raises the very interesting question, what it is about some cases and contexts that makes 'observed frequencies' the relevant kinds of grounds to appeal to, and why 'proportions of alternatives' are to be appealed to in others. The difference has something to do with the difference between the kinds of things we say and do about *objets trouvés* and events beyond our control on the one hand, and the products of manufacture on the other. If all our dice grew on trees, for example, instead of being made by skilled engineers, we might well talk about the chances with dice as much in terms of frequencies as in terms of proportions of alternatives. It is also interesting to enquire why the 'frequency' and 'proportion of alternatives' definitions are so attractive. In part, this seems to be the result of the philosophers' excessive respect for mathematics. The sums we did in Algebra about 'the probability of drawing two successive black balls from a certain bag' were as much *pure* sums as those others about 'the time taken by four men to dig a ditch 3 ft. × 3 ft. × 6 ft.' The former have no more to do with 'probability' and throw no more light on what we mean by the term than the latter have to do with 'time'. But these questions are too large to discuss in detail here.

The attempt to find some 'thing' in terms of which to define the solitary word 'probability', something that all probability-statements can be thought of as really being about, turns out therefore to be a mistake. This does not imply that no meaning can be given to the word : 'probability' has a perfectly good meaning, as we shall discover by examining the way in which it is used in everyday contexts, in such phrases as 'in all probability'. And it is with such an examination that we must begin the philosophy of probability, rather than with questions like 'What is Probability ?' and 'What do probability-statements express ?', if we are not to start off on the wrong foot. To say that a statement is a probability-statement is *not* to imply that there is some one thing which it can be said to 'be about' or to 'express'. There is no single answer to the questions, 'What do probability-statements express ? What are they about ?' Some 'express' one thing : some another. Some are about the weather : some are about my expectation of life. If we insist on a unique answer, we do so at our own risk.

The way in which a false start can queer the pitch comes out if we consider our second point : the problem of 'objectivity' in probability-statements. There are certainly important reasons why the subjectivist's account is deficient, and why we find it natural to describe probability (as Kneale does) as something 'objective', 'independent of thought', which has to be 'discovered'. But as long as we begin by looking for some sort of *designatum* of 'probability', we take it for granted that it is this which must be found if we are to 'preserve the objectivity' of probability-statements. The problem of justifying our description of such statements as 'objective' thus gets entangled from the start with the vain search for the thing we *call* 'probability'. This is quite unnecessary, for the objectivity we require is of a very different kind.

What it is, we can remind ourselves, if we recall how an Insurance Company comes to distinguish between an estimate of probability which can reasonably be relied on and a faulty or incorrect one. If the doctor lies, or the computer misreads the tables, or the data themselves are incomplete, then the estimate which the Company will make of a client's chances of living to eighty will not be as trustworthy a one as they think, nor as trustworthy a one as they are capable of producing. When the error comes to light, therefore, they can distinguish between the client's 'real' chance of living to eighty and their first, faulty estimate. Again we saw how, as the years pass and the relevant factors alter, they come further to distinguish between the best possible estimate which was (or indeed could have been) made when the policy was issued, and the estimate which they see in the light of events would have been more trustworthy. Medicine makes unexpectedly rapid strides and this type of heart disease is mastered, so their client's 'expectation of life' increases : they therefore distinguish the chance he 'actually had' of living to eighty from the chance which, in the first place, it seemed (reasonably enough) that he had. In either case, they do so because it is their business to produce estimates which can be relied on. In either case, what immediately concerns them is the *trustworthiness* of their estimates. Trust-worthiness, reliability, these are what distinguish an 'objective' estimate of the chances of an event from a 'mere' expression of confident belief. And it is in ignoring the need for estimates of probability to be *reliable* that the subjectivist (who talks only about 'degrees of belief') is at fault. What factors *are* relevant, what kind of classification *will in fact* prove most reliable, these are things which Insurance Companies can only discover in course of time, from experience. But whatever the answers to these questions, we certainly need not delay asking them until we have found out definitively what it is that the word 'probability' denotes—if we did, we *never* could ask them.

6. 'PROBABILITY-RELATIONS' AND 'PROBABILIFICATION'

Let us return to the first chapter of Kneale's *Probability and Induction*. I wish to point out how, in seeking to prove that probability possesses the kind of almost tangible 'objectivity' which it neither can have nor needs, Kneale sacrifices even that 'objectivity' which we in practice demand, and which makes the notion of probability what it is.

Kneale sees clearly enough that one cannot treat the probability of an event as an 'intrinsic character', which is possessed by everything which can ever properly be described as 'probable': 'No proposition (unless it is either a truism or an absurdity) contains in itself anything to indicate that we ought to have a certain degree of confidence in it' [1] — after all, one person may properly, though mistakenly, describe as 'probable' what another equally properly says is 'untrue'. He therefore abandons the demand for some *single* 'thing', which can be called '*the* probability of an event'. But, rather than appear to surrender to the subjectivist, rather than give up as vain the search for 'that which all probability-statements express', he cuts his losses, and defines 'probability' as a 'relation' between the proposition guardedly

[1] *P & I*, p. 8.

asserted and the grounds for asserting it. A 'probability-relation' is said to exist between the evidence and the proposition, and the evidence is said to 'probabilify' the proposition to some degree or other.[1] The 'probability' which we talk of an event as 'possessing' is thus still thought of as being in the nature of a 'thing' (*sc*: an 'objective relation'), but it is now any of a large number of different 'things', according to the evidence at one's disposal. And, if this comes as a surprise, that is because 'our probability statements are commonly elliptical' and the particular batch of evidence understood to be relevant 'is not immediately recognizable'.[2]

Kneale's suggestion is an unhappy one, for several reasons. Quite apart from the linguistic eccentricities which it encourages,[3] it leads him to deny to 'probability' the kind of objectivity which really does matter. When an Insurance Company obtains fresh information about a client, and in the light of this information a new estimate is made of his expectation of life, this estimate is commonly spoken of as being a 'more accurate' (*i.e.* more trustworthy) estimate, a closer approximation to his 'actual chance of survival'. This piece of usage Kneale recognizes but condemns : 'Sometimes in such a case we speak as though there were a single probability of the man's surviving to be sixty, something independent of all evidence, and our second estimate were better in the sense of being nearer to this single probability than our first. But this view is surely wrong.'[4] He is forced to condemn this mode of expression because, in his view, after discovering fresh evidence, the Insurance Company must no longer be spoken of as concerned with the *same* 'probability-relation' — and so cannot strictly 'correct' its estimate. And this is only one special case of the general paradox into which his doctrine, that 'Probability is relative to evidence', drives him. According to him, whenever two people are in possession of different evidence, they cannot be said to contradict one another about the probability of an event 'ϵ' — cannot

[1] *P & I*, pp. 9-11.   [2] *P & I*, p. 10.
[3] Cf. Section 2 above.   [4] *P & I*, p. 9.

quarrel, apparently as to how far one should be prepared to act as though, and commit oneself to the assertion that, ϵ occurs — for they are talking about different 'probability-relations'!

Kneale's doctrine is not even free from 'naturalism', though this fact is partly obscured by his terminology. Suppose that he had intended us to regard 'recognizing that a large degree of probabilification exists between (*e.g.*) the evidence that a man of thirty has chronic heart disease, and the proposition that he will not live to eighty' as meaning the *same* as 'coming correctly to the conclusion that, in view of his physical condition, we cannot expect him to live that long (though we must bear in mind that 1 in 1000 of such cases does stagger on)' : in that case, this objection would not arise, for then he would be presenting us with a possible, though roundabout way of defining phrases like 'in all probability'. But this does not seem to be his intention. For, if it were, then one could not even ask the question which, according to him, any adequate analysis of 'probability' must answer : namely, the question, 'Why is it rational to take as a basis for action a proposition [that he will not survive] which stands in that relation [of being highly probabilified] to the evidence at our disposal ?'[1] For this would be to query a truism, as if we were to ask, 'Why need we not expect that which is extremely unlikely ?'

" Probability-relations " are therefore to be thought of as *distinct* entities, coming logically *between* the detailed evidence as to the prospective client's age and physical condition, and the practical moral that he need not be expected to survive (though of course 1 in 1000 does). And at once all the objections to a 'naturalistic' definition recur. Even if there always were certain entities to be found "between" the evidence and the conclusions we base on it, we could presumably only discover *from experience* that, in some or all circumstances, they can reasonably be relied on as a guide to the future, like the green cloud out at sea presaging a gale. And, in that case, 'probability', 'probably', and 'in all prob-

[1] Cf. *P & I*, p. 20.

ability' could no more be defined in terms of them, than they can in terms of 'frequencies' or 'proportions of alternatives', and for the same reasons. Now indeed we could properly ask the question Kneale regards as important (why, when our knowledge is less than we could wish, it is reasonable to rely on 'probability-relations' but not on mere belief): this question would now be no more trivial than the question why, when butter and sugar are short, it is reasonable to rely on margarine but not on saccharine. In each case, however, the question would have to be answered by appeal to experience — or to independent information, such as that margarine contains enough Vitamin D to be a nourishing as well as a palatable substitute for butter, whereas saccharine, though it tastes sweet, has no nutritive value. Does Kneale intend us to regard 'probability-relations' as the vitamins of probability? If so, if that is how he sees them, they cannot provide us with an *analysis of the term* 'probability'. We cannot show what 'nourishing' means by talking only about vitamins, calories, proteins, and carbohydrates. Kneale believes, I think, that there are two substantial inferences between the evidence and the moral, not just one, and certain features of our usage do suggest this : we say (*e.g.*) 'He's got chronic heart-disease at thirty, *so* the probability that he'll live to eighty is low, *so* we needn't reckon on his living that long'. But, if asked what grounds we have for ignoring the possibility of his surviving, we point immediately to his age and physical condition and to the statistics : nothing substantial is added by saying instead, 'There is no need to reckon on his surviving, *because* the probability of his doing so is low, *because* he's got chronic heart-disease at thirty'. To put our reasons like this is to present an artificially elaborate argument, like saying 'Your country needs Y-O-U, and Y-O-U spells *you*'.

7. TWO FINAL POINTS

To finish with, let me make two points about which I am more confident.

o

(1) Kneale discusses very briefly, and dismisses, one traditional treatment of sentences containing words like 'probably', namely, that in terms of 'modes or manners of assertion' — a treatment he calls a 'subjectivist theory'.[1] It occurs to me that he might regard these remarks of mine as in this tradition, so I must just put in a word in defence. His only argument against this treatment depends on his view that 'If I say " It is probably raining " . . . the discovery that no rain was falling would not refute my statement', and this view (as I have already pointed out)[2] is paradoxical, hard to reconcile with our common usage and practice in such situations. There remains for comment only his description of the treatment as 'subjectivist': this seems to me to be mistaken, and the result of a plain misunderstanding. To say '*p*' is to assert that *p*, *not* to assert that you are prepared to assert that *p* (though of course you thereby *show* that you are). Likewise, to say 'Probably *p*' is to assert, guardedly and/or with reservations, that *p*, *not* to assert that you are tentatively prepared to assert that *p*. Either assertion (positive or guarded) is then open to discussion on its merits : neither can be said to be about the 'state of mind' of the speaker. The description of 'Probably *p*' as a kind of assertion can no more be regarded as 'subjectivist' than can the description of '*p*' as an assertion.

(2) Kneale talks of there being 'two species of probability [3] . . . two senses of "probability", one applicable in matters of chance, and the other applicable to the results of induction'.[4] (Professor Urmson too has written recently about 'Two Senses of "Probable"',[5] advocating a similar distinction.) Now it is perfectly true that, when I say 'It is highly probable that if you throw a dice twenty times, the sequence you get will include at least one six', I mean something quite different from what I mean if I say 'It is highly probable that Hodgkin's explanation of the rôle of phosphorus in nervous conduction

---

[1] *P & I*, p. 3.   [2] In Section 2 above.   [3] *P & I*, p. 13.
[4] *P & I*, p. 22.
[5] *Analysis*, Vol. 8, No. 1, pp. 9-16 (1947), reprinted in *Philosophy and Analysis*, ed. M. Macdonald : Blackwell, 1955, pp. 191-9.

is the correct one'. But the differences between these two statements are fully accounted for by the difference between the subject-matters of the two propositions : nothing is gained and something is lost by saying, in addition, that two senses of 'probable' are involved. Of course, if you are considering the correctness or incorrectness of a scientific hypothesis, the evidence to which it is appropriate to appeal is different from that which is relevant if you are concerned with the results of dice-throwing. But, unless we are once again to confuse the *grounds for regarding something as* probable with the *meaning of the statement that it is* probable, we need not go on to say that there are consequently a number of different senses of the words 'probable' and 'probability'. Nor indeed should we say this, for the word 'probable' serves a similar purpose in both sentences : in each case, what is at issue is the question how far one ought to take it that (and commit oneself to the statement that) Hodgkin's explanation is correct or a six will turn up. Suppose instead that I say, '*I know* that Hodgkin's explanation is correct', or '*I know* that if you throw this dice twenty times, a six will turn up at least once'. Would Kneale and Urmson say that I am here using the word 'know' in two different senses ? And in another, if I say (as a matter of mathematics) 'I know that the square root of 2 is irrational' ? And in another, if I say (as a matter of common courtesy) 'I know that I ought not to have made this paper so long' ?

UNIVERSITY OF LEEDS

Chapter IX

PARENTHETICAL VERBS

BY J. O. URMSON

IN this paper I intend to examine a group of verbs which are
not usually considered as a group. Many of these verbs,
including such important ones as *know*, *believe*, and *deduce*,
are frequently misconstrued by philosophers, and their consideration as a group may help to get them into better perspective. None of these verbs is here examined exhaustively ;
in general only that which can be said of all is said of each.
For convenience this group is here called the group of
parenthetical verbs ; no great significance should be attached
to this title. Such significance as it has can more conveniently
be explained later.

Delimitation of the group of parenthetical verbs. In
prose the verb *to read* is used in the present continuous
form 'I am reading' to report a contemporary happening ;
the present perfect form 'I read' is used only to report what
one often, or habitually, does. This is true of most of the
verbs in the language. It has been observed in recent years,
but only, even by philologists, in recent years, that some verbs
do not conform to this pattern, since they either have no
present continuous tense, or, when they have, it is only so in
one out of two easily distinguishable uses. Thus the verb *to
prefer* has no present continuous tense, we never say 'I am
preferring' ; the verb *to wish* can have a present continuous
form, as in 'I wish whenever I pass a wishing-well', 'I am
wishing at a wishing-well', but has not when we say 'I wish
that you would make up your mind'. Here in the third
example the use of 'I wish' is similar to the use neither of
'I wish' nor of 'I am wishing' in the first two examples. It is
clear, then, that these verbs are not simply defective of a present

continuous tense, having only a normal present perfect tense ;
for 'I prefer' and 'I wish' (as used in the third example) are
not used in the way that 'I read' and 'I play' are used.

Some of these anomalous verbs are used normally with a
direct object ; examples are *love*, *like*, *hate*, *prefer* : some are
used normally with a subjunctive or other non-indicative
clause ; examples are *wish*, *command*, *beg*, *beseech*. These
verbs do not fall within the group of parenthetical verbs, and
are not further discussed in this paper, though they are well
worth discussing as groups. I intend to discuss only a special
set of verbs which lack a present continuous tense, which
must now be distinguished from the others.

Let us start with an example. Taking the verb *to suppose*,
we may note that in the first person present we can idiom-
atically say any of the following :

> I suppose that your house is very old.
> Your house is, I suppose, very old.
> Your house is very old, I suppose.

A verb which, in the first person present, can be used, as in
the example above, followed by 'that' and an indicative
clause, or else can be inserted at the .middle or end of the
indicative sentence, is a parenthetical verb. Note that this is
a grammatical distinction, and that these verbs are called
parenthetical because of this grammatical feature of their use.
'Parenthetical' is sometimes used of a piece of information
slipped into another context, but I do not wish to imply that
these verbs are parenthetical in any sense except that they
are sometimes used parenthetically in a purely grammatical
sense ; beyond that 'parenthetical' is merely a convenient
label. In some contexts it will be virtually indifferent, on all
but stylistic grounds, whether the verb occurs at the beginning,
middle, or end of the indicative sentence with which it is
conjoined ; this will not always be so, but when it is the verb
will be said to be used purely parenthetically. Thus in most
contexts 'I suppose that your house is very old' would be
used purely parenthetically, for it would mean virtually the
same as either 'Your house is very old, I suppose' or 'Your

house is, I suppose, very old'; if one person says 'I suppose that your house is quite new' and another says 'Well, I suppose that it is very old', then in the latter statement the verb *to suppose* is not being used purely parenthetically. We shall study parenthetical verbs in their more or less pure parenthetical use for the sake of simplicity; on other occasions most of what we have to say will remain true, but will be more or less far from being the full story. It would be perhaps more accurate to say that the features of parenthetical verbs to which I shall draw attention are one aspect of their use which is relatively more important on the occasions on which we shall concentrate than on others, but it is convenient to talk of a parenthetical use; purists may substitute *aspect* for *use* throughout.

Another preliminary point must be made before we get down to philosophical business. Part of what I design to show is how differently these verbs are used in the first person present and in other persons and tenses. Therefore we shall at first confine our attention to their pure parenthetical use in the first person present. It will be no accident therefore that all examples will be in this person and tense, nor will it be an objection to my thesis that what I say will not be true if examples in other persons or tenses are substituted for the ones given; it will in fact be a partial confirmation of my thesis.

A random and incomplete list of parenthetical verbs might be helpful at this stage : *Know, believe, deduce, rejoice, regret, conclude, suppose, guess, expect, admit, predict.* A few minutes' reflection will enable anyone to treble this list. Some of these verbs, like *conclude*, are always parenthetical, though of course not always used purely parenthetically. Others, like *rejoice*, may be non-parenthetical and have a present continuous tense ; we shall only be concerned with these verbs when they are parenthetical. We shall find easy tests to distinguish their different uses.

Parenthetical verbs are not psychological descriptions. Let us take for comparison three sentences :

(1) I rejoice whenever my sailor brother comes home.

(2) I am rejoicing because my sailor brother is home.

(3) I rejoice that you have returned home at last.

In sentences (1) and (2) *rejoice* is not a parenthetical verb. In (1) the main verb reports the periodic recurrence of a psychological condition, the occasions of which are given in the subordinate clause ; in (2) the main verb reports that something is going on now, and the subordinate clause states the cause. No such explanation can be given of (3), where *rejoice* is a parenthetical verb though not used purely parenthetically. The point becomes even clearer if we contrast a purely parenthetical use with a clearly descriptive verb :

> (A) He is, I regret, unwell.
>
> (B) I am miserable because he is unwell.

Note that it would be absurd to say :

> (A') He is, I am miserable, unwell.
>
> (B') I regret because he is unwell.

'I am miserable' does, 'I regret' does not, describe a psychological condition. In (B), 'because he is unwell' gives the cause of a mental state. (B') is absurd because a cause is given where nothing has been described needing a causal explanation. It should surely be obvious that though we are, in some sense, dealing with psychological or mental verbs, they are not parts of psychological histories as are verbs like *ponder* or *be miserable*. Nor, so far as I can see, is it any more plausible to say that they report dispositions to behave in certain ways. This has, however, not seemed obvious in the case of some parenthetical verbs to some philosophers. For while the difficulty of regarding 'I know' and 'I believe' as if they reported contemporary events (as if we said 'I am knowing' and 'I am believing') has been appreciated, many philosophers tend to treat *know* and *believe* as though they were simply defective of a present continuous tense. Thus 'I know' and 'I believe' have been construed as ordinary present perfects implying, not the frequent truth of 'I am knowing' and 'I am believing', but of 'I am doing this thing and the other thing'. It is an alternative to this mistaken view that will shortly be given.

Implied claims to truth. Whenever anyone utters a sentence which could be used to convey truth or falsehood there is an implied claim to truth by that person, unless the situation shows that this is not so (he is acting or reciting or incredulously echoing the remark of another). This needs an explanation. Suppose that someone utters the sentence 'It will rain to-morrow' in ordinary circumstances. This act carries with it the claim that it is true that it will rain to-morrow. By this is meant that just as it is understood that no one will give orders unless he is entitled to give orders, so it is understood that no one will utter a sentence of a kind which can be used to make a statement unless he is willing to claim that that statement is true, and hence one would be acting in a misleading manner if one uttered the sentence if he was not willing to make that claim. The word 'implies' is being used in such a way that if there is a convention that X will only be done in circumstances Y, a man implies that situation Y holds if he does X.

This point has often been made before, though not always in these terms, and it is, I believe, in substance uncontroversial. I now wish to make the point that when a speaker uses a parenthetical verb of himself with an indicative sentence p, there is not merely an implied claim that the whole statement is true but also that p is true. This is surely obvious in some cases — 'I believe it will rain', 'He is, I regret, too old', 'You intend, I gather, to refuse'. But I think that a little thought shows that it is also true in the case of, say, 'I hear that he is ill in bed', or 'He is, I hear, ill in bed'. We should not and would not say these things if we did not accept the reports on which our statements were based, and by saying them we imply a claim to their truth. The claim to truth need not be very strong, we shall indeed find that the whole point of some parenthetical verbs is to modify or to weaken the claim to truth which would be implied by a simple assertion p; but even if we say 'He is, I suppose, at home', or 'I guess that the penny will come down heads', we imply, with however little reason, that this is what we accept as true.

Positive examination of parenthetical verbs. We make our statements in contexts, social as well as logical. For example, we often have an emotional attitude to the fact we state, or it is likely to arouse emotion in our hearers. To some extent, both by accident and by design, our manner, intonation, and choice of words betray our attitude and prepares our hearers. But this is imprecise and uncertain, and, in writing, is difficult to get right for all but the great stylist. Again, content and manner give some clue to the hearer or reader of how he is to understand the statement in relation to its logical context, but not infallibly. Further, we make our statements sometimes with good, sometimes with moderate, sometimes with poor, evidence; which of these situations we are in need not be obvious to the hearer, and it would be cumbersome always to say explicitly. It is my contention that parenthetical verbs are one of the sets of devices that we use in order to deal with these matters, though not the only set. By them we prime the hearer to see the emotional significance, the logical relevance, and the reliability of our statements. This we do not by telling him how we are moved or how he should be moved by them, nor by telling him how our statement fits into the context, nor by describing the evidential situation, but by the use of warning, priming or orientating signals; we show rather than state. This is the contention which will now be somewhat elaborated.

Suppose that I go to a mother in wartime as a messenger to inform her of the death of her son. I can, no doubt, merely say 'Madam, your son is dead'. But this would be abrupt and harsh, and I would more probably say 'Madam, I regret that your son is dead'. For anyone other than a great actor it is easier to steer a course between callousness and false sentiment as a stranger bearing news by the use of a parenthetical verb in this way than by means of intonation. Clearly

I am mainly bearing news, and the addition of 'I regret' (not necessarily at the beginning of the sentence) shows without it being actually said that it is being offered, and will be received as, sad news. I am not being a hypocrite, even within the excusable, conventional, limits of hypocrisy, if I personally have no feelings on the matter at all — messengers of that sort can rarely have much feeling in wartime about each case. If, for the moment, we turn to a less purely parenthetical use of the same verb, we shall find that the essential point remains the same. If, as a friend of the family, I go to the mother when the death is well known and say 'I much regret that your son is dead, he was a dear friend' then, no doubt, I am no longer mainly bearing news. But I am still not describing my feelings; it is rather that the signal is being made for its own sake as an act of sympathy, the indicative clause giving the occasion of my sympathy. *Regret* and *rejoice* are two of the most obvious examples of verbs which give emotional orientation when used parenthetically.

Another set of these verbs is used to signal how the statement is to be taken as fitting logically into the discussion. 'I admit that he is able' assigns the statement that he is able to the logical position of being support for the opposed position, or a part of the opposed position which will not be assailed — one shows while saying that he is able that this is to be treated as an admission. One is forestalling a possible misapprehension — 'But don't you see, that is part of my point' — one is not reporting the occurrence of a bit of admitting, whatever that may be supposed to be. The parenthetical verb in 'Jones was, I conclude, the murderer' assigns to the statement the status of following from what has been said before, preventing it from being taken as, say, an additional fact to be taken into account. There is no specific activity of concluding. Other verbs which fulfil approximately similar tasks are *deduce*, *infer*, *presume*, *presuppose*, *confess*, *concede*, *maintain* and *assume*.

Another rough group is constituted by such verbs as *know*, *believe*, *guess*, *suppose*, *suspect*, *estimate*, and, in a

metaphorical use, *feel*. This group is probably more con-
troversial than the previous ones, and will require more explanation. This is the group which is used to indicate the
evidential situation in which the statement is made (though
not to describe that situation), and hence to signal what
degree of reliability is claimed for, and should be accorded
to, the statement to which they are conjoined. Thus 'I guess
that this is the right road to take' is a way of saying that
this is the right road, while indicating that one is just
plumping and has no information, so that the statement will
be received with the right amount of caution; 'I know'
shows that there is all the evidence one could need; and so on.
Some of these verbs can clearly be arranged in a scale showing
the reliability of the conjoined statement according to the
wealth of evidence — *know, believe, suspect, guess*, for
example; and adverbs can make the situation even plainer —
'I strongly believe', 'I rather suspect' and so on. We are,
in fact, in a position where we can either make our statements 'neat', and leave it to the context and the general
probabilities to show to the hearer how much credence he
should give to the statement; or, in addition to making the
statement we can actually describe the evidential situation
in more or less detail; or give a warning such as, 'Don't rely
on this too implicitly, but . . .'; or I can employ the warning
device of a parenthetical verb 'I believe it will rain'. If this
is insufficient for any reason (perhaps it is an important matter),
then the hearer can ask why and get the description of the
evidential situation. More will have to be said about these
verbs, but it will be convenient first to introduce another topic.

Adverbs corresponding to parenthetical verbs. I mentioned
earlier that parenthetical verbs were not the only device that
we have for warning the hearer how our statements are to be
taken while making it; it will perhaps make it clearer how
parenthetical verbs are used if one of these other devices is
briefly outlined. We were taught at school that an adverb
modifies a verb; but this is inaccurate, for some adverbs are
quite as loosely attached to sentences as are parenthetical

verbs. Examples are : *luckily*, *happily*, *unfortunately*, *consequently*, *presumably*, *admittedly*, *certainly*, *undoubtedly*, *probably*, and *possibly*. Note that the position of these adverbs is variable in relation to the sentence as in the case of parenthetical verbs ; we can say ' Unfortunately he is ill' or ' He is, unfortunately, ill'. If the word 'modify' is to be used these adverbs can perhaps be said to modify the whole statement to which they are attached. But how do they modify them ? Surely by giving a warning how they are to be understood. *Luckily*, *happily* and *unfortunately* indicate the appropriate attitude to the statement, for example ; *admittedly*, *consequently* and *presumably*, among others, indicate how to take the statement in regard to the context ; *certainly*, *probably* and *possibly*, among others, show how much reliability is to be ascribed to the statement. Perhaps it is worth saying, though the matter should be sufficiently obvious, that no importance should be attached to the grouping of verbs and adverbs into three sets which has been adopted. It has been done purely for convenience in an outline exposition. There are differences between the members of each of my groups and the groups are not sharply divided ; it is easy to think of verbs which might with equal reason be placed in either of two groups. Once again it must be said that our aim is to lay down general lines for the interpretation of parenthetical verbs, not to do full justice to any of them.

Comparison of these adverbs and parenthetical verbs. Provided that it is not construed as a list of synonyms, we can couple these adverbs with parenthetical verbs as follows : happily — I rejoice ; unfortunately — I regret ; consequently — I infer (deduce) ; presumably — I presume ; admittedly — I admit ; certainly — I know ; probably — I believe. This is not, I repeat, a list of synonyms ; apart from questions of nuance of meaning the adverbs are more impersonal — *admittedly* suggests that what is said would be regarded by anyone as an admission whereas *I admit* shows only the way that the statement is to be regarded here. Also it is not possible to say that every adverb has a verb corresponding to

it which has more or less the same import, or *vice versa*.
But it does seem that these adverbs and parenthetical verbs
play much the same rôle and have much the same grammatical relation to the statements which they accompany, and that,
therefore, the comparison is illuminating in both directions.

But now I must meet an objection which will certainly be
made by some philosophers to this comparison ; and I intend
to meet it by a fairly detailed examination of the example
which they themselves would most likely choose.   In doing
this we shall further explain the use of parenthetical verbs.

Probably and I believe. To say, that something is probable, my imaginary objector will say, is to imply that it is
reasonable to believe, that the evidence justifies a guarded
claim for the truth of the statement ; but to say that someone
believes something does not imply that it is reasonable for
him to believe it, nor that the evidence justifies the guarded
claim to truth which he makes.   Therefore, the objector will
continue, the difference between the use of the word 'believe'
and the word 'probably' is not, as we have suggested, merely
one of nuance and degree of impersonality, for in one case
reasonableness is implied and in the other not.   This objection
can be met, but to do so we must first make a more general
point.

Implied claims to reasonableness. Earlier it was said that
there was an implied claim to truth whenever a sentence is
uttered in a standard context, and the meaning of this was
explained.   Now we must add that whenever we make a
statement in a standard context there is an implied claim to
reasonableness, and this contention must be explained.
Unless we are acting or story-telling, or preface our remarks
with some such phrase as 'I know I'm being silly, but . . .'
or, 'I admit it is unreasonable, but . . .' it is, I think, a
presupposition of communication that people will not make
statements, thereby implying their truth, unless they have
some ground, however tenuous, for those statements.   To
say, 'The King is visiting Oxford to-morrow', and then,
when asked why, to answer 'Oh, for no reason at all', would

be to sin against the basic conventions governing the use of discourse. Therefore, I think, there is an implied claim to reasonableness which goes with all our statements, *i.e.* there is a convention that we will not make statements unless we are prepared to claim and defend their reasonableness. With this prolegomenon we can return to the question of the relation of belief and probability.

Defence of our account of belief and probability. We can now say, with less risk of being misunderstood, that when a man says, 'I believe that he is at home' or 'He is, I believe, at home', he both implies a (guarded) claim of the truth, and also implies a claim of the reasonableness of the statement that he is at home. Thus, if our objector points out that 'probably he is at home' implies, in the view of the speaker, the reasonableness and justifiability of the statement, we may answer that this is equally true of 'believe' in the first person present, in such a form as 'I believe that he is at home'. What our objector has failed to do is to notice the vast array of situations in which the verb 'believe' is used. We will now single out some, but only some, of these uses.

(A) Jones says, 'X is, I believe, at home'. Here Jones makes an implied guarded claim (that is the effect of adding 'I believe') to the truth and also an implied claim to the reasonableness, of the statement 'X is at home'. This is the case already examined.

(B) Smith, reporting Jones, says 'X is, Jones believes, at home'. This is *oratio obliqua*, reporting Jones' parenthetical use of the verb. Smith, by uttering the sentence, implies the truth and reasonableness of the statement that Jones has made the statement that X is at home (Jones thereby implying its truth and reasonableness with the conventional warning signal about the evidential situation).

(C) Smith, who has discovered that there has been a sudden railway stoppage, sees Jones making his habitual morning dash to the station, and says, 'Jones believes that the trains are working'. This is a new, and, however important, derivative, use of the verb 'believe'. Note that in this context Smith could not say, 'The trains, Jones believes, are working'. Jones, who has probably not considered the matter at all, is behaving in the way that someone who was prepared to say either 'The trains are running' or 'I believe that the trains are running' would behave (no doubt he would be prepared to say one or other of these things if he considered the matter). We thus, in a perfectly intelligible way, extend our use of the verb 'to believe' to those situations in which a person behaves as a person who has considered the evidence and was willing to say 'I believe' would consistently behave. In this case, but in this case alone, there is some point in saying that the verb is used dispositionally; but note that it is so used with reference to another use of 'believe'. It is also noteworthy that the verb cannot be so used in the first person present. To say 'I believe' in this sense is no more possible than to say 'I am under the delusion that'. 'I believe' is always used parenthetically, though not always purely so. If one recognizes that a belief that one has held is unreasonable, one either gives it up or is driven to saying 'I can't help believing'. This is psychological history, and carries with it no claim to truth or reasonableness.

Thus we see that 'Jones believes p' does not imply the reasonableness of p any more than 'It *seems* probable to Jones that p' does. On the other hand, both 'Probably p' and 'I believe that p' do imply the reasonableness of p. Thus, so far at least as we are concerned with the well-known objection about reasonableness, the parallel between 'probably' and 'I believe' has stood the test without difficulty.

At the risk of digression we may pause to comment on the history of the analysis of belief. Of old, philosophers tried to find a primary occurrent use of 'believe' as a psychological description; but in recent times the impossibility of this has been amply demonstrated, and philosophers have resorted to the so-called dispositional analysis, assuming that if the verb does not describe an occurrence it must describe a tendency to occurrences. There is, as we have seen, some point in the traditionalist reply to this that belief is here

analysed as being the behaviour, if any, which would consistently accompany itself. A recognition that in the analysis
of belief the non-descriptive parenthetical use is primary
seems to me to illuminate and resolve this dispute.

This is all that can here be said about belief. It far from
exhausts even all the relevant considerations, but our aim is
not to examine any one parenthetical verb exhaustively;
rather it is to shed new light on them all by presenting them
as a group. I want to say the main things which may be said
about a set of verbs which are not normally considered
together as an aid to the thorough examination of each which
I do not undertake. Individually, none of these verbs can be
exhaustively treated in their capacity as parenthetical verbs
and I must not be taken as suggesting that they can.

Further consideration of the third group. 'I guess' has
nowadays a colloquial use in which its significance is, at the
best, very indeterminate. But in a stricter use it serves to
warn that what is being said is a guess. Suppose that one is
asked 'Do you know who called this afternoon?' one may
answer 'No, but I guess that it was Mrs. Jones'. Even
here one is making an implied claim that it was Mr. Jones
who called and that this is a reasonable thing to say; if one
had said 'I guess that it was Mr. Stalin' one would have
been making a clumsy joke and not really guessing at all. It
seems to me to be quite impossible that anyone should think
that here 'I guess' reports any mental events or any tendency
to behave in any special way. It is put in to show that one
is making one's statement without any specific evidence, that
it is, in fact, a guess. What makes it a guess is not a mental
act nor a disposition to behave in any way, but, if it is a
genuine guess, its being said without any specific evidence,
and its being potentially silly or lucky, not well-based or ill-
supported. I cannot see that there is any essential difference
between *guess* on the one hand and *know*, *opine*, and *suspect*,
for example, on the other. The epistemological situation is
more complicated in the latter set of cases, and some of them
have special quirks in their use, *know* being a notorious

example, but that is all. They are essentially the same sort of verb.

It might be worth while to compare this view of knowledge with what Professor Austin said in his valuable paper on 'Other Minds'.[1] Among other, less immediately relevant, things, Austin there distinguishes a class of performatory verbs and compares our use of *know* with our use of these verbs. In particular, he compares it with *guarantee*. But Austin is careful not to say that *know* is a performatory verb. He also points out important differences between the two verbs. I agree that the comparison which he makes between *know* and performatory verbs is just and illuminating. Parenthetical and performatory verbs have much in common as against ordinary descriptive verbs. I am not therefore disagreeing with Austin, but trying to locate the verb *to know* in a class which it was not his purpose to consider.

Relation of the parenthetical use of parenthetical verbs to their other uses. We have now distinguished a set of parenthetical verbs and have made the following main points about their parenthetical use in the first person of the present tense :

(i) They occur in the present perfect, not the continuous tense, though their use is different from that of the present perfect tense of verbs which have a present continuous tense.

(ii) Though, in a wide sense, psychological verbs, they are not psychologically descriptive.

(iii) They function rather like a certain class of adverbs to orient the hearer aright towards the statements with which they are associated. The ways in which they do this may be roughly indicated as being aids to placing the statements aright against the emotional, social, logical, and evidential background.

(iv) There is, as when the conjoined statements are used alone, an implied claim for the truth and reasonableness of these associated statements.

[1] *P.A.S.* Supp. Vol. XX (reprinted in L. L., II). Much of my approach was suggested by this paper.

P

But parenthetical verbs are not always used parenthetically in the first person present, to which use we have so far confined practically all our attention. We must now say something about their other uses. First, we may consider the positive analogy. In connexion with point (1) above, there is a positive analogy, though not a very tidy one. The analogy seems to hold completely in the case of some verbs; one cannot say, 'I was believing', 'he is believing', 'I was knowing', 'he was knowing', 'I was suspecting' or 'he was suspecting'. In the case of some other parenthetical verbs, we find a rare and anomalous imperfect tense. For example, we can say that you were admitting something if you were interrupted in the middle of a statement which you were making as an admission; or again, we can say that someone is deducing the consequences of a set of premisses, while he is stating a succession of things as deductions. But these are not genuine exceptions. In the case of another set of these verbs an imperfect is not so strange. At the end of an argument which I have put forth someone might say, for example, 'All the while you were assuming (presupposing, accepting) that so and so'. But this is not like the imperfect tense of ordinary verbs which report the continuance throughout a period of some occurrence. I was not throughout the period continuously doing an act of assumption which I carefully refrained from mentioning. Rather I was arguing as a man would reasonably argue who was prepared to say, 'I assume that so-and-so'; that is to say, I was arguing in a way that required so and so as a premiss if the argument was to be valid. I ought, therefore, to be willing to state so-and-so as a premiss. Thus here, too, the other use has to be understood in the light of the parenthetical use.

We must also note that, in general, these verbs can throughout be used in parenthesis; we can say 'Jones was, Smith admitted, able'. This seems to be so whenever the use is either definite *oratio obliqua* or, at any rate, a fair paraphrase. Some verbs, such as *deduce* and *admit*, seem always to be used in this way. But others, including, as we have already seen, *assume, presuppose*, and *believe*, are sometimes used, not of a man who has said, 'I assume (believe, presuppose)', or words to that effect, but of a man who behaves as a man reasonably would who was prepared to say that. In such a use, which is a genuine descriptive use, the parenthetical insertion (in a grammatical sense) of the verb seems to be impossible.

Continuing with the positive analogy, it seems to follow from the above that, except in some derivative uses, parenthetical verbs are not used as psychological descriptions in other parts of their conjugation any more than in the first person present. And even in these derivative uses, they seem to describe general behaviour rather than to be specifically mental.

The obvious negative analogy is, first, that the adverbs can only be used to correspond to the first person present (see point (iii) above). But this negative analogy is only so in a very limited way. If the adverbs did correspond exactly to the whole conjugation of the verb, then the conjugation would appear to be otiose. But the adverbs can be systematically correlated with the whole conjugation of the parenthetical verbs with the aid of the verb *to seem*. This point is illustrated by these two groups of four sentences : I regret that it is too late — Unfortunately it is too late ; He regretted that it was too late — it seemed to him to be unfortunately too late ; believe that it is lost — It is probably lost ; He believed that it was lost — It seemed to him to be probably lost.

The second obvious negative analogy is that in connexion with point (iv) what is said to be supposed, regretted, believed, etc., by others, or by oneself in the past, is not in general implied to be true or reasonable by the speaker (there are exceptions to this, in each case with a special reason, *know* being an obvious example). But here, again, this is exactly what is to be expected ; while 'He believed that it was lost', if said by me, does not imply a modified truth claim to reasonableness by me for the statement that it is lost, it does allege exactly that of the man to whom I refer. The same would be true of 'He suggested', 'He concluded', and so on. The point of these verbs remains as a kind of orientating signal, but when not in the first person present they report the statement-cum-signal rather than making it.

Beyond this I do not see my way to a general account of the relation of other uses of these verbs to their parenthetical use in the first person present. Such relation is in detail different and more or less close in the case of different verbs. Sometimes the parenthetical use seems to be the basic use and to be requisite for an understanding of the others; in other cases the illumination is of much lower candle-power. I have already indicated, for example, that I regard the parenthetical use as basic in the case of 'believe', and how I regard some other standard uses as being related to it. If the point of 'I know' is, roughly, to signal complete trust-worthiness for a statement made in the best evidential con-ditions, then the point of other uses of the verb may be said with reasonable accuracy to be the assertion that somebody else, or oneself at another time, was in a position in which he was entitled to say 'I know'. This is a different, though equally close, connexion, from that which we found in the case of belief. *Know* is a rather special case, but many parenthetical verbs are very similar to *believe* in this respect. Thus, if to say 'I presuppose that p' is to assert p with an indication that it is to be fitted into the logical context as an unproved premiss, so to say 'He presupposed that p' is either to say that he said p in that way, or, at one remove, to say that he put forward p as one would reasonably do if he were making a presupposition. This last use corresponds to the use of 'he believes that p' to indicate that someone is acting as he would reasonably act if he believed in the sense that he was willing to say 'I believe that p'. *Assume* is the same in this respect. *Deduce, conclude* and *guess* seem to be different again. We would never say that someone deduced p unless we believed that he had seen that p followed, even though it was a possible deduction and he appeared to accept p, which is a difference from the case of belief. On the other hand we can say that someone deduced *p*, where we are not ourselves prepared to treat *p* as a legitimate deduction, which is a difference from the case of knowledge. In the case of still other verbs which have a parenthetical use in the first person present this use does not seem to be at all central, a key to the understanding of other uses, as in the case of the verbs above mentioned. Examples of such verbs are *hear*, *rejoice*, *expect*; it is among these verbs that possible exceptions to some of our generalizations are to be sought.

It is perhaps worth mentioning a fact which will make it especially clear that too much generalization about the relation of other uses to the first person present is not possible. It is possible to manufacture parenthetical uses of verbs which are not normally parenthetical, even in the first person present, by the addition of the infinitive *to say*. Thus the verb 'I am sorry that' is normally a formula of apology or of self-reproach; but we can convert it into a parenthetical verb by the addition of *to say:* 'He is, I am sorry to say, unwell'. 'I am glad' can be treated in the same way, and so can other verbs. It thus becomes abundantly clear that we must not always try to see the parenthetical use as central. It might also be interesting to note at this point that we can use the device of the infinitive to get two parenthetical verbs into association with one sentence. Thus 'I regret to hear that *p*' combines 'I regret' and 'I hear', thereby orientating the hearer in two different ways at the same time. Compare 'I am sorry to conclude'. These points should make it clear that one cannot generalize too much about the relation of parenthetical to other uses of verbs.

Before attempting to draw the threads together, we will anticipate a possible criticism. It may be said that the grammatical feature of being used sometimes in parenthesis, in the grammatical sense, is not a sufficient test of a verb's parenthetical character in my sense. *Guarantee*, it may be said, is a performatory verb, since to say 'I guarantee' is to guarantee, not to orientate the hearer. Similarly to say 'I bet' is to bet, and to say 'I warrant' is to warrant. But we can put these verbs into parenthesis. My answer is that we do not put these verbs into parentheses when we are using them in a performatory way ; to treat 'He'll come to a bad end, I guarantee' as a guarantee, or to ask for the odds or to cry 'Taken !' when someone says 'He'll forget to come, I bet' would be, as Aristotle would say, the mark of an un-educated man. We have here another case of the borrowing of another sort of verb for parenthetical uses. But it must, of course, be acknowledged that grammatical form is likely to be, here as elsewhere, but a fallible guide to the logical nature of a statement. In the end, the feature of being capable of occurring in parentheses is only a heuristic device for picking out a certain class of verbs, which is certainly different from, say, performatory verbs. A little more is said below about the relation of my philosophical thesis to the grammatical fact to which I draw attention.

Another objection which should be anticipated will be made on different grounds. It may be said that I have often given the appearance of conducting a grammatical rather than a philosophical investigation, and that, for example, the point about the lack of a present continuous tense could not be made in many languages. It is true that I have been using the grammatical features of English as a clue to philo-sophical points ; but one can find similar, if different, gram-matical clues in other languages. The actual point about parenthesis seems to apply to French ; and one should try to explain why in French one says 'Je regrette de vous informer que votre fils est mort' and 'Je suis désolé du fait que votre fils est mort'. It would surely be out of the question to say 'Je regrette du fait que . . .'. Similarly, I am informed by those with a better command of German than I have that my point about the similar use of parenthetical verbs and some adverbs is reinforced by the fact that in German the verb would often be most naturally translated by an adverb, e.g. 'I regret' would often be translated most naturally by 'leider'. The fact that one makes use of the clues given by one's own language does not make the thesis inapplicable to other languages which have the same devices. There is, of course, no reason to hold dogmatically that every language has devices closely similar to the use of parenthetical verbs in English.

We may now sum up, and reiterate the point of what has been said in this paper It must be admitted that there are verbs which may be said to describe a mental process, however mental processes have in the end to be analysed. Examples are *meditate, ponder, worry, imagine,* and *work out.* In the case of all these verbs one uses the present continuous tense to say what is happening now. Other verbs such as *wish, command, implore,* or *like, hate, approve, love* are interestingly different from the above and need discussion, but are not discussed here. But there is another class of verbs, different from any of the above, whose peculiarity is that they can be used either parenthetically in the normal grammatical sense, or else followed by *that,* in either case with an indicative clause. Further, they are so used in the present perfect tense, though not with the same dispositional force as are the general run of verbs. These verbs are the ones for which I have invented the technical name of parenthetical verbs. They are important because they include such philosophical war-horses as *know, believe,* and *deduce.* I have tried to show

(i) that when these verbs are used in the first person of the present tense, as is very clear when they occur grammatically in parenthesis, the assertion proper is contained in the indicative clause with which they are associated, which is implied to be both true and reasonable. They themselves have not, in such a use, any descriptive sense but rather function as signals guiding the hearer to a proper appreciation of the statement in its context, social, logical, or evidential. They are not part of the statement made, nor additional statements, but function with regard to a statement made rather as 'READ WITH CARE' functions in relation to a subjoined notice, or as the foot stamping and saluting can function in the Army to make clear that one is making an official report. Perhaps they can be compared to such stage-directions as 'said in a mournful (confident) tone' with reference to the lines of the play. They help the understanding and assessment of what is said rather than being a part of what is said.

(ii) I have further wished to show that in the case of many important verbs an understanding of this use of the verb is basic for a philosophical understanding of them; other uses of the verbs must be explained in terms of it.

(iii) It must, however, be clearly understood that there is a great deal which importantly needs saying about these verbs which has not been said here. I have not attempted to say all that there is to say about *know*, for instance, but only to bring out certain peculiarities which it has in common with a number of other verbs alongside of which it is not normally considered. But we must not be too modest; we have exposed such views as that these verbs report occurrences or tendencies to behave in certain ways. Most philosophers have been obsessed with the idea that verbs always describe some goings on — if not a simple event, then a complicated set of events. I have tried to pick out one class of verbs which do not report any goings on or even patterns of goings on at all. That the present discussion of them has been lucid and accurate, let alone final, may very well be doubted; that the set of characteristics which these parenthetical verbs share is significant and important is, however, something of which I feel very much more confident.

Queen's College, University of St. Andrews

Chapter X

THE RIVER OF TIME

BY J. J. C. SMART

THERE are certain metaphors which we commonly feel constrained to use when talking about time. We say that we
are advancing through time, from the past into the future,
much as a ship advances through the sea into unknown waters.
Sometimes, again, we think of ourselves as stationary, watching time go by, just as we may stand on a bridge and watch
leaves and sticks float down the stream underneath us.
Events, we sometimes think, are like such leaves and sticks ;
they approach from the future, are momentarily in the
present, and then recede further and further into the past.
Thus instead of speaking of our advance through time we
often speak of the flow of time. Sometimes we carry this line
of thought further. Thus there are occasions on which we
feel inclined to say that time flows at an even rate (cf. Newton),
while there are other occasions on which we want to say that
sometimes time flows faster than it does at other times.
'To-day', we may say, 'has just flown past. How different
from yesterday when the time just seemed to crawl.'

These metaphorical ways of talking are philosophically
important in a way in which most metaphorical locutions
are not. They are not the result of some wild flight of poetic
imagination, but are, in some way, *natural* to us ; at first
sight, at any rate, it seems difficult to see how we could avoid
them. 'Time, like an ever rolling stream, bears all its sons
away', says the hymn, and we feel how right the description
is. 'Yes,' we say to ourselves, 'time is like that; it is *just*
like an ever rolling stream. What better description could
there be ?' Furthermore, these metaphors have found a
place in philosophical and scientific writings. I have already

alluded to Newton, and Locke defines duration as 'fleeting extension'. Sometimes, instead of the metaphor of the flow of time, that of our advance through time is found more congenial. Thus Eddington (*Space, Time, and Gravitation*, p. 51) says, 'Events do not happen; they are just there and we come across them. "The formality of taking place" is merely the indication that the observer has on his voyage of exploration passed into the absolute future of the event in question.' Similarly the philosophy of J. W. Dunne (*An Experiment with Time*, etc.) derives largely from the idea of the voyage through time.

The metaphor of time as a river which flows or a sea through which we sail is, therefore, a very natural one. Nevertheless we cannot help realizing that it is a metaphor, though often we try to disguise this fact by using jargon. Sometimes, for example, it is asserted, as if it were one of the hardest of hard facts, that time is 'irreversible'. Now I know what it is for a car or a train to be irreversible; if ever we want it to come back to its starting-point we have to send it on a circular route. Again, I understand the assertion that the flow of a river is irreversible while the flow of the tides is not. It is motion that is or is not reversible. Hence to say that *time* is irreversible is merely to elaborate our old metaphor of the flow of time. This, then, is part of our dissatisfaction with regard to time: we have a metaphor which seems inescapable even though we recognize that it is a metaphor. Still worse, when we subject it to the least scrutiny we see that it is a metaphor which is liable to lead us astray. It is suspected by even the least critical person that when we talk of time as a river which flows we are talking in a way which is somehow illegitimate. 'Time a river!' we say to ourselves, 'a queer sort of river that. Of what sort of liquid does it consist? Is time a liquid? A very peculiar liquid indeed!' This, moreover, is only the beginning of our troubles. We become even more worried when we ask ourselves how fast this river flows. If time is a flowing river we must think of events taking time to float down this stream, and if we say 'time has flowed faster to-day than it flowed yesterday' we are saying that the stream flowed a greater distance to-day than it did in the same time yesterday. That is, we are postulating a second time-scale with respect to which the flow of events along the first time-dimension is measured. 'To-day', 'to-morrow', 'yesterday', become systematically ambiguous. They may represent positions in the first time-dimension, as in 'to-day I played cricket and to-morrow I shall do so again', or they may represent positions in the second time-dimension, as in 'to-day time flowed faster than it did yesterday'. Nor will it help matters to say that time always flows at the *same* rate. Furthermore, just as we thought of the first time-dimension as a stream, so will we want to think of the second time-dimension as a stream also ; now the speed of flow of the second stream is a rate of change with respect to a third time-dimension, and so we can go on indefinitely postulating fresh streams without being any better satisfied. Sooner or later we shall have to stop thinking of time as a stream. Our difficulty, of course, is that at present we do not see very clearly just how we are to stop.

A connected point is this : with respect to motion in space it is always possible to ask 'how fast is it ?' An express train, for example, may be moving at 88 feet per second. The question, 'How fast is it moving ?' is a sensible question with a definite answer : '88 feet per second'. We may not in fact know the answer, but we do at any rate know what sort of answer is required. Contrast the pseudo-question 'How fast am I advancing through time ?' or 'How fast did time flow yesterday ?' We do not know how we ought to set about answering it. What sort of measurements ought we to make ? We do not even know the sort of units in which our answer should be expressed. 'I am advancing through time at how many seconds per — ?' we might begin, and then we should have to stop. What could possibly fill the blank ? Not 'seconds' surely. In that case the most we could hope for would be the not very illuminating remark that there is just one second in every second.

It is clear, then, that we cannot talk about time as a river, about the flow of time, of our advance through time, or of the irreversibility of time without being in great danger of falling into absurdity. Nevertheless, when we think of time we do visualize it as a river which flows past us or as a sea through which we sail. How else are we to think about time? Now it may well be objected that we never do think about time but only about temporal facts, that there is no such thing as time and so we can't think about it, for the word 'time' is not referential in the same way as 'second' is, nor either of these in the same way as 'chair' is. Such an objection is, so far as it goes, perfectly sound. Our trouble is certainly due, at least in part, to our hypostatization of time, to thinking of it as a liquid on which events float, but nevertheless just to point this out is not, by itself, to cure our perplexity. We need to go deeper into the matter. We must ask why we should be so drawn to hypostatize time in just this way; we must put to ourselves the question, 'What features of our talk about temporal facts are analogous to features of our talk about rivers?'

Temporal facts are facts of before and after and of simultaneity. Now we may say, roughly, that it is events that are before and after one another or simultaneous with one another, and that events are happenings to things. Thus the traffic light changed from green to amber and then it changed from amber to red. Here are two happenings, and these happenings are changes of state of the traffic light. That is, *things* change, *events* happen. The traffic light changes, but the changing of the traffic light cannot be said to change. To say that it does or does not change is to utter nonsense. Similarly, the traffic light neither does nor does not happen. We must also resist the temptation to misuse the word 'become'. The traffic light *was* green and *became* red, but the becoming red did not become. Events happen, things become, and things do not just become, they become something or other. 'Become' is a transitive verb; if we start using it intransitively we can expect nothing but trouble. This is part of what is wrong with Whitehead's metaphysics; see, for example, *Process and Reality*, p. 111, where he says that actual occasions 'become'. Broad (*Scientific Thought*, p. 68) agrees that events do not *change* but he says that they *become*, and by this he means that they *come into existence*. Now this use of 'become' is no more applicable to events than is the ordinary transitive use. Events do not come into existence; they occur or happen. 'To happen' is not at all equivalent to 'to come into existence' and we shall be led far astray if we use the two expressions as though they could be substituted for one another. We can say when the inauguration of a new republic occurred and we can say that the new republic came into existence then, but we cannot say that the inauguration came into existence.

With what sorts of words can we use the expressions 'to change' and 'to become'? In the rough statement above I answered this question by saying '*things*, not *events*, change or become different'. Now while I think that if certain philosophers, notably Whitehead and McTaggart, had asked themselves this question and given themselves this rough answer, they would have saved themselves from much gratuitous metaphysics, nevertheless the answer is by no means satisfactory as it stands. It points in the right direction but it does not point clearly enough. As used thus in the abstract, 'thing' and 'event' are woefully vague. Just what expressions are we to count as 'thing-expressions' and just what expressions are we to count as 'event-expressions'? In ordinary parlance a battle is an event, for we might say that the battle of El Alamein was the decisive event of the African campaign. On the other hand a victory might be said to be an event; so also might the changing from red to green of a traffic light. This brings out how rough and ready is the usual classification of 'event-expressions'. 'Victory' and 'changing from red to green of the traffic light' have important logical properties in common which are not possessed by 'battle', in some of its uses at any rate. Thus we can say 'the battle became fiercer' but not 'the victory became fiercer'· We

can indeed say, 'the victory became more probable', or 'the
victory became possible to foresee', but there are peculiarities
about such predicates as 'probable' which are too obvious
to require special mention now, but which are connected with
the peculiarities of some other rather special predicates,
namely 'past', 'present', and 'future', which will occupy
our attention shortly. Similarly, the changing from red to
green of the traffic light can not become anything or stay
anything, if we rule out such things as *probable*, *imminent*,
past, which, as I have just remarked, are somewhat peculiar.
The logical grammar of 'battle' in 'the battle grew fiercer'
has thus an analogy to that of 'traffic light' in 'the traffic
light became green', an analogy which that of expressions
like 'change from red to green' and 'victory' lacks. Compare again, 'journey' and 'arrival'. The journey can become
more pleasant or more tedious, but we cannot say that the
arrival did or did not become or continue to be anything.
Those philosophers, then, who do their thinking in the abstract, who talk in category language about 'events', 'things',
and 'processes', and never give concrete examples, can
scarcely be intelligible to us. Just what, we may ask, is an
event ?

Contrast 'battle' with 'victory', 'journey' with 'arrival',
'running a race' with 'winning a race'. The contrast is one
between two quite different sets of expressions ; it is, roughly,
the contrast which Professor Ryle has made between 'task
words' and 'achievement words'. When you have won a
race you have not gone through two processes (1) running the
race and (2) winning it. You have gone through one process,
namely running, with the result that when you got to the end
of the course no one was in front of you. You might have
gone through exactly the same motions and lost it. So we
must not say that 'winning' is the name of a process in the
way that 'running' is ;· nor must we say either that winning
is something that takes some time to perform or that it is
instantaneous. The difference between winning and running
is not that between a flash of lightning and a roll of thunder.

In Aristotelian language, winning is an actualization, not a process. So also are seeing and understanding as opposed to looking and trying to understand. In the *Metaphysics*, 1048 *b*, 30-4, Aristotle makes this very point; he contrasts 'to see' and 'to understand' with 'to walk' and 'to build'. We can say that we are in the middle of a walk or of a building operation, but what should we think if someone said that he was half-way through seeing that the inkpot had fallen over or that he would soon have finished understanding a certain argument? To use Professor Ryle's words, actualizations, unlike processes, 'can be dated but not clocked'.

I have drawn attention to this distinction because I think it helps to illuminate the use of expressions like 'went' in 'the ball went into the goal', 'reached', in 'the apple reached the ground', 'changed' in 'the traffic light changed from red to green', and 'became coincident' in 'the star became coincident with the cross-wire of the telescope'. We should not normally say that the ball's going into the goal changed or did not change, or that the becoming coincident became or did not become anything, or that the apple's reaching the ground altered or did not alter in any way. We must compare 'to change' and 'to become' with 'to arrive' and 'to win', rather than with 'to journey' and 'to fight'. Changes, becomings, beginnings, endings, reachings, hittings, touchings, and coincidences are like victories, arrivals, and scorings of goals, in being things to which we can give a date but not a running commentary, not even an infinitesimally short running commentary.

Changes, I have said, like arrivals and victories, neither do nor do not change. Someone may perhaps deny this, and say, 'Of course changes change, and so do changes of changes, and changes of changes of changes. . . . The differential calculus is always talking of changes of changes.' Let such an objector pause to think again. It is not changes of changes that change, it is *rates of change* that change. Now 'rate of change' is defined in terms of 'change' but it has quite different logical properties from it. Of course one could no doubt bring up special usages in which we said that changes changed, for language is a flexible instrument and we must not expect that words will *never* be used in a certain way. For example, we could imagine an idiom in which we said 'the becoming grey of his hair became much more rapid'. The use of 'to become grey' in this idiom stands to the use of 'to become grey' in 'when I met him again I was surprised to find that his hair had become grey' rather as the use of 'to win' in 'he was winning all the way' stands to the use of 'to win' in 'he won'. 'He was winning all the way' means some such thing as 'he was in front all the way and it was quite obvious that he was going to win', *i.e.* it uses 'to win' in a more sophisticated way than does 'he won' or 'he is going to win'. We should have to teach a child how to use 'he won' before we could teach him to understand 'he was winning all the way'. Similarly, such an idiom as 'the becoming grey of his hair became quicker' would use 'become' in the first instantiation of this word in a more sophisticated way than it would in the second instantiation of the word, or in a more sophisticated way than does 'he became enraged'. I do not want to legislate as to how people should use 'to change' and 'to become' but I do want to invite them to become sensitive to changes of the usage of these words, because philosophers do not seem to have been so sensitive in the past. The traditional category of 'event' is far too catholic.

A word like 'battle' is not easy to categorize. There are certain differences between the use of 'battle' in (1) 'The battle of Hastings occurred on 14th October, 1066' and its use in (2) 'The battle of Hastings became fiercer'. For although the two uses have many similarities, in its first use 'battle' is analogous to 'change from red to green of the light' and 'victory' in a respect in which in its second use it is analogous rather to 'traffic light', *i.e.* in the second sort of context 'battle' takes on some of the properties of a substance word. This difference in use can be seen if we reflect on the statement, 'The battle of Hastings occurred on 14th October, 1066 and became fiercer as the sun rose in the sky'. Is there

not something wrong with such a conjunction ? We should
want to change the sentence to something like this : 'The
battle of Hastings *began* on the morning of 14th October,
1066 and became fiercer as the sun rose in the sky'. It may
be remarked that although this change of phrasing is a
change for the better, nevertheless, this is merely a stylistic
matter. I want to suggest that this is not *merely* a stylistic
matter, but that the stylistic propriety reflects a logical
propriety.

Let us now, for our present purposes only, classify together
such expressions as the following : 'change' and 'becoming — ' (as in the traffic light example), 'victory', 'arrival',
'coincidence of the star with the cross-wire', 'impact',
'starting', 'stopping', and so on, and 'battle' in use (1)
though *not* in use (2). These all show the same logical property
of not ordinarily being able to be used in conjunction with the
verb 'to change'. They do, of course, differ in others of their
logical properties ; it is only for the purposes of the present
paper, no doubt, that it is convenient to regard them as of
one logical type. This, however, is nothing to be distressed
about. All type classifications are relative only to certain
purposes, though some purposes are of course more important
than others. Type classifications only point out *certain* similarities of logical grammar, while they leave unmentioned
differences which in other philosophical contexts, perhaps,
should not be overlooked. Most philosophers would ordinarily be quite happy to put 'chair' and 'table' in the same
category, but these words have not, *in all respects*, quite the
same logic. Thus 'how large is its seat ?' may intelligibly be
asked about a chair but not about a table.

I may now specify the way in which I propose to use
'event' by saying that all expressions of the class defined in
the last paragraph are event expressions. Thus we shall say
that 'battle' in its use (1) is an event word while in its use (2)
it is not. Again, a person's birth, death, and marriage are
events, but his life is not. I think that this corresponds to
one of the ways in which philosophers have used 'event',

Q

though I do not think that they have clearly distinguished it from other, wider, ways in which they have used the word.[1]

If 'E' is an event expression in the sense just explained, 'E happened' will always be sense and, if we exclude for the moment the peculiar use of 'change' whereby an event may be said to change from being future to being past, 'E changed' and 'E did not change' will always be nonsense. So also will 'E became —' for all fillings of the blank except for the special class of fillings which consists of the words 'past', 'present', and 'future', and of connected expressions. Nor again, can we say anything of the form 'E began' or 'E ended'. We can say that the first world war began at midnight on 4th August, 1914, but we cannot say when the beginning of the war began, unless by 'beginning of' we mean 'early part of'. To say anything of the form '— changed to —' or '— became —' or '— remained —' is to say that something had a certain property and later on either had another property or still had the same property. Thus an event expression will never fill the first blank of such a sentence form; what is wanted, we may say, is a *continuant* expression of some sort. In particular we cannot say that the battle of Waterloo will ever change in respect of being after the French Revolution, nor can we say that it will not so change, for this implies that it might so change but will not in fact do so. It is not false but nonsensical to suggest that it could ever be true at one time to say that the battle was after the French Revolution and also at another time to say that it was not. McTaggart is thus very misleading when he says (*Philosophical Studies*, p. 113) 'an event can never cease

[1] By 'event' some philosophers profess to mean a 4-dimensional entity, for example that of which the 3-dimensional shape of a man at any instant of his life outlines a cross-section. It is not necessary to argue in great detail that if an event (in this sense) may be said to be susceptible of change, say along the time-dimension, this is a usage very different to that in which we say 'the traffic light changed'. It is analogous to that in which we say 'the country changes as you go north' and has nothing to do with our present puzzle at all. The country does not 'really change', *i.e.* it does not change in the sense in which the traffic light does. It is just different in one place from what it is at another.

to be an event' and 'if N is ever earlier than O and later than M, it will always be, and always has been, earlier than O and later than M'.   This is to say that events do not change, but my point is that they neither do nor do not change.   The concept of change is just not applicable to them.   McTaggart also held that Time essentially involves Change.   There is, of course, a sense in which this is true, for if nothing ever became different from what it was before, if things never changed from one state to another or in their relations to one another, we could never say anything of the form 'A became B before C became D' or 'x changed from A to B before y changed from C to D'.   There would be no situations in which the words 'before' and 'after' could be used.   Nevertheless, McTaggart was wrong in proceeding from the true but unilluminating proposition that time involves change (*i.e.* things changing) to the assertion that we cannot use temporal expressions without implying that *events* change. He was hence led to attach quite the wrong sort of significance to the perfectly true statement that we *can* say that events change in respect of pastness, presentness, and futurity, *i.e.* that a statement of the form 'E became —' makes sense if we put into the blank the word 'past' or 'present'.

It therefore behoves us now to consider the special idiom which has just been mentioned, to pay attention to the special class of expressions with which it is legitimate to form a sentence of the form 'E became —' or 'E changed from — to —'.   This class of expressions consists of the words 'past', 'present', and 'future', and of such words as 'probable' and 'imminent'.   It is a characteristic of these words, by the way, that none of them can be used to complete the sentence-form 'the traffic light became —'.   I shall deal only with the cases of 'past', 'present', and 'future'.   The discussion of expressions such as 'imminent' and 'probable' would be on similar lines, though it would have to be more complex.   'Past', 'present', and 'future' are the expressions of central importance, and they were, of course, the ones which fascinated McTaggart.

When we say that the boat '*was* upstream, *is* level, *will be* downstream', we are saying that occasions on which the boat is upstream are *earlier than* this utterance, that the occasion on which it is level is *simultaneous with* this utterance, and that occasions on which it is downstream are *later than* this utterance. That is, a language could be devised in which temporal copulae did not exist, but in which we used the words 'earlier than', 'later than', or 'simultaneous with' in combination with a non-temporal copula and the expression 'this utterance'. This language would not contain words like 'past', 'present', and 'future'. For example 'is past' would be translated by 'is earlier than this utterance'.

In 'the boat's being upstream is earlier than this utterance; the boat's being level is simultaneous with this utterance; the boat's being downstream is later than this utterance' we have three occurrences of 'this utterance' all pointing to the *same* utterance. On the other hand we cannot translate the statement, 'the beginning of the war was future, is present, will be past' in the same way. If we try to do it we get: 'the beginning of the war is later than some utterance earlier than this one, is simultaneous with this utterance, and is earlier than some utterance later than this one'. We can only put in a simple 'this utterance' once. It was once true to say 'the beginning of the war is in the future' or 'the beginning of the war is later than *this* utterance', *i.e.* if a person were to have said it he would have turned out to be right. Later on it became true to say 'the beginning of the war is simultaneous with *this* utterance'. Still later it becomes true to say 'the beginning of the war is earlier than *this* utterance'. The three 'this's', however, point to different utterances.

This shows how misleading it is to think of the pastness, presentness, and futurity of events as properties, even as relational properties. It shows how utterly unlike 'this event was future and became past' is to 'the light was red and became green'.

Substances exist in space. In this sense of 'space', space

is something that endures through time. Thus it makes
sense to talk of a part of space becoming occupied, or of the
curvature of space in a certain region altering. There is, of
course, also a timeless sense of 'space' — the sense of 'space'
in geometry (if we talked of a sphere turning into a cube we
should be going outside the language of solid geometry) or
in which the space-time of the Minkowski world in physics is
a space. Now if we think of events as changing, namely in
respect of pastness, presentness or futurity, we think of them
as substances changing in a certain way. But if we sub-
stantialize events, we must, to preserve some semblance of
consistency, spatialize time. (That is, think of time as a
space that endures. In another sense of 'spatialize time' this
is a most laudable thing to do. Think of the Minkowski
representation. Note, however, that when we talk within
the Minkowski representation all our sentences must be
tenseless and there must be no verbs of action or process.
There is a category mistake involved in certain popular expositions, as when a light signal is said to be propagated
through space-time, or our consciousness is said to crawl up
a world line.) If we spatialize time 'earlier than' becomes
'lower down the stream'. There is a close syntactical similarity between our talk about rivers and our talk about time;
e.g. just as 'earlier than' is transitive and asymmetrical, so is
'downstream of'. By our substantializing of events and our
consequent spatializing of time we make this syntactical
similarity still closer. Part of our language, we may say, has
had its syntax 'shifted', and we can, of course, go on talking
in our new symbolism (with our shifted syntax) indefinitely,
so long as we remain within the area in which all our central
concepts are so 'shifted' or distorted. Trouble arises at the
boundary between our shifted system and the old one, for
example, when we use 'event', with its syntax shifted so as to
behave like 'substance', in combination with 'time' with its
syntax *not* shifted to behave like 'space'. We then get nonsense, such as 'how fast do events float down the river of
time ?', *i.e.* 'how much time$_1$ does it take for events to float a

given distance (time$_2$) in the river ?' Here 'time$_1$', is used in the ordinary way and 'time$_2$' is used in the shifted way.

Shifted syntax is an interesting linguistic phenomenon, and is at the root of most philosophical mythology. Indeed it might be useful to use 'philosophical mythology' just so as to indicate this sort of mythology. This mythology is in a way harmless if, so to speak, we draw a red line round all our 'shifted' talk and carefully avoid mixing it with our un-shifted talk. A comparison will perhaps help to make this clear. Suppose that there are two chess players who have very weak eyesight but very retentive memories. They can, we may suppose, tell quite easily what square a piece is on, and that, *e.g.*, it has just moved diagonally, but cannot very easily distinguish its shape ; they cannot tell very easily by looking at the shape of a piece whether it is, say, a bishop or a rook. Such players might get into the habit of very often identifying pieces solely by their previous moves. They might say to themselves, for example, 'this is a knight because it has just gone one place forward and one diagonally'. Memory, we may thus suppose, largely makes up for deficiency in eye-sight. Now suppose that the two players have been inter-rupted for a moment and that when they resume one takes the shadowy-looking thing, which is in reality one of his rooks, to be a bishop. He will then move it diagonally. The other player will say to himself 'that's a bishop, for it came diagonally'. The game may now proceed perfectly normally, though of course reference to a written record would bring to light a discontinuity, namely the 'metamorphosis' of a rook into a bishop. The two players may have jumped to other conclusions also. As there cannot be three bishops they may take one bishop to be a rook. The metamorphosis of one piece leads to the metamorphosis of others. Our players may enjoy an excellent game ; trouble will only arise if they suddenly look very hard at the supposed bishop and say 'it's a rook', and start wanting to use it from now on once more as a rook, or if, by recourse to written records, they wish to bring the earliest part of their game into relation with the part of the game which succeeded the interruption.

When we talk about the river of time we are like these chess players. What could the chess players do? They could agree to split up the game into separate 'games', and say, *e.g.*, 'I had the best of the first "game", and you had the best of the second, and the third was about evenly contested'. Similarly we can draw a line round our shifted talk about the river of time, and make sure not to mix it up with our ordinary unshifted talk; this is the best thing to do when we want to enjoy a hymn like 'Time, like an ever rolling stream', and there is no reason why we should not sing such a hymn with a clear logical conscience. For most purposes, however, by far the best thing is not to shift our syntax at all, to go on using our bishops as bishops and our rooks as rooks, to avoid the temptation to spatialize time or to hypostatize events.

UNIVERSITY OF ADELAIDE

Chapter XI

TIME, TRUTH, AND INFERENCE

BY D. F. PEARS

I

McTaggart's way of thinking about time leads in the end to paradoxes of reduplication. These paradoxes are the revenge which time takes on philosophers who deprive it of its proper means of expression, temporal verbs. For temporal verbs, when they are banished from their natural logical level, persist in reappearing at a higher logical level. The usual origin of the preference for timeless verbs which generates this regress is an obscure misconception about the eternity of truth. For it is dimly felt that thoughts about the future somehow have eternal truths as their contemporary objects. Thus thought, itself a symbolic reduplication of objects, when those objects are not contemporary with it, generates surrogate contemporary objects. And, since this spurious reduplication is the ultimate source of McTaggart's conception of time, it is not surprising that McTaggart's conception of time led to more and more puzzling reduplications. And McTaggart's argument for the unreality of time, which used that conception and its attendant regress, was only a complicated way of expressing a mistaken prejudice against temporal verbs.

THE sun will rise to-morrow if and only if to-morrow's sunrise is an event which will happen. And to-morrow's sunrise is an event which will happen if and only if to-morrow's sunrise is an event which will become present. These two equivalences, taken together, express McTaggart's way of thinking about time. Now McTaggart went further down this road than most people. But most people follow it in its earlier stages. For it is such a natural way of thinking about time that it is almost unavoidable. 'We may, indeed, say that the hour of death is uncertain, but when we say so we represent that hour to ourselves as situated in a vague and remote expanse of time, it never occurs to us that it can have any connexion with the day that has already dawned, or may signify that death — or its first assault and partial possession of us, after which it will never leave hold of us again — may occur this very afternoon, so far from uncertain, this afternoon, every hour of which has already been allotted to some occupation.'[1]

But, although McTaggart's way of thinking about time is almost inevitable, it leads in the end to puzzling reduplications. For it suggests that the death becomes present in the same way that the man dies, that the sunrise becomes present in the same way that the eastern sky becomes pale. And, if this suggestion were correct, we could ask how quickly the sunrise becomes present. But, as Smart pointed out, this question could be answered only by someone who possessed a second time-scale.[2] And we can neutralize the suggestion which led to the question by pointing out that temporal predicates are not like non-temporal predicates, that 'present' is not like 'pale'.

McTaggart's way of thinking about time also suggests that time causes the sunrise to become present in the same way that the spinning of the earth causes the eastern sky to become pale. Now time is usually made into a cause only when it is difficult to name an ordinary cause for an event 'Hans Castorp's hair and nails grew too, grew rather fast. He sat very often in the barber's chair in the main street of the Dorf, wrapped in a white sheet. . . . First time, and then the barber performed their office upon him.'[3] But, if time is ever a cause, it is always a cause. And, if time is always a cause, then wherever we succeed in finding another

---

[1] Proust, *Remembrance of Things Past*, tr. Scott Moncrieff, Vol. VI, p. 3.
[2] Smart, 'The River of Time', Chapter X, above.
[3] Mann, *The Magic Mountain*, c. vii.

cause we shall have two causes on our hands. But this is an idle reduplication of causes. And we can neutralize it by pointing out, as Smart pointed out, that events are unlike things, that the sunrise is unlike the eastern sky, so that it is impossible for a cause to alter the sunrise in the same way that a cause alters the eastern sky.

Now to point out that temporal predicates are unlike non-temporal predicates and that events are unlike things is to neutralize the suggestions contained in the second equivalence; that to-morrow's sunrise is an event which will occur if and only if it is an event which will become present. So it might appear that it is this second equivalence which is solely responsible for the two reduplications.

But in a way which is almost too obvious to be noticed the two reduplications are also partly the fault of the first equivalence : that the sun will rise to-morrow if and only if to-morrow's sunrise is an event which will occur. For this equivalence throws the main verb into the present tense, and relegates the future tense to a subordinate clause. And this transformation in itself contains the suggestion of a falsehood. It suggests that to-morrow's sunrise is somehow a contemporary thing. And, though it does not go as far as the second equivalence goes, though it does not suggest that to-morrow's sunrise is a genuine thing which genuine causes alter with genuine celerity, yet the suggestion which it does contain, that to-morrow's sunrise is somehow a contemporary thing, is much more primitive and fantastic.[1] For, if to-morrow's sunrise were a contemporary thing, then one of its contemporary properties would be that it would happen in the future : it would be about to happen in the same way that at a later date it would be happening. Yet, at the time when it was still only about to happen, an inventory of relevant contemporary items would contain at the most a man be-

[1] Cf. I. Silone, *The Seed Beneath the Snow*, tr. Frances Frenaye, p. 352 : 'With the use of the infinitive' (instead of temporal verbs) 'everything becomes present; there is no more past or future, only a sense of the infinite. Even in speaking of an event long since gone by, or of a future action, as if by magic the past repeats itself and the future becomes imminent.'

lieving that it would happen, his belief, perhaps the words in
which his belief was expressed, and the evidence and memories
on which it was based. Contrast the man who believes that
the sun is actually rising. If he is correct, he can have before
his eyes the rising sun, or, if he wants an event, the sunrise.
Only he will not find this reduplication in the presence attractive. For, as Wisdom has pointed out,[1] the sunrise is only a
sort of logical shadow of the rising sun ; and who would care
about the shadow when he has the thing which casts it ? But
the other man, who believes that the sun will rise, cannot
have the thing which cast the shadow. And, since beliefs
about contemporary properties of contemporary things are
the most likely to be correct, he consoles himself by pretending that the logical shadow, which is timeless, is really a
contemporary thing, and that one of its contemporary properties is that it will happen in the future.

For most of us the surrogate contemporary things which
duplicate the past are less imposing. This is partly because
there is memory, and impersonation of the familiar is more
difficult ; and partly because the future is in a practical way
more interesting. But for McTaggart, who followed this
way of thinking to what he believed to be its conclusion, the
past was impersonated by timeless events just as much as the
future. Languages show how exceptional this disinterested
thoroughness of McTaggart's was. For according to Jespersen, the way in which many languages form their future
tenses makes them less independent of the present than their
past tenses are.[2] For, though it is true that the perfect tense
expresses what has happened by its effects in the present, the
other past tense usually stands on its own feet. Contrast the
future tense, which often expresses what will happen by its
causes in the present. English and French use the idea of
motion : 'It is going to', 'Il va'. English and Modern Greek
use the idea of volition : 'It will', 'θa'. And English and
Italian use the idea of obligation : 'I shall', 'Scrivero' (from

---

[1] 'Logical Constructions II', *Mind*, 1931, p. 460.
[2] Jespersen, *The Philosophy of Grammar*, pp. 260-61 and p. 269.

the Romanic form scribere-habeo, I have to write).   Perhaps
the reason why these future tenses are not detached from the
present is that they are referring to the present signs of future
events on the principle that a statement which is based on
flimsy evidence ought to contain a reference to that evidence.
For in a way the going to be, the wishing to be, and the being
obliged to be are contemporary evidence.   Or perhaps these
future tenses should be regarded as impostors which desperately misuse anthropomorphic ideas in order to build between
the present and the future the sort of logically unshakable
bridge which Hume showed to be logically impossible.   For
sometimes the future tense does impose on us in this way.

But anyway McTaggart's conception of time does not
depend on a projection of present evidence beyond the bounds
of logical possibility into the future.   It uses another device,
which is in a way the opposite of this one.   This is the device
of making the timeless shadows of the future (and the past)
into contemporary things.   And this is achieved by making
the timeless present tense refer to any time when really it
refers to no time.   This misconception about the eternity of
truth is so bizarre that it must have been thrown up by a
strong desire to know the future.   For if I say, 'That sunrise is
an event which will occur', it is obvious that the main verb is
timeless and that the indication of the time of the event has
been delegated to the subordinate verb, which must change
its tense with the time of utterance.   After all, if the main
verb really referred to the present time, it would be premature.
For 'being an event' is a sort of ontological diploma awarded
to a possibility which has been successful in the competition
for actuality;   and the award must await the result.   The
main verb, by detaching itself from the time of the event, has
not left itself free to be attached to the time of utterance.
When it shuffled off its only proper time it shuffled off all time.

Now 'being true' is another ontological diploma of success, like 'being an event':   only, unlike 'being an event', it
is awarded not to possibilities but to the sentences and propositions which describe them.   And, if I say, 'It is true that

the sun will rise to-morrow', it is equally obvious that the
main verb is timeless, and that the indication of the time of
the event has been delegated to the subordinate verb, which
must change its tense with the time of utterance. Now
Tarski's equivalence, 'The sun will rise to-morrow if and only
if it is true that the sun will rise to-morrow', makes no attempt
to conceal its ascent to the timeless heaven of logicians. For,
unlike an event, a truth is quite overtly a timeless logical
shadow. A truth does not even masquerade as a substance.
It is merely a lucky substantival clause. Yet it is the eternity
of truth which lies beneath McTaggart's conception of time
and its attendant reduplications. This comes out very clearly
in his celebrated argument for the unreality of time.[1] For
he claimed that events have properties which do not change.
His example was the death of Queen Anne. '. . . That it
has such causes, that it has such effects — every characteristic
of this sort', he claimed, 'never changes.' And this claim is
a conflation of two sentences. The first is : 'The death of
Queen Anne is an event which was caused by Γ and which
caused Δ'. And the second is : 'It is true that Queen Anne
died because γ, and that because she died δ'. Only McTaggart
failed to put the subordinate verbs in his compound sentence
into the past tense. He said 'That Queen Anne's death *has*
such causes, that it *has* such effects . . .'.

The largest block capitals in the world would not over-
emphasize this mistake of McTaggart's. It is the most important point in his argument for the unreality of time. And
I shall use it as a pivot on which to turn his whole argument
upside down, and show that his conclusion ought to have been
not the unreality of time but the unreality of timelessness.

McTaggart showed that the subordinate verbs which
link temporal predicates to events must change their tenses
with the time of utterance ; that, for instance, in the twentieth
century we can only say that Queen Anne's death is an event
which was future. And he showed that, if we want to relieve
this subordinate verb of the duty of changing its tense with

[1] McTaggart, *Philosophical Studies*, c. v.

the time of utterance, we must drag in another subordinate verb to perform this duty.[1] This co-opting of another subordinate verb is achieved if we say : 'There is a moment, at which Queen Anne's death is an event which is future, and which is past'. And in this sentence the fourth 'is' is temporal, and must change its tense with the time of utterance. And McTaggart showed that this fourth 'is' can be made timeless only if we enfold the whole sentence in yet another logical wrapping : 'There is a moment, at which . . . , and which is present'. And here again the last 'is' is temporal. And this, he said, quite rightly, is an infinite regress.

But what drove McTaggart down this infinite regress ? He was haunted by the mistaken idea than an event possesses timelessly the three incompatible characteristics, pastness, presentness and futurity. And he realized that he could escape this spurious contradiction only by making the subordinate verb, which linked a temporal predicate to an event, change its tense with the time of utterance. But he thought that making this verb temporal was tantamount to saying, for instance : 'There is a moment at which Queen Anne's death is an event which is future, and which is past'. And he thought this only because he had an obsessional preference for timeless verbs. And this obsession created the spectral contradiction which pursued him down the infinite regress. For this spectre, when it had been exorcized from one logical level, only reappeared on the next higher logical level. He thought he could free an event from the factitious contradiction inherent in its timeless possession of the three incompatible temporal predicates only by transferring this factitious contradiction to a moment : and that he could free this moment only by sacrificing another moment ; and so *ad infinitum*.

But the spectre was only the creation of his prejudice against temporal verbs. And the regress was only the result of attempting the impossible operation of freeing from temporality the subordinate verbs which link temporal predicates

[1] Cf. Broad, *Examination of McTaggart's Philosophy*, pt. i, p. 314.

to events. Now McTaggart failed to see that this operation
cannot be performed even on the verbs which link non-
temporal predicates to events. And he failed to see this
because he made the crucial mistake of saying 'That Queen
Anne's death HAS such causes, that it HAS such effects —
every characteristic of this sort never changes'. But it *is* not
caused in a certain way: it *was* caused in a certain way.
And McTaggart made this crucial mistake because, like most
logicians, he was too preoccupied with adjectives to pay any
attention to verbs. For, when the predicates are non-temporal,
the alleged incompatibility cannot lie in the predicates, but
only in the verbs which link them to events : whereas, when
the predicates are temporal, the alleged incompatibility can
lie in the predicates. But this difference is only the result of
making events into substances, so that what was previously
expressible only by a temporal verb can now be expressed by
a temporal predicate. And why should one be worried by an
alleged incompatibility of predicates, and not by an alleged
incompatibility of verbs ?

And, if McTaggart had realized that the operation of
freeing from temporality cannot be performed even on the
verbs which link non-temporal predicates to events, he might
have seen that the regress is not peculiar to temporal predicates. And, if he had seen this, he might have realized that
his whole argument against the reality of time is only the
expression of a general prejudice against temporal verbs.
And, if he had realized this, he might have abandoned this
prejudice and accepted in its place the natural tendency of
ordinary people to use temporal verbs. And, if he had done
this, his conclusion would have been not the unreality of
time, but the unreality of timelessness.

Now, because McTaggart was a disinterested metaphy-
sician, he treated the past just like the future, and he did not
try to reintroduce his timeless shadows into the present
moment. But most people are metaphysicians who are not
disinterested. And it is because they want to have the future
somehow in the present that they try to make timeless shadows

into surrogate contemporary things. But the unreality of timelessness baffles all their attempts to reach into the future and drag something out of it into the present. For they only succeed in grasping more and more absolutely transparent logical wrappings, which will not be noticed in the future when they clothe things, and which cannot be seen when they have got them into the present where there is nothing for them to clothe. For who, in the presence of the thing, would bother to say: 'There is a moment, at which . . . , and which is present'? And who, in the absence of the thing, would say it with as much conviction as he would say it, if he bothered to say it, in the presence of the thing?

The reason why McTaggart's way of thinking about time leads to reduplications is that it springs from the very nature of thought, which is itself a sort of symbolic reduplication of reality. For beliefs in a way reduplicate objects. And those beliefs which are contemporary with their objects are the most likely to be correct. Hence those beliefs which are not contemporary with their objects, in a spirit of rivalry, treat timeless shadows as if they were contemporary objects.

A perfect example of this self-deception is cited by Aristotle in the *De Interpretatione*.[1] He there presents and refutes the argument that, if to-day it is true that there will be a sea-battle to-morrow, then there will be a sea-battle to-morrow: but that to-day it is either true or not true; and so that we must either accept determinism or reject the law of excluded middle. Few people are deluded by this overt argument. For it is difficult to believe that one could determine the whole future if only one could utter true sentences sufficiently quickly. And it is easy to see that truth is not a contemporary property of sentences like being chanted. But it is easy to be deceived when the same argument is put more covertly, as in: 'If I knew the future it would all be determined', or in: 'If I could see future events they would be bound to happen'. For people want to be deceived. They want to have the future in the present. But they can only

[1] 18 a 33 ff.

have its shadow. And, since one reduplication leads to another, they find that they have not only shadow-things but a shadow-time and a shadow-cause. This is time's revenge.

II

This conclusion, that the truth of a sentence is a timeless shadow and therefore cannot determine the event which the sentence describes, can be extended so as to apply not only to categorical sentences, but also to hypothetical sentences, both singular and general. But in the case of hypotheticals, if ' determine' means not ' make the opposite logically impossible' but ' make the opposite causally impossible', there is something which can determine the event described in the consequent, and that is the event described in the antecedent. To say this is to speak anthropomorphically, but anthropomorphism is harmless so long as it does not confuse causal and logical necessity. And it is important to be thoroughly anthropomorphic and not to forget that the verb in the antecedent which describes the determining event is temporal. For failure to realize this generates one of the puzzles of determinism.

The suggestion that the truth of a categorical sentence determines the future event which it describes is unconvincing. For one event can be determined only by another event, and not by a timeless shadow. And the mistake in the argument cited by Aristotle is the mistake of taking the same inference twice over, once as a deductive inference, and once as an inductive inference. And this is yet another of the illicit reduplications which spring from McTaggart's conception of time. No inference can lead to a novel conclusion with logical certainty. And anyway 'making the opposite logically impossible' is a degenerate case of determination. It is completely effective, and yet its effect is never felt. In fact the event might be described as self-determined if we were not too jealous to extend this description to events whose seats

R

are not persons but things. For, if there is nothing to determine an event except the truth of the sentence which describes
it, there is no lever in the present which could move the event
in the future. And this applies not only to categorical
sentences but also to hypothetical sentences.

However, the suggestion that the truth of hypothetical
sentences determines the future events to which they apply,
though equally false, is less unconvincing. It is less unconvincing because in the case of some hypotheticals there is
something to do the determining; there is the antecedent
event. Now we should not say that the antecedent event
determined the consequent event unless we believed that the
hypothetical was true. But from this it does not follow that
it is the truth of the hypothetical or the truth of any other
sentence which determines the consequent event. Nor could
it follow. For the timeless cannot determine. Nor does
'determine' here mean 'make the opposite logically impossible', but 'make the opposite causally impossible'. For
the inference now leads to a novel conclusion and therefore
forfeits logical certainty and affects to follow the track of
causal necessity. But what is causal necessity? This is a
difficult question. For whereas logical necessity achieves
nothing in a way which can easily be described, causal
necessity achieves much in a way which defies description.

For in the case of a singular hypothetical the antecedent
event either is made to happen by us, or is made to happen
by some other event, or just happens (since we do not know
that every event has a cause). And, however it happens, it
is a lever in the present, which, we say, moves the consequent
event in the future. But we should say that it was logically
impossible for the consequent event not to happen only if
we had been given not only the truth of the antecedent, but
also the truth of the hypothetical. But unfortunately we never
are given the truth of the hypothetical until we have been
given the truth of the consequent (I omit consideration of
those queer cases where the antecedent is false). So, though
we have a lever in the present, we have no fulcrum until the

future event has happened.   And then the lever and fulcrum
are no longer needed.

And a general hypothetical is an endless conjunction of
singular hypotheticals, only one of which applies to a particular future event.   And, though we have not yet been given
the truth of this or any other singular hypothetical which
applies to a future event, often we have been given the truth
of many of the others which apply to past events.   And it is
easy to overlook the incompleteness of the particular singular
hypothetical which interests us, since so many of the others
are already complete.   But unfortunately we shall not have
been given the truth of the general hypothetical until we have
been given the truth of this particular and singular hypothetical
and per impossible that of all the others too.   So, though
we may have a large set of levers, they are no use to us.   For
each one either has no fulcrum, or else the event which it was
to move has already happened anyway.   The universe is like
a signal-box constructed by Kafka, and we are the signalmen.   We desperately try to alter the signals, but always the
rod on which the levers are pivoted is just not quite long
enough to reach the particular lever which we want to use.
And, by the time that we have succeeded in extending it so
that it will provide this lever too with a fulcrum, the signal
which we wanted to alter has already altered itself.   And,
even if we were signalmen living in the sort of utopia in
which all the levers moved themselves, they could never move
quickly enough to be any use.   Yet the extraordinary thing
is that, if the lever is the last of a long row of levers, it seems
to us that it moved as if it already had a fulcrum.

This description of causal necessity, like any other description of causal necessity, is a ghost story.   If a real signalman told it we should call him superstitious.   We might ask
him if he really thought that someone was holding on to the
lever at its pivotal point.   Superstition, as Wittgenstein said,[1]
is the belief in the causal nexus.   But we say this only when
we compare causal with logical necessity.   And this is all

[1] *Tractatus Logico-Philosophicus*, 5·1361.

that my analogy does. It pretends to mechanize logical necessity in a way which suggests that it competes in the same field with causal necessity. And it ensures that causal necessity will lose in this unreal competition by making it work in an uncanny way. After all, if causal necessity is a poltergeist, logical necessity is the sort of traditional ghost which very conspicuously does nothing.

But, quite apart from superstition, this description of causal necessity is anthropomorphic. However, such anthropomorphism is natural and harmless so long as it does not confuse causal and logical necessity. But, if we are going to adopt this anthropomorphic manner of speaking, we must be thorough about it. We must realize that, when one event determines another, this determination, or making the opposite causally impossible, is something which happens in time. And that those events, whose causes, if they have any, are unknown to us, for all we know determine themselves. And that, once an event has been determined by another event or has determined itself, no subsequent event can determine it any further. For failure to grasp these three points leads to a curious puzzle.

The puzzle is this. An objection might be made to my assumption that only the earlier determines the later. For it might be urged that this is a mistake, since, wherever there is a causal inference, we say that the event which is the sufficient condition of the other event determines that other event ; and some sufficient conditions are later than the events which they are said to determine. And from this it would follow that the future determines the past, or, dropping the reference to the time of utterance, that the later determines the earlier. But this is absurd. Therefore the whole anthropomorphic presentation of causality must be abandoned. And I failed to see this only because I confused the consequent with the subsequent.

But the objection and the puzzle which it presents are both ill-considered. For those who say the future determines the past forget that 'the future' is a phrase of success which must not be used prematurely. And they forget that determining is something which is done in time, and so should properly be described with a temporal verb. The very most that they could be entitled to say — and in a few moments we shall see that even this is too much — is that what will happen, when it happens, will determine what has happened. But will it happen? In a way the future tense can be an impostor. For it suggests that there is something now happening which guarantees that something else will happen. And this suggestion becomes almost irresistible when the task of indicating the time of the event is delegated to a phrase of success, like 'the future', and the main verb is made timeless, like 'determines'. Now of course the suggestion might be correct. It might be the case that some third event was a sufficient condition of the particular future event. But, if this third event were past, and had happened at an earlier date than the other past event, then, though we might say that the future determines the past, we should also say that the pluperfect determines the future, and so that, indirectly, it is really the pluperfect which determines the past. Or, dropping these timeless distortions and the elaborate system of reference to the time of utterance, we should say that the earlier event, as always, determined the later event, but indirectly, through an even later event.

But, supposing that either there was no present or past event which was a sufficient condition of the future event, or that there was but that it was not earlier than the original past event, what should we say then? Surely in both these cases we should be driven to say that the later event determines the earlier event? Well the very most that we can say at the time when the earlier event happens is that the later event will determine it. But even this is too much. For, when an event has already happened, either it has already been determined by an earlier event or it has already determined itself. And in either case there is no determining left for its later sufficient condition to do. An event cannot have done more than have happened. And there is something very odd about saying that a later sufficient condition will make it causally impossible for it not to have happened. For one cannot obey a perfect imperative in the same way that one obeys a present imperative. After all, if the event had already not happened, the most that its alleged sufficient condition could achieve by happening would be to falsify the relevant general hypothetical and so prevent itself from being a sufficient condition. In short if we are going to describe this situation anthropomorphically, we must be thorough about it and take account of temporal priority. We must say not that the later event will make it causally impossible for the earlier event not to have happened, but that the earlier event made it causally possible for the later event to happen. Of course we might say both. But we cannot really mean both. For, if we did, we should be taking the same causal nexus twice over : and this reduplication, which is yet another remote result of McTaggart's conception of time, would defeat the whole purpose of anthropomorphism, which is to locate the responsibility for an event.

Curiously enough it is easier to accept this thorough anthropomorphism when the later event is a necessary condition. Yet the two cases are precisely symmetrical. For, when an event has already not happened, there is no determining left for its later necessary condition to do. An event cannot have done less than not happen. And there is something very odd about saying that a later necessary condition, by not happening, will make it causally impossible for it to have happened. After all, if the event had already happened, the most that its alleged necessary condition could achieve by not happening would be to falsify the relevant general hypothetical and so prevent itself from being a necessary condition. In short, here, too, it all depends on which comes first, and consistent anthropomorphism should lead us to say that the earlier event, by not happening, made it causally possible for the later event not to happen ; and not that the later event, by not happening, made it causally impossible for the earlier event to have happened ; and not both.

It is this anthropomorphism which lies beneath the traditional distinction between ratio essendi and ratio cognoscendi.
But unfortunately this distinction is not quite sharp enough,
and so does not succeed in developing anthropomorphism to
the point at which it is free from puzzles. For it is easy to
say that conditions of events, both sufficient and necessary,
are rationes cognoscendi and rationes essendi when they
precede their events, but that, when they follow their events,
they are only rationes cognoscendi.   But someone might
object, in the spirit of Hegel, that surely all rationes cognoscendi must also be rationes essendi even when they are subsequent to their events.   For surely the gerund 'essendi' is
timeless, and can refer to past time so that the event can precede its condition.   And, if this objection were made, it could
be countered only by the introduction of a new kind of ratio,
ratio efficiendi.   Then ratio cognoscendi would always also
be ratio essendi, but not also ratio efficiendi unless it preceded
its event.   For, though the gerund 'efficiendi' is timeless, the
meaning of 'bringing about' ensures that it can only refer to
a time previous to the event.   And thus the anthropomorphic
weltanschauung is made consistent and impeccable.

The chief source of the puzzle about the future determining
the past is the old mistake of tampering with temporal verbs.
And the temptations to make this mistake are in this case
many and insidious.   First there is a general prejudice against
anthropomorphism because some philosophers have misused
it against Hume : but this misuse is avoidable.   Secondly,
logicians generally deal in truths and falsehoods, and so
readily forget that the truth of the antecedent of a singular
hypothetical, though a timeless shadow, is nevertheless the
timeless shadow of a temporal event : but, if it were not, there
would be nothing to do the determining.   Then, more particularly, all inductive inferences can be cast in a form in
which there is an element of deduction, and logical necessity
cannot figure on time's stage because it is not that sort of
ghost : but there is always also an element of induction, and
causal necessity can figure on time's stage.   And finally, all

inductive inferences depend somehow on an open general hypothetical, and open general hypotheticals are expressed timelessly : but this is only because they are in a way too full of time to express it in one verb.

Russell said [1] that time's arrow is irrelevant to determinism. And, if I am right, his arguments for this thesis illustrate the mistakes which I have been trying to expose. He dwells on the fact that inductive inference often runs counter to time's arrow, and claims that therefore later events can determine earlier events. And, in the only other sense of 'determine', the sense in which it means 'make the opposite logically impossible', he claims that the future is as determined as the past : for, though what has happened has happened, there is an equally good tautology about the future, that what will happen will happen. Now the first of these two claims would be valid if the second was. For, unless past events had already been determined in some sense in which future events had not already been determined, future events would sometimes be able to determine past events. But according to the second claim past events are not determined in any sense in which future events are not also determined. But this second claim is erroneous. For 'What will happen will happen' only says '(x) (x will happen $\sqsupset$ x will happen)' : and this is only a general sentential function which could be completed in various ways so as to yield a series of tautological singular hypothetical sentences about future events. But, if the future events described in the consequents of these hypotheticals are only determined by the future events described in their antecedents they are only self-determined. For the two sets of events are identical. In fact it is just like saying that there will be a sea-battle to-morrow if it is true that there will be a sea-battle to-morrow. And, if they are only self-determined, since they are future events it is more correct to say that they *will* be determined when they happen. And this future tense is important. For past events, which in a similar way are only self-determined, *have been* determined

[1] 'On the Notion of Cause' in *Mysticism and Logic*.

already. And this difference in tense is an important difference between the two tautologies. Russell ignored it only because, like McTaggart and most logicians, he was preoccupied with adjectives and neglected verbs. But it is a sufficiently important difference to invalidate Russell's second claim. And, since his second claim is false, his first claim is false too.

The timeless heaven of logicians has been lifted above the world of temporal happening. But this elevation is merely the work of thought. And, though traffic in truths and falsehoods is usually harmless, it can sometimes be dangerous. It is dangerous when people descend again from the logicians' heaven to the world of temporal happening without making it clear that they are descending. This is what Russell does when he uses 'determines' timelessly. The remedy is to take the particular sentence which has a timeless verb and rewrite it with a verb which does indicate time. And this simple transcription is all that is needed against McTaggart, who makes the same mistake on a much larger scale and much more tendentiously. For the reinstatement of temporal verbs is the best possible, indeed almost the only possible vindication of the reality of time. Moore said that there are temporal facts. Anyone who is thorough about the reinstatement of temporal verbs is really saying that there are no non-temporal facts.

III

Enquiries into the source of this temporal weltanschauung never progress very far. Either they reach the unexciting result that we use temporal verbs because events happen in time: or else they go a little further and come back with definitions of the past and the future. But these definitions, which ought to be very important, are curiously inadequate. The reason for the baffling inadequacy of this result is that time is a category.

When Russell said that what will happen will happen, it seemed not quite enough to answer very loudly 'Yes, but what has happened *has* happened'. Something more than mere emphasis of temporal words seemed to be needed. For instance, it would be more satisfying to know why we talk like this. And it is not good enough to say that we talk like this because events happen in time. Some more detailed reasons are needed, perhaps some definitions. For, if we could produce some good definitions of the past and future, we should be able to say that we could not talk about the past or future unless we could also talk about their definientia : and that we could not talk about their definientia unless we experienced them. And this might represent some progress. For it would enable us to point to those features in our experience which are Necessary and Sufficient conditions of the use of temporal verbs (I use capital letters to indicate conditions which are not causally necessary or sufficient, but logically Necessary or Sufficient).

Now Russell [1] admitted that 'we all regard the past as determined simply by the fact that it has happened'. But he immediately neutralized this admission by suggesting that 'but for the accident that memory works backward and not forward we should regard the future as equally determined by the fact that it will happen'. But this suggestion either does not go far enough, or else, in a self-frustrating way, it goes too far.

The way in which it would not go far enough is this. Russell may have meant that we might have no memory of the past, but that we might have instead some faculty for knowing the future which was in every other way just like memory, say precognition. And then, he suggested, we should say that the future was determined. Now I waive the difficulty that if we could not remember the past we should not say anything, if 'waive' is a strong enough word for this difficulty. For I want to concentrate on the difficulty concealed in the words 'in every other way'. Precognition

[1] *Loc. cit.* p. 202 (1921 edition) or p. 190 (Pelican edition).

cannot differ from memory only in telling us about the future.
For, if it tells us about the future, it tells us about something
which usually has not yet been determined ; whereas memory,
which tells us about the past, tells us about something which
has always already been determined. Of course this might
be called part of the same difference. But in that case this
difference is big enough to ensure that we should not say that
the future was determined. And so Russell's suggestion
would not go far enough.

And the way in which it would go too far is this. Russell
may have meant that we might have no memory of the past,
but that we might have instead, in the fullest sense, memory
of the future.[1] But now there is a difficulty concealed in the
words 'in the fullest sense'. If we really remembered the
future it would not be the future but the past. For one good
definition of the past is 'what it is logically possible to remember'. Now this is not *the* definition of the past, since
there may be others equally good. But, even if it is only one
definition among many, being something which it is logically
possible to remember is at least a Sufficient Condition of
being past. And so Russell would have made the toy soldier
turn right about only by turning the toy parade-ground right
about ; and in this self-frustrating way his suggestion would
go too far.

Bradley once executed a similar manœuvre and overshot
the mark in a similar way.[2] He said that we necessarily look
forward to the source of events in the same way that fishes
necessarily face the direction from which their food comes.
And that events come from the future, just as fishes' food
comes from upstream. And he suggested that, just as a river
might flow backwards, so in the Absolute the direction of the
flow of time might be reversed ; so that events would come
from the past, and consequently we should look forward to
the past. Now enough has been said about the general
difficulties of this metaphor. Here there is an additional par-

---

[1] Cf. Lewis Carroll, *Through the Looking Glass*, c. v.
[2] *Appearance and Reality*, p. 189.

ticular difficulty, which is that, whereas it is only a contingent
fact that a river flows in a certain direction, it is not a contingent fact that events come from the future. For one quite
good (but not very good) definition of the future is 'the source
of events'. And so events would not come from the past
unless the past became the future. And, if we are like fishes
at all, we are like fishes which can never see either the bed of
the stream or its banks. There is little left of the river of time.

So far my enquiry has led to two definitions : that the
past is what it is logically possible to remember ; and that the
future is the source of events. But neither of these definitions
is very satisfactory. For memory itself can hardly be defined
without some reference to the past : and we can explain the
phrase 'the source of events' only by saying that the events
meant have not yet happened, or had not yet happened, or
will not have yet happened. And other definitions of the past
and future seem to lie along the circumferences of equally
small circles. Suppose, for instance, that we tried defining
the future as what our wishes (and other things too) can alter.
Now there is something wrong with saying that the future can
be altered, since the future is necessarily the successful survivor of alterations whose victims are only possible futures.
The future cannot be altered in the way in which a man cannot
change his clothes until he has dressed ; whereas the past
cannot be altered in the way in which, when he has dressed,
he cannot now succeed in having changed his clothes then.
However, we can evade this difficulty by saying that our wishes
can make the future different from what it would have been
without them. But then we are beset by another difficulty.
For making is causal efficacy : and temporal priority is a
Necessary Condition of causal efficacy. And thus we here
come round a circle which has a circumference which is only
a very little longer than the others.

Now Russell and Ramsey were worried because no
attempts to push this enquiry further have met with any
greater success. Russell complained that it is a mere tautology
that our wishes can cause the future to be different from what

it would have been without them. And Ramsey said : [1] 'It
is, it seems, a fundamental fact that the future is due to the
present, or, more mildly, is affected by the present, but the
past is not. What does this mean ? It is not clear, and, if we
try to make it clear, it turns into nonsense or a definition.'
I shall now try to discover the precise deficiences of these
definitions or tautologies, and the reason for them.

Now first of all we have no right to complain because our
enquiry has led only to definitions. For definitions are not
always adopted capriciously, but are often firmly based on
contingencies. For instance, if we noticed that a certain substance always exhibits a certain property, we should be
justified in making that property a defining property of the
substance. But, though there is nothing wrong with definitions in general, definitions of the past and future are peculiarly
inadequate. For, whereas the defining properties of a substance can themselves usually be defined without reference to
that substance, the definientia of the past and future themselves immediately involve again the past and future. Now,
as Wisdom has shown,[2] one of the things which metaphysicians do is to seek definientia which in no way involve their
definienda. But it is impossible to define the past and future
in this way because, whereas gold and its melting-point are
separately observable, time and its definientia are not. For
time figures in all our experience without ever obtruding
itself. In fact it is a category.

And, because time is a category and figures unobtrusively
in all our experience, it is possible to define the past and
future in many different ways and yet none of these definitions
is very convincing. For the sentences which give the logical
relations of temporal words exhibit a curious feature. They
are not synthetic *a priori*, but they are, as it were, weak
tautologies. And they are weak tautologies not only because
we are so accustomed to using temporal words correctly that

[1] *The Foundations of Mathematics*, p. 249.
[2] 'Metaphysics and Verification', *Mind*, 1938, p. 465 ff. (reprinted in John
Wisdom, *Philosophy and Psychoanalysis*, Blackwell, 1953).

we need no strong reminders, but also because their structure is peculiar. For most tautologies are constructed like columns, by placing terms squarely one on top of another like marble drums. But the tautologies which give the logic of temporal words put their terms together like the stones of a vault. No single conjunction of terms is indispensable or could stand alone. But together they form the vaulted ceiling on which the fresco of knowledge is painted.

And, because time is a category and figures unobtrusively in all our experience, it gives logicians no room to manœuvre. Russell thought that memorability is something which is necessarily connected with being determined, but only contingently connected with being past. But, on my second interpretation, he was wrong, since it is also necessarily connected with being past. And Bradley thought that being the source of events is something which is necessarily connected with being what we look forward to, but only contingently connected with being the future. But he was wrong, since it is also necessarily connected with being the future. And we cannot even say that these definientia of the past and future, like the definientia of gold, were originally discovered to be attached synthetically and only afterwards attached analytically. For time is not an object of discovery, but a sort of elusive atmosphere in which discovery is done. And, since the definientia of the past and future never were attached synthetically to the past and future, if we try to detach them, we are embarking on a gedankenexperiment which can only end in one of three ways. Either, like Russell on my first interpretation, we choose something which is only synthetically connected with being past, and then, through this looseness in the apparatus, the experiment never really begins. Or — and this is what happens to most people — the experiment begins, we do some indescribable violence to our concepts, destroy the vital atmosphere of thought, and come out with our heads reeling. Or else, like Russell on my second interpretation and like Bradley, we succeed in shifting the definientia of the past and future, but only by shifting the past and future with them.   In short, temporal tautologies are so firmly based that it is impossible that we shall ever succeed in dismantling them and exposing their foundations.   Of course we can always say that temporal tautologies are based on the fact that events happen in time : but this is no more informative than saying that the foundations of a building go down into the site on which it stands.

But how exactly does time figure as an unobtrusive category in all our experience ?   If we look at the words which report this experience we find that time is expressed predominantly by the tenses of verbs.   For even other ways of expressing time are usually reinforced by temporal verbs. Now one of the things which Aristotle meant by a category was a mode of verbs.   And it is partly because the category of time is the temporal mode of verbs that it is so elusive. For most logicians [1] have concentrated on nouns and adjectives and have neglected verbs except where they can be reduced to present participles attached by a timeless copula. And this neglect of tenses is now so natural to us that we do not recognize that tenses can play an important part in tautologies.   Yet, if we replace tenses by temporal nouns or adjectives, though the tautologies which we get are much more fashionable, they are somehow not sufficiently closely connected with ordinary language.   For people do not talk about the future and the past nearly so often as they use temporal verbs.   Nor do people, for instance, learn the meaning of 'past' explicitly and separately ; that it is no good crying over spilt milk *and* that the past cannot be altered.   But this particular inadequacy of temporal tautologies, though real, is the result of an illusion.   For tautologies which depend on temporal verbs are as good as those which depend on temporal predicates.   And so there is no need to replace 'what has happened' by 'the past' or 'what will happen' by 'the future', no need to adopt inadequate versions of temporal tautologies.

But the other ways in which the categorial nature of time

---

[1] Reichenbach is a conspicuous exception. Cf. *Elements of Symbolic Logic*, c. vii, § 51.

is responsible for the inadequacies of temporal tautologies are in no way illusory. For we cannot make temporal tautologies less circular, stronger or easier to dismantle. We must accept that in these three ways temporal tautologies cannot be improved, and we can console ourselves with the reflection that we have a good name for the source of this limitation—the categorial nature of time.

Corpus Christi College, Oxford

Chapter XII

COULD SPACE BE FOUR DIMENSIC

BY H. BROTMAN

THERE are at least three possible ways of asking v
space might not under certain circumstances be four
sional.

The first way is : Could we imagine something else
to length, breadth, and height but none of these ? Intui
this seems impossible. The second way is : Can we sup
that more than three straight rods could meet mutuall
right angles ? To this one might say that it is analytic
necessary that only three straight rods can meet mutuall)
right angles, if we consider what is meant by 'straight' a
'90°'. The third way is : If we speak not about leng
breadth, and height but merely about position, might not the
be circumstances in which we could use four co-ordinates t
determine position ? Let us see what this implies. We migh
say that we find it convenient to characterize the position of
objects by three co-ordinates rather than two for the following
reasons. When an object goes behind another it disappears
from view at different times for different observers. One
might say that it is inconvenient to speak of objects disappearing at different times for different observers, and that is
why we speak of the object going behind and speak of its
position in terms of three co-ordinates and not two. Similarly
if it were the case that the ordinary objects of our acquaintance
disappeared at different times for different observers we would
similarly find it convenient to say that they had gone in some
manner that was analogous to going behind, rather than speak
of them as disappearing, and for the same reason we would
find it convenient to characterize their position by four co-
ordinates.

I am going to outline an example which comprehends all these three possibilities, but I shall begin by considering the second way. Here then I am going to enquire whether it is analytic that only three straight rods can be put mutually at right angles. I agree indeed that it does depend on how one interprets 'straight' but I want to give a possible interpretation that might be accepted, but would allow us to say that four straight rods could be placed at right angles. Suppose we take what looks like a straight rod, that is, one that is judged to be straight by the eye, and we lay another rod crosswise on it, so that the figure obtained looks symmetrical. In ordinary parlance we would say that the two rods had made a cross and that each arm of the cross enclosed a right angle. Let us say that any two half arms of the cross enclosing what we call a right angle, should be called a square angle. I do not want to call it a right angle because I wish merely to refer to the shape of a physical object. A square angle can be obtained by laying down one's rods in a manner involving a judgment of symmetry. In ordinary experience, however, one can make a test for symmetry. We find we can take two square angles and first of all lay one on top of the other so that they fit. Fitting here is something to be determined by sight and touch. Then one of the square angles can be turned over, so that the backs of the square angles touch each other but the bases make what looks and feels like a straight line.

This will be as in Fig. 1. Here, let me emphasize that the criterion of straightness is the look of the thing. This then

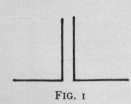

FIG. 1

gives a method of settling when in practice we might speak of a square angle. An angle is square, we could say, given the condition that its base can form a straight line together with the base of another angle if the backs of the two angles are placed together, provided also that this other angle can be made to fit the first angle. This, in our ordinary mathematical terminology is

to say that the two angles that together make a straight line and are equal to each other, are right angles.

With this operational definition of a square angle it is now an empirical fact that only three lines can be put mutually at right angles, for we can discover experimentally only, that if we have two square angles AÔB and CÔD, then there is but one way in which they can be placed so that one arm of each angle touches the other, and the other two arms together contain a square angle in a plane perpendicular to the touching arms. Consider for instance, how one might place two L shapes on a table, with the backs of the Ls touching, there would be but one way of placing them so that the two bases of the Ls made a shape on the table, which, if copied in cardboard, would obey the tests of coincidence and straight line forming that are the empirical tests of a true L shape.

If we accept that such a physical criterion of a square angle is permissible, then it is *not* mathematically necessary, but only empirically true, that three rods only can be put mutually at square angles.

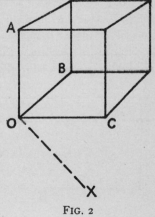

If it is empirically true only, then we can imagine something different.

Suppose we have three rods, O_1A, O_2B, O_3C, mutually at square angles at O, and then a fourth rod, O_4X is fitted at an angle to the other three.

One must imagine this to be like the corner of a box, the edges of the box that meet at the corner being like O_1A. O_2B, O_3C, as in

FIG. 2

Fig. 2. Then OX juts out from the box. Then normally we would suppose the rod OX does not make a square angle with all the other three rods.

Suppose, however, that we test each angle that OX makes with the other rods in turn, to see if it is a square angle. We could test each angle by comparing it with AÔC, for AÔC is a perfectly good square angle. Suppose we find, for instance, that the angle OX makes with OC, when it is unfixed and compared with AÔC, fits it. Then we shall say that the angle OX makes with OC is a square angle. But then suppose we find that the other two angles that OX makes with OA and OB also conforms to the same test, when compared with AÔC by unfixing and bringing up close, what shall we say then? There are two possibilities. First one can say that in moving the angles about, they have become distorted, and that is why all three angles, XÔA, XÔB, and XÔC, appear to coincide with AÔC when brought up to compare. One might say, for instance, that in two of the three cases, although we have not noticed, in moving the angles up to be compared, they have opened out slightly. On the other hand we might say that no such distortion took place, and then in that case one would, I think, be committed to saying that, odd though it may seem, we have four rods mutually at square angles.

Thus we have a twofold choice, either we can declare that the rods have become distorted, or we can speak about four rods mutually at square angles. The plausibility of this example might be enhanced if I illustrate how the same choice lies before us in a two dimensional framework. Imagine a

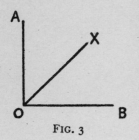

FIG. 3

surrealist film showing two lines, OA and OB at square angles, as in Fig. 3. Someone comes along and sticks a third line OX at an angle to the other two. Then suppose the people *in the film* start playing with the angles OX makes with OA and OB. They start with AÔX and they compare it with AÔB and it fits, then they compare BÔX with AÔB and it fits too. What are we to say? That BÔX and AÔX are not really square angles at all; but as BÔX and AÔX are moved up to AÔB they change shape, and that is why they fit? Are we to say that the projection on a vertical screen of a square angle in a horizontal plane is a different shape or the same shape as the projection of a square angle in a vertical plane on to a vertical screen ? I want to make it quite clear that there lies before us a *choice* of whether we are to speak of distortion or not, for the test of what is a *real distortion*, what is *really* a change of shape is not a simple matter of sense experience.

If we can accept this, then we must be prepared to admit that given certain behaviour in nature, four rods could be said to be at square angles; and perhaps now there will be no objection to calling these right angles.

This can now be applied to the question of whether we can imagine a fourth thing like length, breadth, and height. In a picture of a cube, for example, one can have three lines meeting at a point, to represent the corner of a cube, and these can be imagined as the directions in which one would measure length, breadth, and height, although as far as the picture surface is concerned, sense can be attached to only two of these terms. However, we do not consider the lines of the cube as lying on the surface of the picture but as having depth, and in this case, sense can be attached to the third of the terms, length, breadth, and height. Can we not equally suppose that when one has four rods at square angles, these represent the length, breadth, height, and something else of a four dimensional cube. Let us again appeal to the analogy of a film or a photograph.

One can have on a two dimensional surface, the picture of a cube, like Fig. 4. This is a picture where one is looking into the cube. LMNO is the back wall, and ABCD the front wall. Now by a well-known analogy, we can likewise construct a picture, in three dimensional space, of a four dimensional cube. Fig. 5 is the view into a four dimensional cube. The analogies in the figure are clear.

Fig. 4, considered in two dimensions, consists of one square inside another, at the corners of which there are three lines

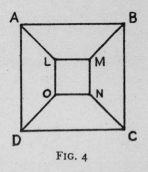

FIG. 4

meeting, only two of which are at right angles. In Fig. 5,
if considered in three dimensions, we have one cube inside
another, at the corners of which four lines meet ; only three
of which are at right angles ; but, just as Fig. 4 represents a
cube, where the front square and the back square, LMNO
and ABCD are *really* squares, and the three lines meeting at
the corner, AD, OD, and CD are *really* mutually at right
angles, so we can interpret Fig. 5 in such a way that we have
what we call a four dimensional cube. Then we would say
the small inside cube, *lmno l'm'n'o'* is really the same size as
the big cube *abcd a'b'c'd'* ; that the curious trapezoidal-like
shapes at the sides, such as *aa'll' oo'dd'* are cubes ; and the
lines meeting at a corner, say, *la, da, a'a* and *ba*, meet really
at right angles. Now it becomes clearer how my previous
demonstration of four rods at right angles is to be applicable.
Just as, in a film, a shape that looks like the angle $A\hat{D}O$ in
Fig. 4 can be interpreted as a right angle, provided it under-
goes the necessary transformations either as the camera moves
or it moves ; that is to say that when placed vertically it becomes right-angular in two dimensional space ; so in ordinary
space, if four lines are placed as are placed the lines at the
corner *a* of Fig. 5, that is, *la da, aa'* and *ba*, and then undergo
the type of transformation I outlined above, when I was explaining how one could have four rods at square angles, then
we would say that they are four rods at right angles, and of a
complete figure in three dimensional space, such as I have
indicated in Fig. 5, provided the necessary transformations
occurred as we moved or it moved, then we would be prepared
to call movement along the oblique lines *la, l'a', m'b'*, etc., as
movements in the direction of the fourth dimension analogous
to height, length, breadth, just as the oblique lines AL, etc.
in Fig. 4 give us the third dimension of length. In this sense
then we could imagine a fourth dimension analogous to length,
breadth, and height. We can now elucidate our third way of
speaking about the fourth dimension in the light of this. For
instance in Fig. 4 if the thing is three dimensional, then we do
not normally see the back face of the cube LMNO until we

move to the side of the cube, and then it appears. Moreover, if the cube itself is moving in front of us, then the back face disappears at different times for different observers. Similarly in Fig. 5 we would say that such a construction was a four dimensional cube, if the small cube *lmno l'm'n'o'* became visible outside the big cube as *we* moved ; and, moreover, if as the whole figure moved, the small cube reappeared from the inside of the big cube at different times for different observers.

Then again, just as when in Fig. 4 we get round to the back face LMNO then this becomes the bigger square and ABCD of the front face, the smaller, so, if in Fig. 5 we were to call it a four dimensional cube, then there would have to occur transformations such that the inner cube became larger than the outer cube and this we would call approaching it in the

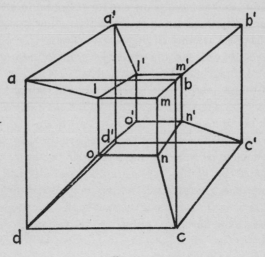

FIG. 5

fourth dimension. Moreover, when we measured the two cubes with measuring rods, they would not be different in size, because the measuring rods would be undergoing a transformation when moved from the inner cube to the outer cube, such that *ad* and *lo*, for example, would, by measuring rod standards, be the same size.

There is one important remaining phenomenon that we must expect to happen if we are to call this cube four dimensional. In Fig. 4 it is the case that a line drawn on the front face of the cube can be coincident with a line drawn at the back face of the cube when we consider it from a two dimensional standpoint, but when considered from a three dimensional standpoint, there are *two* lines, one behind the other. Moreover, we should be led to describe it in this three dimensional way if as the figure moves, or we move, the two lines separate out ; for then, as we say, the front line no longer obscures the view of the back line.

Now if we are dealing with a four dimensional cube we must expect an analogous thing to happen. In this case, a plane surface lying in the small inside cube which is *coincident* with a plane surface lying on the larger outside cube can be said to be merely obscured by it, and we must expect the two surfaces to separate out as the figure moves.

It is best to consider this example in the following manner : In Fig. 4 a diagonal line drawn from A to C in the large square obscures, that is, is in front of, a diagonal line drawn from L to N in the small square. When one moves round to the side, this line separates out into two lines. In Fig. 5 the analogy to the large and small squares are the large and small cubes. We now draw a diagonal plane in the large cube from *aa'* to *cc'* and this coincides with a diagonal plane in the small cube ; drawn across from *ll'* to *nn'*, but, they do not *really* coincide, and we must expect them to separate out as we move.

This last consideration helps one to see more clearly how the problem of solidity is to be overcome. When one is considering Fig. 4 then there is a jump from considering it as a plane surface to considering it a filled-in solid which it seems we cannot make in Fig. 5 ; for here, although we have a solid, what is a super solid to be like ? If, however, one is satisfied that the notion of solidity in Fig. 4 can be obtained by imagining that every line on the surface has a disposition to separate out into a multitude of lines, or a plane, as one moves, so too one can imagine that the notion of super solidity in Fig. 5 is to be obtained by envisaging that each plane in the solid has a disposition to separate out into a multitude of planes, or a solid, as one moves.

This then is my example of how things would have to behave in order that we should call space four dimensional.

It is a world in which four rods can be put mutually at right angles ; objects disappear into other objects at different times for different observers, and are thus obscured from view, and objects change apparent size and shape, either as they move or as the observer moves. Four co-ordinates are required to measure position, and we have another direction besides length, breadth, and height.

One most important point, though, that this example brings out is that in order to say space is four dimensional one must not only imagine objects behaving in a curious sort of way ; that is, suffering these distortions that I have described, apparently single surfaces becoming double and so on ; but one must not describe these distortions as though they are distortions.

It will be remembered that we could speak of four rods meeting at right angles only if we supposed that none of the angles were distorted when we attempted to measure them. That is to say we would not *call* them distorted. Similarly, we would have to say that the two cubes of our four dimensional cubes are *really* the same size however they may look. The fact that the one seems smaller than the other is due to the phenomenon of four dimensional perspective.

This, then, is the example complete. I would like to make one comment about its use. One of the chief difficulties in examining this problem occurs in that we do not know properly how to use the words 'space' or 'dimension' in the proposition 'space is three dimensional'. The use of analogy does, I consider, overcome this difficulty ; for the similarities between the analogy and its prototype seem to warrant the claim that the words 'space' and 'dimensions' are being used in much the same way, in so far as it is possible to do so.

It is now time to ask whether a similar example can be constructed which would make us say that space is two dimensional. Now here, there seems to be an asymmetry, because in our construction of a four dimensional example, we asked that one should imagine objects in this world behaving in a curious fashion, whereas, it is difficult to see what, in a two dimensional world, would have to be the behaviour of objects before we decided to call this world two dimensional. However, in the four dimensional example, not only do we have to imagine curious behaviour of objects; but we also have to change our language; so that what we normally call distortions, are not called distortions, and so forth.

Now this at least does have a similarity to the case where we might say the world was two dimensional, for we might say that we could call the world two dimensional provided we changed our language. That is to say : if our language were such that the words 'far', 'near to', 'behind', and so on had no meaning, and we were prepared to say that only two straight lines could ever be put mutually at right angles, this would be to describe the world in a two dimensional language; and if the language was two dimensional, then perhaps we would say that the space of the world we are describing is two dimensional also.

I shall illustrate how this two dimensional language works. For instance, we shall no longer talk of objects being far away or near to. This is to be described by saying that an object is smaller or larger. Progress towards one by an object will be described as the object swelling, and progress away from one will be described as the object diminishing. One object going behind another will be described by saying the object vanishes; and when an object is behind another, it will be described as being only dispositionally there.

Moreover, movement by an observer is to be described not as movement by him; but as making the object change shape. 'I walk across the room' is to be described as 'I have kinaesthetic sensations in my legs which makes the objects around me change shape'.

This at least is precisely analogous to the way one's language was to differ if one is to call the world four dimensional.

Thus, if in our ordinary world we do have cubes, one inside the other, then this is to be described as being the same size, but one is further away than the other, where the language is four dimensional.

A solid described as swelling or diminishing in size in our three dimensional language, is, in a four dimensional language, to be described as moving nearer or farther away (here of course I mean nearer and farther away in the fourth dimension analogous to our left, right, up, down, in front, and behind directions).

A solid described as disappearing into another in our three dimensional language is to be described as going behind another in the four dimensional language. And a solid described as dispositionally vanished into another solid in the three dimensional language, in our four dimensional language is described as merely being behind.

Moreover, a general distortion of objects in our three dimensional world is to be described as movement by the observer in our four dimensional world.

Thus, we can show that the same curious phenomena that I have outlined can be described in a three dimensional or four dimensional language ; and likewise the world as it is can be described in a three dimensional or a two dimensional language.

This, however, raises the apparent asymmetry of it ; cannot we describe the world as it is in a four dimensional language without having to suggest that objects undergo these odd distortions ; just as we have to make no assumption about the behaviour of objects in order to describe the world two-dimensionally ?

Now this is precisely analogous to asking whether we could not describe a film of two dimensional objects in a three dimensional language. How could one, for instance, describe

the first part of 'Fantasia', where there are only two dimensional shapes appearing on the screen, in a three dimensional
language ? The answer is that one could ; but one would not
have anything to say. These are, one could say, merely surfaces dancing around in a three dimensional world ; but it is
only if the shapes underwent the type of distortion that is
characteristic of the two dimensional projection of a three
dimensional solid that one would have any need to use a three
dimensional language. That is to say, that a three dimensional
language would be too rich to describe a film in which the
appropriate distortions do not occur.

Similarly, it would be possible to suggest that we should
describe the world as we know it in a four dimensional language ; but unless by accident it so happened that it was the
case that some of our objects did start to swell or distort in
the way that I have described ; then the use of a four dimensional language would be too rich.

Now, it is also the case that when we do describe the
three dimensional world in a two dimensional language, the
language is too poor. For instance although we *can* talk about
an object having dispositionally vanished when it has gone
behind ; nevertheless, we cannot describe what is happening
to it when it *has* dispositionally vanished ; although we can
perfectly well speak about what is happening to an object
whilst it is behind another. One might sum up this situation
by saying that if objects behave in the way I have outlined in
the beginning of this article, then we would describe space
four dimensionally and thus say 'space is four dimensional'
whilst if objects behaved in the same way that the shapes in
'Fantasia' do, then we would speak of space two dimensionally, and say 'space is two dimensional'.

It is not, of course, strictly accurate that it is the behaviour
of 'objects' we are concerned with. My examples are built
up from mathematical analogies and only seemed plausible
because I referred not so much to the movements of the *rods*
but simply to the movements and distortions of lines, trusting
that one would believe these lines to have some physical in-

terpretation. Thus the possibility of describing Fig. 4, that is, the picture of the three dimensional cube, in two ways, depending on the behaviour of it, was only plausible provided I confined myself to speaking about the behaviour of the lines making it up, and similarly the possibility of one's finding something in the world one would describe as a four dimensional cube was really only made plausible by suggesting that the planes and lines in a three dimensional world behaved in a curious fashion.

So far as I can see, the only possible physical interpretation of planes, lines, and points is something like mere visual sensations; and from such sensations a world with a quite different Gestalt quality would be built up.

All I have attempted to show is how such a world might be envisaged, and in the course of my analysis to clarify some of the ideas behind the statement 'space is three dimensional'.

THE END

PRINTED IN GREAT BRITAIN BY
LOWE AND BRYDONE (PRINTERS) LIMITED, LONDON, N.W.10

Date Due

DEMCO NO 295

JAN 2 3 '6 CANISIUS				
MAR 26 '65				
APR 19 '6				
26 '66				
JAN 19 '67				
APR 5 '67				
MAY 13 '67 CANISIUS				
MAY 25 '67